This book is due for return on or before the last date shown above; it may, subject to the book not being reserved by another reader, be renewed by personal application, post, or telephone, quoting this date and details of the book.

HAMPSHIRE COUNTY LIBRARY

Flying
Between
the Wars

By the same Author

THAT NOTHING FAILED THEM

BUILDING AEROPLANES FOR
'THOSE MAGNIFICENT MEN'

Flying
Between
the Wars

ALLEN WHEELER

G T FOULIS & CO LTD
Henley-on-Thames
Oxfordshire

First published 1972
© Allen Wheeler, 1972

ISBN 0 85429 137 7

Printed in Great Britain
by Alden & Mowbray Ltd
at the Alden Press, Oxford

CONTENTS

ILLUSTRATIONS

FOREWORD

by Marshal of the Royal Air Force Sir Charles Elworthy, G.C.B., C.B.E., D.S.O., M.V.O., A.F.C.

When Allen Wheeler asked me whether I would write a foreword to this book I wondered why he had picked on me. Though we had both joined the Royal Air Force as 'University Entrants' from Cambridge, he had done so ten years before I did and the five years covered in his story were ended before I had learned to fly. Indeed our paths never crossed until after the war.

When we came to know each other we found that we had both suddenly cast aside planned professional careers to take commissions in the Royal Air Force. We did so simply because we both had a passion for aeroplanes and the prospect of flying them. We were young and had few responsibilities so the inevitably bleak financial future was no real deterrent. To be able to fly and to be paid for doing it was something too good to be missed.

Though in our early Service years we had the same general enthusiasm it was only Allen who throughout the rest of his Service career managed to remain closely in touch with flying. His speciality was the art of flying and the development of aircraft perhaps more as flying machines than as weapons of war and for this his natural brilliance as a pilot and his engineering qualifications well suited him. Happily, on retirement from the Royal Air Force, his infectious enthusiasm for flying and for aircraft remained undiminished and he has applied his restless energy to the benefit of aviation in general and to the Shuttleworth Collection of vintage aircraft in particular.

I have deliberately strayed from the last half of the nineteen twenties, which is the period covered in this book, in order to put things into perspective. No reader of this book should be deluded into believing that the author, however light-hearted his record, was, as a junior officer, so irresponsible or even so undisciplined that he should quickly have been removed before he could break any more aircraft and waste more of the tax payers' money. I am not suggesting for one moment that junior officers could today behave in the same way and not just because forty to fifty years ago they had only a two thousand pound aircraft strapped to their backsides as opposed to one costing two million pounds today, but because in those early days the best piloting techniques and the best characteristics to be built into an aeroplane could, to a large extent, only be discovered by trial. Pilots who were sufficiently daring deliberately to subject their aircraft to unknown stresses and aerodynamic effects sometimes advanced flying techniques or aircraft design, sometimes they merely broke their aircraft and sometimes, notwithstanding what the author describes as the 'forgiving' qualities of the aircraft of those days, they killed themselves. Nowadays such experimentation as is necessary is immensely complex and scientific and has to be conducted accordingly. The point I want to make is that the inquisitive, imaginative but sometimes somewhat harum scarum Allen Wheeler of the nineteen twenties is an essential element of the highly responsible Allen Wheeler of today.

Even so some readers may feel that his story reveals a lack of serious dedication to what should have been the prime function of any fighting Service—defence of the realm. But the story begins only six years after the end of the 'war to end all wars', by which time with no apparent threat to the security of the country, the Royal Air Force had been reduced to a mere shadow of what it had been in 1918. Its parents, the Royal Flying Corps and the Royal Naval Air Service had their origins only a few years earlier. Without history and tradition like those of the Army and the Navy, the Air Force was having to feel its way and develop its own personality. With hindsight we can be thankful for the emphasis that was placed upon the retention of such skills as had been acquired during the war and their further development and thankful too for Trenchard's great contribution to his Service namely the supporting organisation geared to the future as a foundation which could be built upon when need arose.

Allen Wheeler's personal story reveals many of the growing pains of the young Air Force and the cheerfulness with which they were borne. It also makes the point that life was not all flying—there were ground jobs too—and out of both, to a large extent performed in turn by the same people, understanding grew and efficiency with it. Those may have been years of seeming irresponsibility but they were certainly formative.

Governor's Office
Windsor Castle
18 August 1971

INTRODUCTION

This book is a record of our day to day life in the Royal Air Force from January 1925, when I joined and learnt to fly, till November 1929, when I was posted overseas.

In the book I have described these events as seen at the time through the eyes of a very junior officer, not as seen in retrospect through the eyes of a retired Air Commodore! If, therefore, a certain amount of happy irresponsibility appears to be revealed in our outlook, particularly on a few lamentable breaches of discipline, well, that was how many junior officers viewed them at the time. Life then was a lighthearted affair for most of us, and a short one for some of the 30 pupils who came to Digby with me to learn to fly. One in six was killed flying within five years. The casualty rate would have been much higher if the aeroplanes we flew had not been so forgiving. But if we had joined the Air Force seven years earlier the ratio would have been reversed – only one in six might have survived.

It is difficult now, after nearly half a century, to remember and appreciate the attitude of the country generally towards the Royal Air Force in 1925. At that time politicians were vying with one another to abolish it or most of it, the Navy and Army were hoping to appropriate those bits of the Air Force which the politicians did not destroy: large sections of the more influential members of society considered that officers in the Royal Air Force were rather low grade irresponsible individuals. Very few had a good word to say for us.

Fear and the sudden realization of the imminence of war in 1937 produced a change in public opinion and by 1945 the Royal Air Force had come into its own—again. But in the late 1920s we could not foresee that happening.

If many of us did not take a very serious view of our responsibilities in the late 1920s it was a view shared by many in the older generations who had—or should have had—enough experience to have known better.

But we loved the life the Royal Air Force gave us and we did our job far better than might have been expected in the circumstances.

This story is not exclusively about flying because life in the Royal Air Force as a junior officer during those years was not by any means all flying: there were administrative jobs to be done and they affected our lives. I have recorded them so far as they were interesting and amusing. They were part of our life and, taken the right way, they were often an exciting part.

Throughout the story I have used the real names of characters mentioned except where some embarrassment might result from the identity being revealed: in those cases I have disguised both the name and the identity effectively.

Memories are traditionally unreliable, but I believe the facts were exactly as recorded. Dates, where given, are absolutely accurate since they are taken from my flying log book.

My thanks are due to Mr L.A. Jackets (now retired) of the Air Historical Branch and to Air Chief Marshal Sir Theodore McEvoy for information on the ADGB organization in 1927; to Wing Commander T.E. Guttery, M.B.E., in charge of Historical research in the Shuttleworth Collection, for the performance figures on those aeroplanes mentioned which were in operational use during the years 1925 to 1929, and also for other information on Service procedure during those years: to Flight International for photographs of aircraft: also to the Irvin Airchute Co., for information and pictures of early parachuting methods; to Mr Nayler, the Royal Aeronautical Society Librarian, to the RAE Librarian, to the Royal Air Force Henlow, the Imperial War Museum, to Wing Commander Turnbull, Charles Brown, M.V. Handscombe and many others who earnestly searched records for the required illustrations, including *Flight* and Mr Bateman of the Air Historical Branch in the Ministry of Defence who was able to provide some of the rarer photographs.

I am particularly grateful to Marshal of the Royal Air Force, Sir Charles Elworthy who read this book in typescript and has written the Foreword to it which puts the story as told into perspective with the present day attitude to the Defence Services.

Last but, by no means least, I have to thank Captain D.J. Turner of British European Airways who read the book for me in its early typescript form and made many invaluable suggestions and essential corrections.

A.H.W.

Whistley Bridge Field
October 1971

I Arrival at Flying Training School

On 17 January 1925 an event took place on the Royal Air Force Station at Digby in Lincolnshire which, had it been noticed in the world, might have caused elation or consternation amongst England's friends or foes abroad. Whether the elation would have been amongst our friends and the consternation amongst our foes, or the other way round, I am not in a position to judge since I took part in the event. It was the arrival of the latest draft of Acting Pilot Officers (on probation) who aspired to become officers and pilots in the Royal Air Force. We were a pretty mixed lot.

Whatever the views might have been abroad amongst our friends and foes, the Station Adjutant had no doubts at all about us when he interviewed one group of six pupils. His view was perhaps accentuated by the fact that one of our number's first question on arrival was whether he could have two days' leave to settle some important financial matters. The Adjutant looked us over, his glare particularly fastening on the leave-applicant: 'Scum' he assessed us collectively, but perhaps a little unfairly. He went on: 'We know what you're like . . . can't get another job . . . bankrupts . . . unsuccessful motor salesmen . . . black sheep . . .' He went on to list most of the dubious reasons which drove men into the French Foreign Legion in those days. Then he brightened up:

'But we'll sort you out. Some of you may make the grade.'

His expression belied that optimism.

'For the rest, we'll get rid of you quick enough. A quick look at a Bradshaw and a bowler hat . . .'

This was not a particularly encouraging reception to those of us who had joined the Air Force because we wanted to serve and wanted to fly. But we were, and he was right in this, a pretty mixed lot. The occupations of 'unsuccessful motor salesmen' and 'bankrupts' was not far short of the mark for a few, and it was certainly true that a high proportion of that draft had tried and failed to get any other job. I was not quite in that category since I had just got my engineering degree at Cambridge and had been offered a job as maintenance engineer looking after the dough-mixing machinery in a bakery at the princely salary of £200 per annum. I had decided that learning to fly would be more exciting.

The adjutant's welcoming remarks to our group did not particularly discourage me since I, and the three other university entrants in that draft, had already had six weeks' probationary attachment to a Royal Air Force Squadron where we had become imbued with the really deep and sincere dedication of most of the Air Force personnel in those days. Also we had already been accepted as suitable candidates for a commission, so our chances of that quick glance at a Bradshaw and a bowler hat were fairly remote — so long as we could learn to fly. None of us, I think, doubted our ability to do that. We also enjoyed an antedate for promotion which would make us Flying Officers after six months, that is, halfway through the training course at Digby.

Of the other three university entrants, one had come from Dublin University, one from Bristol and the third from Cambridge, like me. Since the Cambridge man had taken his degree in biology we had not met there. We had first met when we were both sent to No. 2 Squadron at Manston for our six weeks' probation.

Apart from the four university entrants on the course, there were two Army officers on secondment and an ex-army officer, married and a little older than all of us, who even supported the two war medals 'Mutt and Jeff' on his uniform. He, inevitably from his age and married state, became known as 'Daddy' Holmes. He was also a County cricketer in the Sussex team.

The remaining 23 members of that course entry were composed — apart from the adjutant's accurate assessment of a few — of seventeen to nineteen-year-olds almost straight from school and a few around twenty years old who had tried their hand at one or two jobs near their homes and then found that the Air Force offered good pay, a rather glamorous job, and excellent facilities for sport and games.

At that time the Air Force was definitely a glamorous job with then, as now, its smart sky-blue uniform, and the popular image of the 'daring bird man'. Some elements in the other two Services affected to look down on the Air Force as 'not quite the thing', but the serious elements accepted us as an essential force in the country's defence services and acknowledged the almost fabulous traditions which the Royal Flying Corps and later the Royal Air Force had built up in the four years of war between 1914 — 1918.

If some of the younger members of our course were a little discouraged by the reception they got from the Station adjutant, their morale was restored quickly by a more inspiring reception from the Commanding Officer of the Station. He gave us a brief but heartening talk on what sort of a Service we had joined and what he expected of us in that Service. His name was Wing Commander

Royal Air Force Digby, 1925

Tedder, known to the world a quarter of a century later as Marshal of the Royal Air Force Lord Tedder — a good friend to me on many occasions.

During the morning of the first day we were sorted into two main groups which would alternate between flying instruction in the morning, and ground instruction in the afternoon, thus not over-loading the instruction staff in either. We were also sub-divided into smaller groups for flying instruction and allotted to individual instructors. I and three others were allotted to Sgt George Lowdell, who was one of three other instructors in the Avro 504K flight under the Flight Commander, Flt Lt Fogarty, now retired as Air Chief Marshal Sir Francis Fogarty. Amongst the pupils on the course were also some corporals and sergeants who had been selected to train as sergeant pilots.

In the afternoon we were issued with our flying clothing, which consisted of a Sidcot suit as the main item, a fur-lined flying helmet, fur-lined triplex goggles and fur-lined gloves. In the open cockpits of the Avro and on the cold January days, we needed all those fur linings during our half-hour instruction flights: the seven thicknesses of the Sidcot flying suit were also much appreciated for the same reason. We were also issued with a pair of Service overalls for use when we were learning technicalities in the workshops or helping to wash the castor oil off the Avros after flying.

For our theoretical (ground) instruction we were issued with the various Service manuals on flying and all associated technical

3

problems. Last but not least, we were issued with the Manual of Air Force Law and the massive King's Regulations and Air Council Instructions, with an almost equally massive bunch of amendments to it which we had to insert early on in the course. In fact the King's Regulations was quite good reading — for the first time — and I found the Manual of Air Force Law fascinating, indeed stimulating when one read of the more serious offences which carried the penalty of '. . . . death or such less punishment . . ' I wondered whether the Station adjutant had that in mind as a final resort if he couldn't arrange for the 'Bradshaw and bowler hat'. But a streak of human kindness and sympathy in the Air Council's outlook was revealed in at least one paragraph in King's Regulations. It acknowledged that if one was killed, pay would continue up to and including the day one was killed!

Apart from these arrival formalities we were given a medical check-up which, amongst the whole course, spread over a few days, and we spent our leisure and meal times studying our fellow pupils. Dinner in the Officers' Mess was compulsory for four days in the week, but pupils, for the first few months, were not required to wear Mess Kit, since it was considered that it might turn out — for some of us — to be an entirely unnecessary expense — as prophesied by the Station adjutant.

During the first six months we were given intensive drill on the parade ground. It was the Chief of the Air Staff, Sir Hugh Trenchard's policy that the Royal Air Force must be able to drill as well as the Brigade of Guards, and our Sergeant Major certainly made every effort to achieve that standard. From my point of view there was no great problem since I had learnt my drill in the Eton OTC. under a Guards Sergeant Major, and again gone through drill in the Cambridge OTC, but strangely for those days, many on the course had never drilled before in their lives. Another reason for my finding drill no problem was that I had injured a foot and was excused drill on medical grounds. Although the Squadron Leader Admin. thought I might be 'swinging the lead' over this foot, the senior Medical officer supported me and it was admitted by the Sergeant Major that I was one of the few who really needed no instruction in drill. The two Army officers were exempt anyhow.

PT, in the cold grey light of a winter's dawn, was a different thing since that was supposed to make us healthy and alert for the rest of the day. My foot saved me from a lot of that. Later in the course the Flt Lt on the staff who was supposed to give us PT found it rather tiring, getting up at 7 am every week-day morning, so he appointed one of the Army officers as his deputy to do the job for him. We soon perceived the weakness in this system and ceased to turn up ourselves for PT, encouraged thereto by the fact that the Army officer often failed to turn up himself. One morning, in a fit of dedication to duty, the Army officer did turn up and found no one on PT at all. He put all our names in to the Flt Lt, who told us he would consider what disciplinary action he would take next day. The next morning, punctually at 7am we threw the Army officer into a cold bath and intimated that the same thing would probably happen to the staff Flt Lt. The latter complained we were 'letting the side down and not playing the game' but that was the end of PT in the morning. So far as I know the Squadron Leader Admin. never turned up himself to check PT attendance, and the Flt Lt was in no position himself to report us. I don't remember that our health or alertness suffered: the Army officer was certainly very alert with a healthy complexion at breakfast that morning.

The training course at Digby was to last for one year, divided up into two periods of 5 months, each with a four week leave at the end. At the end of each 5 month period one entry was passed out and a new entry came in. In many ways we were fortunate in our senior course since they were a relatively civilized lot, albeit fairly wild, particularly on the monthly guest nights when it was a tradition that no one should go to bed until the last guest had left. The penalty for infringement of this tradition was extraction from repose and immersion in a cold bath. There were, however, no traditional initiation rites and certainly no organized bullying, as was reported from the Royal Air Force College at Cranwell, in those days, which was just down the road from us. Many of the young new arrivals had still to find out how much alcohol, if any, they could take and still behave like 'officers and gentlemen'. Again the rough justice of a cold bath was meted out to those young pupils who overestimated their capacity for alcohol and underestimated its effect on their ability to behave as tradition required.

2 Flying the Avro 504K

It is recorded in my Pilot's Flying Log Book (Air Ministry publication Book 425) that my first flight with my instructor, Sergeant Lowdell, was at 9.10 am on January 23 1925. Presumably the arrival formalities or bad weather had prevented flying earlier. According to the *ab initio* flying training syllabus for those days, we were supposed to be given 2 hours air experience before serious instruction began so we did not have to count that time as dual instruction in our, and our instructor's, endeavour to get off solo as quickly as possible. In fact I had already had 9 hours 35 minutes air experience in the back seat of a Bristol Fighter, but with no dual controls, during my six weeks' attachment to No. 2 Squadron, so I went straight into instruction from the first flight. How lucky I was with my instructor George Lowdell! Apart from being a magnificent pilot he was the most inspiring teacher one could have to initiate one into the art and mystery of flying, and it was both an art and certainly a mystery to us in those days. George Lowdell's enthusiasm for flying and his sheer joy in it was transmitted to his pupils, giving them those two factors, enthusiasm and confidence, which are so helpful, indeed necessary, to a pupil. It was a great pleasure to me, forty years later, to enlist George Lowdell's help when we were making the Twentieth Century Fox film 'The Blue Max', in which George flew with my team of pilots.

My first flight with George was therefore called 'air experience', although it was mostly instruction since I was shown the operation and effect of the controls. The Avro 504K as an aeroplane was very easy to fly and very forgiving to pupils' mistakes, even to the extent of (usually) not killing them when they spun it into the ground. The problems facing a pupil learning to fly on the Avro 504K in those days will probably be best appreciated by a reader today if I digress at this point to describe the main characteristics of the Avro, and particularly of its engine.

To start off with, and for some reason I could never understand, the Avro seldom seemed to catch fire after a crash even though its rotary engine seemed to be vomiting flames out of its open exhaust ports and spraying fuel in all directions. Its fuel tank was situated immediately behind the engine. The lateral aileron control was soggy

6

by modern standards; the rudder and elevator were more positive but varied in 'feel' considerably according to whether the engine was on power or off as one would expect, and the force required to operate the controls varied very much according to speed. The available speed range varied (according to load) between a stalling speed of about 30 m.p.h. and a maximum attainable speed of about 140 m.p.h. in an almost vertical dive when the controls became almost as solid as those of our early supersonic fighters when they were diving at transonic speeds. So far as my experience went in the Avro I only once, later in my training, got into this rather unhappy state by trying to fly upside down. As we only had seat belts we had to cling on to the bracing wires under the seat with one hand to keep ourselves in; this left no hand on the fuel lever. In the ensuing confusion which started in an inverted dive and developed into an attempt to pull out as though finishing a loop — but with the engine full on — I think I achieved the Avro's TV (terminal velocity) but by dint of hard pulling on the control column the Avro ultimately regained level flight. The cruising speed of the Avro varied between about 65 m.p.h. and 70 m.p.h. according to the condition of the Avro. A new one with a new engine — seldom trusted in the hands of a pupil — might do a good 70 m.p.h. whereas an old one with soggy fabric on the wings and oil-soaked fabric on the fuselage, with dents in the cowlings and near time-expired engine would do well if it cruised at 65 m.p.h. Instructors could view the hazards involved in the handling of such an Avro by an inept pupil with comparative equanimity. Indeed we used to be told of one Commanding Officer of a Flying Training School who was so skilful in crashing that he would frequently 'roll up' an old Avro scientifically so that the damage resulting exceeded the 50 per cent figure laid down by the Air Ministry for justifying a 'write-off' and thus provide his unit with a brand new Avro from the depot.

The pilot had virtually no control over the cruising speed of the Avro since the Mono engine was either full throttle or shut off in cruising flight. The most convenient speed for going into a loop was between 80 and 90 m.p.h. attained in a dive. The Avro would do half rolls and stall turns quite impressively with the use of a lot of rudder, but the ineffective aileron control and the large biplane span made it almost impossible to do a reasonable roll. A 'falling leaf' looked particularly dramatic because the Avro fell from side to side and lost height comparatively slowly. No lateral control is needed for this manoeuvre since it is merely a stall to right and left alternatively. It would go into a spin and come out again very easily but it gave very little warning, if a pupil stalled it carelessly, before it started spinning. For this reason all pupils were taught to spin and recover before they were allowed to go on their first solo.

The first part of our training, very similar to the procedure today, was to try the controls and see what each one did. After that the instructor would usually look after the rudder control, which was rather sensitive, whilst the pupil got used to the lateral control and the elevator. When he had mastered all three controls flying level he would proceed to turns, then climbing and gliding turns and perhaps attempt a few landings and take-offs, but with the instructor watching the engine handling all the time. All this time the pupil was himself trying to master the engine control, which was the most important and the most difficult part of flying the Avro. It was essential to be able to handle the engine properly before attempting taxiing and take-off by oneself.

The engine in the Service Avro 504K was a Monosoupape rotary engine (Mono for short) which, as its name implies, had only one valve in each cylinder head which served both as an exhaust valve and an (air) inlet valve. The fuel mixture found its way in through the hollow crankshaft on which the whole engine rotated. The flywheel effect of this large rotating mass gave wonderfully smooth running when everything was working properly. The fuel inlet was controlled by the pilot by a single lever which was called the 'fine adjustment', and the pilot had to ensure that the right amount of fuel went in to obtain the right mixture. Apart from the position of this control lever the amount of fuel that got into the engine depended on how high one was, how fast one was going and — very important — how much pressure there was in the fuel tank, the pressure being applied by a windmill pump on a centre section strut and controlled by a release valve in the cockpit. For all these reasons it was advisable to ease the fuel lever (fine adjustment) back every now and then to ensure the mixture was not getting too rich. If it did get too rich the engine slowly lost power and black smoke would trail behind the Avro although the pilot could not see it. Very soon the engine would give a despairing cough and cut out. Thereafter the immediate corrective action was to close the fuel lever down completely and WAIT. After perhaps 8 seconds, which seemed like 10 minutes with the Avro necessarily in a steep glide towards the ground to maintain flying speed, the engine might come on again but, in the pupil's mind, there was the worrying thought that the engine might have cut because it was short of fuel. Thus many a pupil would push the fuel lever forward again hopefully after about 5 seconds and accentuate the trouble. This indecision usually resulted in the necessity for a forced landing with the pupil ill-prepared to select a suitable field since he had been concentrating on trying to get the engine going again. A common sequence of events after that was for the pupil to

8

An Avro 504K, powered by a 100 h.p. rotary engine This photograph, taken in 1971, shows American astronaut, Neil Armstrong,
flying with the author at Old Warden aerodrome

select a field hurriedly when he was only about 400 feet up and try
to position himself for landing in it into wind. He had very likely
forgotten which way the wind was blowing. Before his final approach
to the field he probably closed the fuel lever again to prevent the
engine coming on suddenly and spoiling his landing. If he had judged
his approach correctly and was well placed for a landing in a suitable
field, the engine would have been slowly 'unchoking' itself and, at
the moment of touch down, would have come on with a full throttle
roar, carrying the Avro a long way up the field. The pupil would then
decide that all was well after all and the engine was all right,
forgetting that he had closed the fuel lever. As the Avro approached
the far hedge the engine then cut again and the ensuing embarrassment usually cost the Air Ministry quite a lot in Avro repairs. But so
far as the pilot was concerned the Avro was very forgiving.
Sometimes the same sequence occurred except that the pilot might
have misjudged his approach to the field of his choice and as he
was about to drop on to the near hedge the engine came on for its
brief burst of power and then cut out to allow him an apparently
well judged landing in one field or the other. If he then described his
action with more imagination than accuracy he might achieve an
'above the average' assessment in his instructor's and Flight Commander's minds. But that probably did not last for long!

Lincolnshire's flat open country with large fields and low hedges
was ideal country for pupils with engine trouble, pupils who got
themselves lost, pupils who ran into bad weather, and indeed

Engine speed indicator

Oil drip feed visual indicator

Hand pump for fuel pressure

Control column with 'blip' switch on top

Air pressure release

'Bubble' (lateral level)

Compass

Fuel pressure guage

Air–speed indicator

Fuel cock

Engine switches

Throttle control (2-lever Le Rhone one-lever for Mono)

Rudder pedal

The cockpit of an Avro 504K

instructors who had fallen in love — perhaps only for the time being — with some farmer's daughter living nearby.

On the whole we were so well schooled in engine handling before we were sent off solo that most of us were well aware of the dangers of choking the engine and could manage it well enough. A few pupils never really mastered it and one was so unreliable that the pupils and many of the airmen used to look forward with pleasurable anticipation to every occasion when he was due to take off on his own. There was always the prospect of seeing that tell-tale trail of black smoke behind his Avro, followed by that despairing engine cough and then the anxious silence whilst the pupil's instructor threw his flying helmet on the ground and jumped on it, raising despairing hands to Heaven and calling witness to the fact that, 'God knows', he'd done his best for that inept pupil. By this time the pupil, despairing of a successful take off, would close the fuel lever instinctively to save running into the aerodrome boundary. If we were lucky that day the engine would recover with a roar and the Avro would end up in the hedge. When such events were pending it was considered anti-social if one did not call all one's friends out of the hangar to enjoy the spectacle.

This one particular pupil was so well known for his ability to provide us with what W.S. Gilbert termed '. . . . a source of innocent merriment . . .' that I once heard the Flight Sergeant of the Avro flight call out to a crowd of waiting and watching airmen: 'Now then you men, get back into the hangar. No need to stop work just because Pilot Officer Chokem is going to take off'. One could see the airmen didn't agree with him.

With a mastery of the engine handling and a fair ability in making the Avro do what one wanted in the air, the final pre-solo stage was reached when one perfected — or at least made reasonably reliable — one's ability to take-off and land. For some reason I found the take-off more difficult than the landing. This may have been partly due to an exceptional preoccupation with the engine handling, which was not a problem during the landing since one merely shut it off and left it windmilling. On take-off, after lining up into wind with the engine slightly starved of fuel and also controlled by 'blipping' on the ignition switch, one eased the fuel lever forward to the normal running position and there was then only a short run of some 50 yards into a light wind before one was airborne. One pushed the 'stick' forward to raise the tail and as it came up to take off position the gyroscopic forces of the rotating engine gave a slight kick to the right which had to be corrected on the rudder: only a slight kick but quite enough for the pupil to need to correct it, then he might overcorrect it, then overcorrect the overcorrection, etc. If this got

11

too bad it was advisable to abandon the take-off, particularly if the Avro had turned out of wind and was going towards the hangars or some major obstruction. Although many of my take-offs by this time — after a total of about 4 hours dual — were good enough, the odd one was a bit snakey. George, who was a psychologist as well as a brave man, (in this case particularly) decided that if I really felt I was on my own I would concentrate so hard that I could and would take-off straight. On one take-off, therefore, he turned round and knelt on his seat facing me and said: 'Now it's up to you. If you don't do it properly you'll kill us both'. The take-off was as straight as any Avro ever did! I never forgot that lesson.

I found landing the Avro fairly easy when I had once got firmly in my mind that the art of landing properly depended on holding the Avro as close to the ground as possible but holding it off the ground for as long as possible. If this was done with precision a good landing always resulted. The standard approach technique for the Avro was to shut the fuel lever and therefore cut the engine completely at about 800 feet on the cross-wind leg before turning into wind. One then did a series of gliding turns always towards the aerodrome and keeping it in sight. The last gliding turn should be finished at about 200 feet as one turned into wind close to the aerodrome fence. One should then still be a little too high to allow for eventualities so one side-slipped the Avro to lose the spare height, levelled out at 20 feet from the steep approach glide and flew smoothly over the grass with the wheels about 6", but not more than 1 foot above it. As the Avro slowed down one pulled the control column slowly back until the tail skid and wheels touched together. If the wheels touched first one was all right so long as one did not try to pull the tail down too soon. When firmly on the ground one pushed the fuel lever forward and the engine, still spinning because of its great rotary inertia, would come to life again with a bit of a roar. It could then be controlled by the magneto 'blip' switch on top of the control column until one had adjusted the fuel lever to a very weak mixture, after which it would attain its rather erratic idling speed with the cylinders firing in short bursts. Some of the very experienced instructors would practically never use the 'blip' switch from start to stop since they knew the exact position for the fuel level for slow running and taxiing, but this sort of familiarity with the Mono engine was not achieved by pupils.

I should emphasize here that the relative difficulty I experienced as between achieving reliable landings and take-offs, was not by any means common to all pupils. Some found landing easy, take-offs difficult; some found take-offs easy, landings difficult; some never mastered either and quickly qualified for the adjutant's 'bowler hat'. The variations and permutations were almost infinite. I knew of one

12

pupil whose every landing from his first was almost perfection and he never lost the art. Another, 'Daddy' Holmes on our course, mastered the landing technique very quickly and then lost it just before he was due to go solo. It delayed his solo by some four hours, after which he suddenly mastered the art again and never looked back. Fifteen years later he was Chief Instructor at the Central Flying School.

The final stages of instruction, just before solo, consisted in learning to spin and come out of the spin, side-slip on the approach, try one or two forced landings with simulated engine failure with particular emphasis on the need to put the Avro immediately into a steep glide if the engine failed irrespective of what was in front of one. The Avro, like all the biplanes with the light wing loadings and high drag of those days would stall within a few seconds of engine failure if one did not push the nose down quickly to maintain flying speed. Indeed if one happened to be climbing at a slow speed at an unusually steep angle it was not possible to push the nose down quickly enough to avert a momentary stall, but that did not necessarily end up in a spin if one handled the controls properly. After this, I think necessary, digression, we return to the main story.

By 6 February, a fortnight after I had started learning and after 5 hours 45 minutes instruction plus 1 hour 40 minutes 'air experience', I was pronounced ready for a solo test, which was always done by the Avro flight commander, at that time Flt Lt Fogarty. This was always a pretty thorough test and mine lasted for 35 minutes. It was a standard procedure and acted as a double check on the pupil's fitness to fly solo. There would obviously have been a number of serious questions to be answered if a pupil were killed on his first solo — then as now. I passed this solo test and was sent off to the medical officer for a superficial check-up: this was also standard procedure before a first solo. The Senior Medical Officer affected embarrassment when I told him I had come for the solo check-up. 'I've been signing chits to say you can't drill and can't do PT and now you come and say you're fit to go off solo?'

'Well that's rather different, Sir.'

'And I suppose running all the way here from the Flights is different too?'

'Oh yes Sir. You see I can sort of hop off the bad foot when I'm running. Flying isn't like marching about Sir. And when we're doing PT, Sir, we have to twist our feet all the time, Sir.'

I knew the SMO had his tongue in his cheek, but I thought it as well to put up a case, also I hoped to preserve my immunity from drill and PT for a bit longer.

'All right, come along here after your solo and I'll look at that foot again. Good luck.'

13

An Avro 504K airborn

George took me on a couple of circuits to give me, and him, confidence and then climbed out of the front seat of the Avro, fastening his seat belt very carefully so that it could not foul the front control column. I kept the engine running slowly with the fuel lever at a very weak setting and a bit of blip switch. The Avro was already positioned for a straight take-off and George waved me away. It was a worrying moment for both of us, but an exhilarating one for me. I knew I could fly the wide circuit required on a first solo, but I had got used to the reassuring sight of George's head in front of me. When I left the ground I stopped worrying: there was a lot else to think about. As I passed over the far hedge I became aware that the engine was running rough so I eased the fuel lever back to be sure I wasn't choking it. The engine gave to me a reassuring splutter proving it was not choked, but to George it probably gave near heart failure. I then realised that during the brief idling period whilst George got out and tied up his seat belt one plug must have oiled up. The Mono still had plenty of power for a circuit with one of its nine cylinders not working, but one didn't want another to go out as well. I did an extra wide circuit to gain height before turning to do a gliding turn into wind if the engine gave more trouble, but it kept going well on eight cylinders and I came in for a normal approach and, as often happens under stress, made a good landing. George climbed in and told me to taxi in. He seemed pleased. One cylinder cutting out on a Mono was not considered to be a crisis whatever a pupil might feel about it on his first solo.

It was traditional in those days to give one's instructor some small present when one had gone solo. In some cases it would take the form of a bottle of champagne, but I felt the event called for a more permanent memento so I gave George a silver cigarette case engraved with his initials. I wonder if he still has it? If he kept such mementos from all the pupils he has sent off solo he would have quite a houseful. Perhaps, after all, it should have been a bottle of champagne!

3 Ground training—Administration—Courts Martial

Education in all the complementary subjects required by an Air Force pilot, apart from flying, continued on a parallel course to our flying training. This covered such diverse subjects as aerodynamics, navigation, meteorology, airframe rigging, engine overhaul, armament, W/T and R/T, as we termed the then rather primitive radio, although it was not fitted in any of the aeroplanes at the FTS, Air Force Law, administration, drill and other minor subjects on which we had lectures from outside lecturers. Aerodynamics, navigation and meteorology were dealt with by straightforward lectures. Airframe rigging and engine overhaul combined theoretical work in a lecture room and practical work in the Aircraft Repair Section (ARS) and Engine Repair Section (ERS). During the year we were at the FTS we were expected to assemble and rig an Avro 504K completely, including installing its engine. The great day came, at the end of the course, when this Avro, after a very thorough inspection by skilled airmen, was test flown by one of the staff. The test flight was usually done by a great character on the staff, Flt Lt E.L. Barrington. He had lost one eye playing hockey and was therefore due to be retired from the Service on medical grounds. He received notice of this from the Air Council during our time at Digby and delighted in the fact that on the same day that he received the Air Council notification that he was no longer considered fit for flying duties he received another letter from Group HQ notifying him that a Vickers Vimy twin-engined bomber had been forced-landed in a small field and they wanted him to fly it out since they considered he was the most able and experienced pilot in the Group.

Another rather tragic anecdote he told revealed all too clearly to us the desperate measures taken at training schools during the war to try and fill the front line squadron in France after the ghastly casualties they sustained. Barrington himself had passed out top of his course in the training school and was thus given 48 hours extra leave before joining his squadron in France. When he got there and reported to the Adjutant he asked where he could find the other two new pilots who had come to this squadron from his course. He was told they were 'missing', and the Adjutant added in explanation that they '. . . had of course arrived in the Squadron two or three days

16

ago.' Barrington drew his own conclusions as he calculated his chances, but he made up his mind that he was going to survive. I think we learned more from Barrington about the Service in general than from almost any other officer at Digby. For one thing, he mixed freely with the pupils and talked to us in a relaxed and friendly way, which some of the other instructors seemed to find difficult.

The work in the engine repair shop was a messy business since the rotary engines were lubricated by castor oil, which seemed to change into a black, treacly and unwashable mess when partially burnt in a time-expired engine. The standard way of washing the engine parts was to boil them in caustic soda, itself a fairly unpleasant substance. We tended to avoid ERS except when overhauling the Rolls-Royce Falcon engine, which was an inspiring job since it was foremost in design to a formula which continued for the next quarter of a century.

Armament training included learning to shoot with the 0·303 Service rifle and to strip, clean and clear stoppages in the Vickers and Lewis machine guns which were then the standard armament for all Service aeroplanes. Administration was chiefly concerned with discipline and the Service stores procedures, whereby everything which belonged to the Service had to be on someone's charge and, if anything was lost, someone had to pay for it. Our training chiefly concerned learning how to avoid having anything on one's own charge.

Drawing equipment from stores and returning it was done through a fairly complicated system of vouchers. We were impressed with the importance of knowing how the system worked so that we could avoid costly losses, or at least avoid paying for them if the loss occurred. There were intriguing, but probably apocryphal, stories of officers who had apparently lost complete aeroplane hangars at the end of the war — probably because they had never been built after the armistice — but converted them on a Form 673 from 'Hangars Aeroplane' to 'Hangers Coat' and then certified on another appropriate form that 'through fair wear and tear' the coat hangers (Vocabulary price 9d) should be written off. I personally studied the system with great attention and, in 30 years, I don't remember ever having to pay for anything, although I had quite a few near misses.

Air Force Law involved us in a few interesting lectures. We were also made to attend any Courts Martial which took place on our Station or at another Station nearby. Our first Court Martial concerned one of our own number, who may be called P/O Hand. He was a harmless individual but happened to commit an indiscretion early on in the course. He had, in fact, described a corporal in what

17

many of us thought were accurate, but the corporal thought uncomplimentary, terms. The occasion was just before a lecture started on a rainy day, and many of the pupils were waiting outside the locked door of the lecture hut, whilst a corporal with the key of the hut refused to unlock it until the lecture was due to start. There were still a few minutes to go and the corporal was adamant about not unlocking the door. Other pupils came up and joined the wet and impatient group and asked them why they liked standing outside and getting soaked. P/O Hand explained the situation:

'We don't like it but this — corporal won't unlock the door.'

The corporal took exception to the adjective, which admittedly was heard perhaps more frequently in the London Docks than in the precincts of a lecture hall, and reported the incident to higher authority. P/O Hand was unlucky in the fact that the incident occurred at a stage in the course when the staff was beginning to know which of us were likely to make the grade and which were likely to be sub-standard. They had also decided that since the course was beginning to get a bit unruly it would be a good idea to make an example of one of us. So they looked for some convenient indiscretion. They would not have had to wait long anyhow, but they selected P/O Hand's remark about the corporal, perhaps because they considered him to be expendable, and also because it was a suitable offence to illustrate the workings of those two much-used sections in Air Force Law dealing with '. . . conduct unbecoming an officer and a gentleman . . .' and '. . . conduct prejudicial to good order and discipline.'

P/O Hand was placed under close arrest and the case against him was prepared. The rest of us were detailed to take turns on 'escort duty' to ensure he did not run away. Eventually we were all detailed to attend the Court Martial 'under instruction' and the President, a Squadron Leader from Group Headquarters, advised by a barrister from the Judge Advocate General's office, presided over proceedings. When any suitable opportunity occurred the Court was closed and we were told about the finer points of Law. On the whole the case was a dull one only briefly livened up by the defending officer's cross-examination of the corporal, the chief prosecution witness:

'Now Corporal Jones, what did the accused call you?'

'Ee called me a "something" corporal.'

'A "something" corporal? There's no harm in that?'

'Well 'ee didn't say "something".'

'I thought you said he did?'

'Well Sir, I don't like to say what he did say.'

'Come, come corporal, the Court must know what was said. Don't be afraid and speak up. What did the accused say?'

18

The corporal looked embarrassed, and then came out with the offending word. Everyone knew what it was going to be anyhow, so the defending officer affected no astonishment.

'Well corporal, you've heard that word before in the barrack-room haven't you? After all, taken the right way, it might just mean you had an affectionate nature.'

'P/O Hand didn't mean it that way Sir. I didn't like an officer and a . . . and a . . .and a . . . , well an officer, Sir, using a word like that to me. We weren't in no barrack-room Sir, and even there we don't say those sort of things.'

Perhaps Corporal Jones was right. The Court Martial came to an end. P/O Hand was dismissed from the Service — *pour encourager les autres* — and a week later we were attending another Court Martial on a somewhat similar charge. This time it was on an airman — 'conduct prejudicial . . . .' — who on being told by his Sergeant to sweep up the floor of the barrack-room had said he was not going to do it, and (offending words) 'That bloody Sergeant can do it himself.' The Sergeant took exception to that adjective. The President of that Court was a dear old Squadron Leader who specialized in Court Martial activities. Before the final summing up, in closed court, he explained to us that we must not be shocked by such words used in a barrack-room. Although, he said, we were doubtless not accustomed to using, or even hearing, a word like 'bloody' it was not uncommon in the barrack-room. We listened to this discourse, so complimentary to us, with astonishment and some amusement. Only two weeks before one of our number had had his commission abruptly terminated for using another word which Corporal Jones had assured us would never be used in a barrack-room.

Courts Martial were a never-failing source of interest to me, perhaps due to the fact that my father had been a practising barrister and used to tell us about fine legal points when his (later) responsibilities as a local JP produced interesting cases. This early knowledge certainly helped me in later years in the Service when I was often selected as President of some Court Martial. Claiming, very humbly, an outlook which seems to resemble that of the Lords of Appeal today, I used to take delight in finding some good legal point for mitigating the sentence on some erring, but otherwise good-hearted offender. In this I often found myself in fairly violent disagreement with what used to be common advice from the representative of the Judge Advocate General's office in those days. Some of these representatives used to emphasize to the Court members that his office, the JAG's, in considering the sentence later, and before promulgation, could reduce a sentence but not increase it, and therefore the Court should not err on the side of leniency. I always considered this advice entirely wrong in principle since if Courts worked on it they might tend always to impose the maximum sentence so as to give the JAG's office a free hand, and the JAG's office had not the advantage of seeing the witnesses and hearing the evidence first hand. Many of the Judge Advocates were good and sound lawyers, but during the years I am now describing we often thought that some of them were barristers who had failed to make a living at the Bar and sought less exacting, less rewarding, but more secure employment in the Services. But who were we to judge the Judge Advocates — except the potential sufferers from their 'blind' justice!

4 More flying on the Avro 504K

After four months from the start of the course we were all flying alone with around 20 hours solo on our log books. I was venturing on more sophisticated forms of aerobatics and also practising forced landings in fields with simulated engine failures, but we were not allowed to land. Spinning was encouraged and I usually stalled the Avro once or twice on each solo flight to get the feel of it before it 'dropped' and occasionally let it go into a full spin but pulled out again fairly quickly! We used to have checks by flying dual with our instructors at frequent intervals of about one in three flights at first, but these became less frequent as we progressed. After four months my dual checks were at the rate of about one in seven flights, but if one was observed doing something stupid a few quick checks were imposed. By then I had more or less perfected looping, but occasionally 'lost' the prop: *i.e.* the engine failed to start on levelling out after the loop. One must remember that in looping the Avro one had to shut the fine adjustment as one came down in the vertical dive to stop the engine over-speeding, the heavy engine then kept rotating as one pulled out of the dive but if one was a bit slow in pushing the lever forward again when flying level the engine would slow down and stop and one was faced with the rather embarrassing sight of a stationary propeller. The immediate action then was to dive steeply to reach a speed of about 110 m.p.h. when the engine would start turning again and start up — if one had not choked it with fuel in one's attempt to get it going before. The height needed for this manoeuvre was only about 400 feet, but a pupil was wise to allow 1000 feet so that he had something in hand to select a forced landing site if he failed to get the engine going.

I had, in fact, attempted a loop on my second solo flight, partly because other pupils had said they were going to and partly because I thought it would give me confidence and raise my prestige having done it. It was an untidy and almost unclassifiable manoeuvre that resulted; it gave me no confidence at all, George Lowdell was scornful about it and few, if any, other pupils were foolish enough to try.

As mentioned before, flying inverted was very difficult in the Avro, since we had only seat belts, no shoulder straps of the Sutton

21

Fighting Harness type, nor had one in those days any parachutes in any of the Service aeroplanes. They were introduced for fighter aircraft first about 2 years later and a great reassurance they were when we had them. One was not so worried about an aeroplane breaking up in the air or getting out of control, but most of us had a very considerable awareness of the dangers of fire if one happened to be too high up to be able to land quickly. We had all heard stories of this type of disaster.

By this time most of the more accomplished pupils were gaining confidence. One particularly brilliant pupil, 'Scruffy' Purvis, cousin of the famous 'Bruin' Purvis, claimed one day in the Mess that he had flown under the telegraph wires of the Lincoln road that morning. We all expressed disbelief and said we would appoint a witness to watch him do it next day to prove his story. He said he had only said he *had* done it, he did not say he would do it again. But we all ganged up on him and next morning he was followed by the appointed witness: sure enough he did it. This and other exploits, or alleged exploits, inspired one of our number, P/O Rank, to do something daring a few days later to celebrate the fact that it was his 21st birthday. He was one of those pupils who normally took no risks and was therefore hardly qualified to try anything out of the ordinary. The particular deed of daring he selected — although for reasons to be appreciated later he was rather hazy about his intentions after the event — was a series of what he called 'spot landings'. We were never quite sure what he meant by this unless it was intended to be a landing where the whole operation was completed in one spot. This he achieved since he went in almost vertically. He had made the approach in an ever tightening turn and finally got into a spin and went straight into the ground. The Avro, as I have indicated earlier, was very forgiving: so long as one was in the back seat, from which all pupils flew, and so long as one remained in the spin right down to the ground. If P/O Rank had been a better pilot he might have been in a steep dive after recovering from the spin. That probably would have been fatal. This degree of safety does not apply in modern aeroplanes unfortunately, but in P/O Rank's case, after all the twanging of wires and crunching of wood was finished, he crawled out of the wreckage completely unhurt. The accident was observed from the aerodorme and the usual convoy of Ambulance and Fire Tender was sent out. P/O Rank was put in the Ambulance and taken to sick quarters. This was normal routine since he had had a serious accident. Arriving at the sick quarters he had to wait a few minutes to see the Medical Officer, and, understandably, took the opportunity to go to the lavatory. It was here the real injury occurred. When he pulled the plug, which was one of those typical 1925 designs which had a high cistern with a heavy cast iron cover to it, the cover came off and landed on his head. He was knocked unconscious for a few minutes and sustained a large cut and bruise which made him look like a wounded aviator. In some ways this was a great embarrassment to him when next he went on week-end leave and met his girl friends and relatives. He tended to redden somewhat when his female admirers said: 'You poor bird-man: that cut on your head? Was it a terrible crash? Tell us how it happened. You mustn't ever risk doing this again.'

It was about this time that one of the instructors in the Avro flight decided to give a thrill to a farmer friend and his family nearby and told them that he was going to fly between two young poplar trees in a hedge near the house. He took the precaution of pacing out the distance between the trees very carefully to make sure there was enough room, and as an additional precaution, he placed a stick midway between the trees to give him the centre line. The next morning, during the normal testing period of Avros before the pupils arrived to fly, the instructor took off and flew over to the farm. On arrival overhead the distance between the trees seemed to have grown much smaller, but he had told the family he was going to fly between, so pride and prestige forced him to go on with the scheme. As he approached the trees the distance between seemed even smaller than from above — much, much smaller than when he measured them on the ground. But a small stick was showing in the middle so it must be all right, unless — awful thought — he had got the span of the Avro wrong? As a slight precaution he flew almost level with the top of the poplars where the gap was widest and the poplar trunks only a few inches thick. He took the Avro through at about 65 m.p.h. followed by the admiring gaze of the farmer and his family: this gaze turned to consternation as the Avro's outer wings hit both poplar trees and neatly chopped the top off them. The Avro shuddered slightly, but flew on with broken leading edges on all four wing tips. The instructor had flown between the wrong two trees, and, by an extraordinary coincidence, there happened to be a small stick in the hedge midway between these two as well as the others.

The Avro was repaired hurriedly and secretly and the Flight Commander told the instructor that it was a very bad example to the pupils — not checking up the trees properly! The Flight Commander himself was one of the best 'crazy flying' pilots we ever had and he was not above rather similar exploits himself. On the whole the flying instruction staff took a fairly lenient view on mildly irresponsible acts by pupils but came down very heavily on foolhardy ones. I think the instructors' greatest concern was over the uninspired pupil who had little or no joy in flying and was, in fact, rather frightened of it, rather more frightened than all the imaginative ones amongst us were. It was, of course, this slight but constant awareness of danger (if that is fear) which kept us alive.

I remember only one case of a pupil losing his nerve, as the phrase is, which usually seems to mean that an individual suddenly becomes aware of the danger in what he is doing. Although there must also be individuals who appreciate a danger but force themselves to keep going until perhaps a breaking point comes. This could well happen in war but was less likely in peacetime training. In this one case the critical point seemed to come when my instructor was teaching another of his pupils to side slip off surplus height before landing. The pupil did not level off from the side slip soon enough and although George took over immediately, putting the engine on, he was too late to avoid the undercarriage hitting the ground sideways and breaking up. George flew the Avro round the aerodrome for some time to use up fuel and also to ensure that the fire tender and ambulance were ready. By the time his fuel was almost used up we had all collected on the aerodrome to see what happened. George did two or three passes over the grass near the hangars to indicate exactly where he was going to land and then came in as for a normal landing. Some pilots thought that it would have been better to have come in more slowly and dropped it a few feet, but George rightly decided that, with broken struts below him, it was better to ensure scraping them clear rather than risk their coming up through the fuselage. The landing was perfect and for a second it seemed as though the Avro might slither to a standstill on the remains of the undercarriage, but whilst still doing about 15 m.p.h. — it was a calm day with little wind — the Avro nose sank to the ground and dug in so that the aeroplane started to somersault: fortunately it only got as far as standing almost vertically on its nose and then it fell back the right way up. The pupil appeared to come right out of the rear cockpit as the Avro tipped up and then he disappeared completely back into the cockpit as it fell back. Neither George nor his pupil were hurt at all. A wonderfully unimaginative comment was made by a pupil watching on the ground:

'But if he knew his undercarriage was broken why did he land?'

It was this pupil who was watching on the ground who then, perhaps for the first time, realised that when things go wrong in the air other things start happening very quickly and many of them are inevitable. At his own request he abandoned flying for a quieter and less exciting life — but this accident was not really a very bad one by comparison with some we had later. The operational types we were to train on later, like the Bristol Fighter and the Sopwith Snipe, were not so forgiving of human errors as the Avro 504K.

24

By modern standards when engine failure is very rare indeed, the rotary engine was unreliable. When one considered that it was one of the earliest designs of successful aero engines and a completely revolutionary design from any type of engine ever built before, it was astonishing how well it kept going. It is true that plugs used to oil- or soot-up and that inexperienced pilots used to choke it by mishandling of the fine adjustment fuel lever, or on the near time-expired engines oil used to spew out on to the ignition slip ring behind the engine and thus cut it out, but there were very few mechanical failures on the Mono. Personally I never had an engine failure on the Mono in my Service career, although I did one or two precautionary landings because of unusual noises or vibrations. One of these occurred after I had done just under 5 hours solo flying. I had taken off on a day with a light wind intending to do side slips and half rolls, but at about 200 feet I became aware that the engine was running rough and making a very peculiar noise. I turned down wind quickly and, since the aerodrome was clear, landed down wind. George Lowdell was out in a flash and asked me what I was doing since I still kept the engine going so as to taxi in. I told him that the engine was behaving rather oddly so he told me to stop it. He then looked it over and felt all the cylinders: this was the standard way to find out if they were all firing. He remarked that all the cylinders were hot so we had better give it another air test together. Then he suddenly said:

'Oh no we won't. Come and look at this.'

The cowling which enclosed the engine (see photograph on page 9) was discontinuous at the lower part to allow the exhaust gases and the cooling air to escape: to hold the cowling together there was a steel tie rod across the gap. This had come adrift at one end and had bent back into the rotating engine damaging all the push rods and valve gear. It was quite a marvel that the engine had kept going at all.

Cases had been known of rotary engines throwing complete cylinders off and still keeping running, but they were rare. On one occasion a Mono was being run on the ground on test to check it for roughness. One of our instructors was standing watching it from the side to see whether it might be running eccentrically due to worn main bearings on which it rotated. When he was satisfied with that he moved to the front of the engine and, as he moved, one of the cylinder valve assemblies blew out of a cylinder. With the force of the explosion in the cylinder and the centrifugal force of the rotating engine it went straight past where he had been standing and through the corrugated iron cladding of a hangar door. After that the instructor said it was the Flight Sergeant's job to check vibration in

Monos. The Flight Sergeant said that in all his 10 years of looking after rotary engines he had never been such a bloody fool as to watch them running from the side.

5 Inspecting–and being inspected

Concurrently with our flying instruction and ground instruction in aeronautical subjects, we were being initiated into other duties of an officer, such as airmen's kit inspections, checking on airmen's meals and advanced drill wherein we were taught to drill a squad ourselves as opposed to being drilled. Not far ahead of us loomed the annual inspection by the Air Officer Commanding (AOC). We were regaled by stories from the senior course as to what he would expect and what would happen to all of us if he did not get it.

Airmen's kit inspection was fairly straightforward but, as in the other similar jobs (including flying), we 'went dual' in instruction first before being allowed off solo. Kit inspection in each airmen's hut was done by the officer in charge of the hut, assisted by a sergeant or flight sergeant who could deal with any situation in which a young officer's inexperience rendered him at a distinct disadvantage. Senior course pupils were put in charge of individual huts and junior course students followed them round on inspections. There was a definite order for laying out kit and bedding and when one had got this firmly in one's mind one could see at a glance if any item was missing. Any item away for repair had to be replaced by a 'chit' recording the fact. The airmen 'stood by their beds' and were called to attention as the hut inspection started. Even for a young officer there were seldom any causes for embarrrassment in this job.

Inspection of airmen's meals was not quite such a precise affair. For instance, even in a restaurant, one is often faced with a difficult decision as to whether a piece of fish is eatable or uneatable. In the airmen's Mess in those far off days the decision was much more difficult since on some stations the airmen's (and indeed the officers') food was often almost uneatable. And one would expect this when officers in charge were virtually untrained in the art of catering and many of them disinterested in it as well, having joined the Air Force to fly. On the whole the actual quantity of food provided by the rations was quite adequate in bulk. On my first round of airmen's dinner, under instruction with a senior course pupil, I witnessed what was perhaps a time-honoured trick by airmen, but not very popular with sergeants. The duty of inspection of meals devolved on the Orderly Officer of the day, and he was accompanied by the Orderly Sergeant of the day, who called the dining room to attention as they entered. The Orderly Officer then called out 'Carry on' and the inspection began. They had already been through the kitchens. As the Orderly Officer and Orderly Sergeant approached each table the airmen stood up and the Orderly Officer asked:

'Any complaints?'

If one kept moving fairly quickly the airmen had little time to think up frivolous complaints and anyhow the Orderly Sergeant's eye (much less sympathetic than a young Orderly Officer's eye) was on the airmen. At one table we came to with four airmen standing up at it, one of the airmen, a large ginger headed Irishman, pushed forward a heaped up plate of 'stew and two veg.' and said:

'Excuse me Sir, but do you think that's a fair meal for one man?'

The young Orderly Officer answered quickly — too quickly for the Orderley Sergeant to intervene:

'Yes, I think that's a fair meal for one man.'

'Well Sir, it's supposed to do for all four of us.'

The airmen had heaped all the helpings onto one plate.

The situation was an embarrassing one for my 'instructor' of the senior course, but not for the Orderly Sergeant who clearly knew the airman and spoke very loud and clear:

'A/c2 Haggarty, report to me at 6 o'clock this evening at the Guard Room.'

We moved on and there were no more complaints within earshot of that incident.

As years went on up until the present time, these meal inspections have been brought more in accord with modern trends in discipline. Airmen are not called to attention and do not have to stand up as the officer goes to each table. If a very Senior officer, perhaps the AOC is going round a little more respect may be shown and this may include the time honoured reply to the VIP's question 'Any complaints' of 'None at all *today* Sir. I wish you'd come round *every* day Sir!'

The day of the AOC's inspection dawned bright and clear — which was a pity since a good solid and continuous downpour of rain can cover a multitude of sins and omissions. A slight tarnish on brass buttons can pass unnoticed seen through a thick film of moving water; badly wound puttees tend to tighten up with wet; ceremonial parades can never be expected to look very good in driving rain and if, as sometimes occurred, the parade was held in a hangar, then the more difficult drill manoeuvres like wheeling in line could not be done for want of space. But, alas, the day was bright and clear. We arose early and started the complicated business of getting into the (then) No. 1 dress of the Royal Air Force, which included breeches and puttees. I would still like to know where the man who invented puttees is buried so that I could go and jump on his grave, but they were probably invented so long ago that the man who did it may, with justice, have been burnt at the stake. They were fiendish things to put on, terribly uncomfortable and inhibiting to the circulation to wear, and almost always worked loose when one was marching. In addition to his other unattractive features, the inventor of puttees probably had cylindrically shaped legs since, even with the unscientifically designed bias woven into the puttees, they would never adjust themselves to any normal calf muscles I have ever known or seen, still less when those muscles are flexing as one drilled and marched. The art of putting on puttees, so far as there could be one, consisted in starting them round the ankles over the top of the boots and taking two or three turns there to establish stability for the spiral which then coiled up the calf. If one wound it too loose it worked still looser, came undone, trailed behind one when marching and when the rear rank on parade trod on it one fell on one's face. If one wound it too tight it inhibited the circulation of one's legs and one got cramp in both legs and was carried off parade in agony. A compromise was indicated but if achieved it was essential for the puttee to end up just below the knee on the outside of the leg. This was difficult in the case of one puttee and nearly impossible in the case of both if they were to match. Puttees as a form of dress for the Air Force were abolished, with no regrets, in the early 1930s, but in 1925 they were very much the thing.

Having got our puttees on and checked our brass buttons we had breakfast and assembled near the parade ground to be formed up as a second section of the officer cadet wing which was about a fifth part of the whole Station. We then marched on to the parade ground and took up our allotted place in front of the saluting base to await the arrival of the AOC when we would be called to attention for the General Salute and thereafter be inspected in detail before going through certain specified drill manoeuvres. By that time most of us were fairly proficient in drill but we had a few unreliable elements amongst us. There was 'Scruffy' Purvis, who was a magnificent pilot but always seemed to get castor oil on everything he wore, including his No. 1 dress. He was also psychologically unable to resist looking up when any aeroplane was heard overhead. He was put in the rear rank and not being very tall it was hoped he would escape notice. Another even more unreliable element was P/O Auckland-Wood who had spent most of his youth overseas where his father was reputed to be an eminent pro-consul in our eastern Empire. Auckland-Wood had a permanent inclination to stoop and it was generally accepted by us

29

that this resulted from living with his father and trying to share the intolerable responsibility of the 'White man's burden'. The stoop was a defect which was usually controllable for the relatively brief period of one ceremonial parade, but another defect of Auckland-Wood's was an almost uncontrollable tendency to turn his head from side to side. We ascribed this idiosyncracy to the necessity, in the regions of his father's domains, to watch out for tigers and dodge snakes, or — less exciting — just to shake off mosquitos and tse-tse flies. Perhaps, as in the case of the stoop, he was merely following another of his father's habits of looking from side to side so as not to miss friends and acquaintances who were trying to catch his eye on ceremonial occasions. However, on this particular ceremonial occasion Acting Pilot Officer (on probation) Auckland-Wood occupied a less exalted and, we hoped, less obvious position. It was, therefore, agreed by all, including Auckland-Wood, that he should join Purvis in adorning the rear rank, but being fairly tall (when not stooping) he had to be placed behind other taller pupils. This meant being at one end or the other of the line, and this ran the risk of giving the AOC an edgewise glimpse of him. With these defects in the make-up of a really rather charming personality, it was inevitable but regrettable that P/O Auckland-Wood should have been given the nickname of Awk-Wood. However he answered to this name with his usual charm and good nature.

There were other unreliable elements besides these two but they were intermittently unreliable, not chronic certainties like Pilot Officers Purvis and Auckland-Wood. One rather intense but fragile young officer had been known to faint on a parade — probably from trying too hard which was a failing few of us suffered from. There was great competition amongst us to be next to him in the line, since if he fainted it was traditional for the man on each side to carry him off the parade ground and if one took the responsibility to its logical and pleasant conclusion one would escort him on to the sick quarters, thus missing the rest of the parade. Although this sort of behaviour might have come under the general term of scrounging, we satisfied our conscience by asserting that it was part of our training as an officer since we could then appreciate all the tricks that airmen might get up to. In fact, of course, all these dodges must have been invented generations before, certainly they were used in the Roman Legions.

Exactly on time the AOC's car drove up to the saluting base and the great man got out and took up his position. We gave the General Salute in the approved style and the AOC descended from the dais with a little difficulty, since he had a wooden leg, having lost one leg in the War. He then started the detailed inspection. He hobbled across the parade ground making an unexpected and disturbing bee-line straight towards our section; he went round behind the front rank and stopped in front of Auckland-Wood. 'What's your name?' 'Auckland-Wood, Sir.' 'Heh. I think I know your father.' We never quite understood this apparently irrelevant remark. No more was said about Auckland-Wood but as the AOC walked on down the rear rank he turned to the Commanding Officer as he passed Purvis and said:

'Do many of your cadets wipe the castor oil off Avros with their No 1 dress?'

Air Vice Marshal Bonham-Carter never missed much. He was such a martinet, and known for it, that it was always said of him that his own children were subjected not only to full military discipline, but also to the full 'stores' procedure in the nursery. It was said that when they wanted to play with a toy they had to draw it out of the nursery store on a RAF Form 674 and when they had finished playing with it they could either return it on a Form 675 or, if they wanted to play with another, they could exchange it on an exchange voucher Form No. 673. Presumably no toys were lost that way. This story may not have been absolutely accurate!

Soon after this our first term came to an end. We were all assessed according to our flying ability in grades 'Exceptional', 'Above Average', 'Average', 'Below Average'. The grade 'Exceptional' was very rarely given at the Avro training stage since there was a fear that it might lead to overconfidence, with sad results. About half the course, now reduced to 27 in number, were assessed as 'Average', about 6 were assessed 'Above Average' and I managed to get into this group; the rest were considered 'Below Average'.

At this stage I had achieved a total flying time of 60 hours 15 minutes of which 42 hours 35 minutes were solo on the Avro 504K.

6 Operational aeroplanes

In the middle of July 1925 we reassembled at the Royal Air Force Station, Digby after a month's leave. We were all excited to know to which flights we had been posted — Bristol Fighters or Sopwith Snipes. If one went on Bristol Fighters it meant that one would probably be posted to an Army Cooperation Squadron like No. 2 Squadron in which I had done my probationary period before going to Digby. Army Cooperation work was interesting at first but the practices became so boringly synthetic that keen pilots tended to long for the freedom and exhilaration of a single-seater fighter. That was my ambition anyhow, so I was somewhat disappointed to find that I was in the Bristol flight instead of the Snipe flight. There was quite a large difference of opinion amongst the pupils concerning the reasons for selecting pilots for one flight or the other. Pilots who were selected for the Snipe flight had a theory that only the very best pilots were chosen for fighters because the Snipe was a delicate aeroplane to fly. They said the sort of ham-fisted, uninspired average — or below average — pilot who might 'get away with it' in a Bristol Fighter would only survive a day or two in a Snipe — if that long. Thus the worst pilots went to the Bristol flight.

On the other hand, we in the Bristol flight maintained the theory that since pilots selected for that flight were those who would ultimately go on Army Cooperation work, it was essential that the Army should only see and meet the absolute *créme de la créme* of the pilots so as to uphold the prestige of the Air Force. We also put forward the theory that the selection was largely made on humanitarian grounds: the Bristol Fighter being a two seater normally carried an Observer. It would have been sheer murder to put these unfortunate observers in the back seat of an aeroplane flown by some irresponsible, inept, sub-normal, below average moron who never appreciated from one moment to the next if he was stalling, side-slipping or even up-side-down.

The truth in the selection had a little bit of both theories in it. It was a fact that the below average pupils could not have handled the Snipe very safely and indeed even the best pilots on the course found it tricky at times. I was fortunate, as recorded later in this chapter, since I managed to get into the Snipe flight after finishing the Bristol

Fighter training and thus got a chance to compare the handling characteristics of both. In some respects the Sopwith Snipe had characteristics not dissimilar to the Avro 504K. Both had rotary engines and both were light and fairly sensitive on the controls, but the Snipe had a power and performance which exaggerated and emphasized a pilot's error far beyond anything the 'forgiving' Avro did. The Bristol Fighter was heavy on the controls but effective. Its Rolls-Royce Falcon engine was as easy to handle as any modern piston engine — very different from the rotaries. Thus after a 'below average' pupil had got used to the Bristol Fighter, so long as he did not try to do anything 'clever' he would probably survive. Apart from the flying ability required on either type it was a fact that the Air Force at that time was very concerned with maintaining a first class image with the Army. This involved being meticulous in the inter-Service exercises, looking smart at conferences and maintaining the Air Force point of view at discussions without, if possible, offending the Army's diehard exponents of the Cavalry tradition. This tradition even in the 1920s, still contended that horses were more useful in war than aeroplanes. They said aeroplanes were nasty smelly things unlike a horse which, even in its stable, presumably smelled sweeter than woodland violets! Perhaps I should add here that I am personally very fond of horses and some of my happiest days in the Air Force were spent on the polo field.

There was also the consideration that flying for the Army often involved taking quite senior Army officers up in the back seat. Understandably they preferred to fly with good pilots rather than bad ones, or even with those 'full out blokes' as we called them, who usually found their way into Fighter Squadrons for a brief spell before moving on to the other World. Thus it was that a complicated system of selection settled our fate for the second half of our course and the factors concerned involved flying ability, flying enthusiasm, temperament, presentability as an officer and a general sense of responsibility.

Having found out which flight we were allotted to and commiserated with our friends on going to the other one, we reported to our respective flight Commanders. I reported to Flight Lieutenant Gardiner who told me that he himself would be my instructor. This was not a surprise to me since he had given me two half-hour periods of dual instruction on the Bristol Fighter at the end of the previous term. I had then hoped that this did not mean I was to go to the Bristol flight. I heard some time later that this was, in fact, inevitable since the report I had had after my early attachment to No 2 (Army Cooperation) Squadron had kindly intimated that the CO there would be very glad to have me posted back to his squadron after my

A Bristol Fighter, powered by a 275 h.p. Rolls-Royce Falcon
engine

year's training at Digby. It was kindly meant but my real love was for
fighters. It took two years and two 'Air Council Displeasures' before
I got to a fighter squadron.

Flt Lt Gardiner was a great martinet in all respects. He himself was
always well turned out with clean white overalls when he was flying.
He affected white gloves and a white silk scarf and all the Bristol
Fighters in his flight were clean and polished as if for an AOC's
inspection; we were all impressed right from the start with the idea
that we were now handling a magnificent aeroplane with a
ROLLS-ROYCE engine and there was not going to be any
irresponsible fooling about. On the whole it did us all good to have
that sort of morale booster. I think it was partly done to offset the
Snipe flight's remarks about ham-fisted bus drivers. To emphasize the
almost incredible smartness of the Bristol flight I may mention here
an episode which occurred a few weeks later when the AOC flew in
for an unofficial interim inspection, concerned only with the flying
operations. He arrived in a Bristol Fighter and proceeded first to the
Avro flight where work proceeded normally, albeit with somewhat
exceptional zeal as befitted the occasion. He then went to the Snipe
flight and was friendly and complimentary. When he came to the
Bristol flight he was perhaps a little irked by the Flight Commander's
obvious self-satisfaction with the splendour of the turn-out and it
was only human to search rather harder than normal to find some
defect. He found it at the end of the line of gleaming Bristol

34

Fighters; the last one was not at all up to the Digby standard. The AOC stopped before it:

'Flight Lieutenant Gardiner, next time I come I shall expect *all* the aeroplanes to be properly maintained'.

The Flight Commander opened his mouth in expostulation, then shut it again and preserved a discreet silence. He could hardly tell the great man that that could only be done if he himself arrived in a clean one! We did however leave the AOC's Bristol Fighter in exactly the same place: when he climbed into it he must have realised that the laugh was on him.

Before dealing with our training on the Bristol Fighter, and particularly the incidents which occurred during our training, it will be as well to give a brief description of the Bristol to indicate its handling characteristics. To start off with it was about as different in the air from an Avro as a rook is from a butterfly. In the case of an Avro the pilot asked it to do something and, in its own good time, it did it. In the case of the Bristol Fighter the pilot decided what he wanted to do and then he MADE the fighter do it — and it did it very well.

So the Bristol Fighter was quite a revelation after the Avro. It had a 275 h p Rolls-Royce Falcon engine, controlled by a normal throttle as with any engine today. The first thing impressed on us was respect for the engine — no 'blipping' for instance. One opened up the engine gently and it always seemed to give its full power. The water coolant

A Bristol Fighter of No. 2 Squadron, RAF Manston, 1926

temperature had to be watched, and controlled with the radiator shutters.

The pupil's chief worry on the Bristol Fighter was the pressurization system for the fuel tanks. There were two fuel tanks, one in front of the pilot and one under the rear seat. There were three air pressure pumps — one engine driven, one windmill and one hand pump. There were two pressure release valves, one automatic and one manually operated on the hand pressure pump. There was a pressure indicator gauge on the dashboard in front of the pilot. The pressure lines from all these met on a sort of small brass control panel on the dashboard so that immediate action could be taken by the pilot in the case of any emergency arising from a variation of pressure (see illustration on page 50).

In the unlikely event of the pressure going too high, it could be released either by tapping the release valve in case it had got stuck, by operating the manual release on the hand pump, or by turning off the pumps. In the much more likely event of a loss of pressure below the standard 2½lb the first action was to turn off the pressure line to the fuel tank not in use at the time and give a few supplementary strokes on the hand pump. If the pressure still dropped, one turned off the line to the pressure release valve since that clearly was not needed at that moment, and gave a few more hand pumps, but one had to remember to turn it on again when and if things returned to normal.

Thereafter, by a process of elimination, one could probably establish where the fault lay; at the worst one was left with all lines turned off except pressure to the tank in use and the hand pump, which was operated energetically until one could land at an aerodrome. We always took off on the front tank because it had a slight gravity feed effect when full, thus a sudden loss of air pressure would probably not cause a dead cut from the engine.

The pre-take-off check was fairly simple. After running up and checking oil pressure, water temperature, both magnetos, and take-off revs, one merely set the 'cheese-cutter' tail adjustment, wiggled all the controls to their full movement to check that they came to 'meet the stick' in every case lest some mechanic had replaced one since the last flight and crossed the wires, and then one taxied out. Any repair or replacement in fact always involved a full test flight by one of the instructors.

Taxiing in a light wind was fairly easy. There were no brakes, but the tail skid gave enough braking effect to need significant engine power before the aircraft moved, thus ensuring a fair slipstream over the rudder. Taxiing down wind was more tricky but use of the ailerons augmented the rudder control very effectively if they were operated as for a normal turn in the air. In this way the following wind acted on the 'down' ailerons and helped the rudder. Taxiing into wind required aileron operation the other way.

Take-off was absolutely straightforward, with very little tendency to swing, and the Bristol Fighter flew itself off in a quietly graceful way which was a joy to watch and hear, and still is today when one sees and hears it flying at the Shuttleworth Trust Aerodrome in Bedfordshire. It was very stable with rather heavy controls all round. We were told that the elevators were made specially heavy since the specification called for a maximum diving speed at 400 m.p.h., and light elevators at that speed could have been embarrassing. I doubt if the Bristol could have reached such a figure even in a vertical dive, but it certainly picked up speed very quickly in a shallow dive at full power — as for a loop, which one entered at speeds between 120 and 140 m.p.h.

Its spin characteristics were normal, but a lot of height was lost during recovery owing to the steep angle of spinning and the aircraft's relatively heavy weight. One of the most impressive aerobatic manoeuvres practiced in the Bristol was the flick roll, induced by adjusting the speed to approximately 85 m.p.h. in level flight and pulling the stick hard back with full rudder; it then did an impressive one turn of a spin horizontally, following which the pilot quickly normalized the controls to prevent it starting another. A 'falling leaf' was also possible, and quite neat, but one had to use a little engine power during the change-over to keep the manoeuvre symmetrical. As in the Avro a slow roll was virtually impossible owing to the very heavy ailerons; furthermore, we only had lap straps in the Bristol Fighter.

Approach and landing was very straightforward. It stalled at 42 m.p.h. and the approach correction was greatly assisted by the wonderful control one had in even the steepest side-slip. We looked upon the Bristol landing run as rather long — all of 100 yards on a calm day — but the grass aerodromes we operated from as pupils usually gave a landing or take-off run of at least 900 yards, often much more. In operational squadrons we were expected to operate from 400 yard strips with reasonably clear approaches.

But much of this was yet to be learnt by the pupils. After we had mastered the difference between the Bristol Fighter and the Avro the actual flying of the Bristol was easy enough although I met an unusual problem on my first solo after 5 hours 45 minutes dual. The apparently large amount of dual for this conversion to another type was due to the requirement in those days for a pupil to be practised in recovery from stalling and spinning — spinning being a much more frightening experience on the Bristol Fighter than on lighter types —

and also the need to get a pupil to a state of familiarity with the Bristol so that he had a reasonable chance of forced-landing it successfully if the engine failed. In fact the reliability of the Rolls-Royce engine was so good that engine failure was very unlikely, except for the risk of pressure failure in the fuel system. As mentioned, it was essential for pupils to understand fully the immediate action to be taken if this were suspected.

On 31 July 1925, Flt Lt Gardiner decided I was fit to be sent off solo. I was much more confident on this one than I had been on the Avro. All went well until I came in to land with what seemed to me to be a perfectly normal approach in speed and height; but the Bristol floated right across the aerodrome and showed no sign of wanting to land. I put the engine on and went round again, deciding that I must have come in too fast. On my second approach I paid particular attention to my speed and, if anything, was on the slow side. Again the Bristol floated right across the aerodrome and again I put the engine on and went round again wondering whether the Air Speed Indicator and my own sense of feel were both at fault. I could imagine Flt Lt Gardiner's state of mind whilst he watched my performance. I was not unduly worried myself since I had made up my mind that if I simply could not land within the aerodrome at Digby – which was big enough in all conscience – then I would fly over to Cranwell only six miles away where the aerodrome provided a mile or more of clear landing space. On my third attempt, again with considerable attention to the speed of approach, I could sense that the same thing was going to happen again and as I passed in front of the hangars I glanced apprehensively towards the Flight Commander's office to see whether he was, as I suspected, jumping up and down with fury and anxiety. In glancing towards the hangars I inadvertently let the Bristol's wheels touch the ground and the Bristol bounced several feet into the air: fearing that I would then stall and drop with a bump I gave a burst of engine and then shut the throttle again smartly. The Bristol settled down for a perfect landing and the mystery was solved. As one closed the throttle on the Bristol there was a stiff point just above the idling position where the throttle movement also retarded the ignition; on my first solo I had been particularly light handed on all the controls, including the throttle control; thus when I thought I had closed the throttle the engine was still giving about 20 per cent of its power, but the Falcon engine was so quiet that one did not notice it and this 20 per cent power was quite sufficient to keep the Bristol floating right across the aerodrome. When I had given the engine a burst of power and then shut the throttle smartly I had instinctively over-riden the stiff point and closed the throttle completely. Flt Lt Gardiner must have recovered his confidence in me after my explanation since he only gave me a perfunctory 10 minutes dual check before sending me off again on a 40 minute solo flight followed by another long solo flight without a dual check in between.

Within three weeks from first solo most of us were doing all normal aerobatics and had started practising cloud flying. One had of course no sophisticated instruments in those days for blind flying. One kept the angle of climb or descent reasonably constant by watching the Air Speed Indicator and kept the aeroplane level laterally partly by trusting to its own natural stability provided by a generous dihedral angle of the wings and partly — but very doubtfully — by reference to the 'bubble' which worked on the ordinary builders' level principle, but the bubble tube was curved to make it less sensitive to minor deviations. Since this 'bubble' instrument was very sensitive to accelerations due to flat turns one was never very sure in a cloud whether it was indicating a side slip or a flat turn. Keeping straight was supposed to be achieved by watching the compass but a pupil in a cloud very soon got the compass swinging round so fast that he could hardly read the cardinal points on the compass card as they passed in front of his eyes. For these reasons, in our early cloud flying practices, we wisely selected very thin layers of cloud, flew as fast as the Bristol would go just below the cloud and then pulled up to a good climbing angle hoping to emerge above the cloud before losing control. As confidence increased we tried flying level in cloud and surprisingly became fairly good at it. But even experienced pilots hesitated to go into cloud unless the cloud base was high enough above ground level to allow for recovery from a spin after emerging. Aeroplanes in those days had the advantage that they were stressed to be able to dive vertically and pulling out of a very deep dive, even in a Bristol Fighter, could be achieved in under 1000 feet if one pulled hard enough.

On one of these cloud flying and navigational practices I flew south west from Digby to Grantham and then climbed above a layer of cloud and flew north until my wrist watch told me I ought to be over Lincoln. It was quite a thrill to me, as I think it is to anyone, to emerge above and see the flat layer of white woolly cloud stretching away on all sides as far as one can see. I had been above the clouds before down at Manston when I was attached to No. 2 Squadron, but only once. Whilst in the Avro flight there was little opportunity to climb through the clouds since the Avro climbed very slowly and there was a lot of urgent practice to be done below them. I was rather pleased with myself at climbing through successfully and elated at the really glorious sight of the bright sun shining on the cloud layer. I gave this spectacle rather more attention than I gave to my compass and my watch. Regretfully I glanced again at my watch and descended through the cloud layer to find myself above a countryside I had never seen before. I decided on no very good evidence that I must be west of Lincoln and a little short of it, so turned north east and flew on looking for Lincoln. After fifteen minutes I saw a fairly large town and flew round it trying to convince myself that it was Lincoln, but regretfully I had to admit to myself that unless they had pulled down the Cathedral and re-aligned the railways there within the last week I must be over some other town. On still flimsier evidence I decided it must be Newark and therefore flew on in a wandering but mainly north easterly direction. The cloud cover got thicker above me and the ground below looked dark and strange with rather limited visibility. I was flying on the rear petrol tank and did some earnest calculations to work out how much fuel was left in it. By the time I had finished these calculations and come to a somewhat worrying conclusion which persuaded me to turn on to the front (main) tank again, I looked out and down again, hoping to see Lincoln. All I could see around me was sea. I turned 180° very hurriedly and made for land which was only about 2 miles back, but it looked like most of the North Sea to me then. I flew back on the reciprocal bearing and found the large town again. Not far from it was a large stubble field in which I landed and was greeted by a group of admiring children, who all asked me to take them up, and an elderly man who did not share their ambition to be flown out of a strange stubble field by a pupil who had lost himself, but he did tell me that the town was Louth. He also indicated, with a generous wave of his arm through an arc of about 80° in which direction Lincoln lay. I worked out a course on my map, thanked the man, apologised to the children for disappointing them, and took off again. This strictly was against the rules for pupils, who were supposed to stay on the ground if they were forced to land for any reason, but I convinced myself that I had not been 'forced to land'. I also guessed, correctly as it turned out, that the Flight Commander would be less displeased with me if I brought his Bristol back safely than if I rang up from some remote place and said I had lost myself. After a quarter of an hour's flying I calculated Lincoln should have been in sight, but it wasn't so I landed again in a field where I was greeted by more children and three farm hands. They were all delighted to see me and told me that Lincoln was 'just over there' and if I looked I could see the top of the Cathedral. No sight was ever more welcome to my eyes, and it was probably a low smoke haze that had obscured Lincoln when I was flying, or perhaps it was my preoccupation with trying to find another field to land in that had diverted my attention and prevented my noticing Lincoln in the distance. I did not waste much time getting into the air again since I knew fuel was running low and even leaving the engine 'ticking over' on the ground was using the precious few gallons left. I turned south short of Lincoln since I was then over known country and took the shortest way home. I had already been away from the aerodrome for 2½ hours and that was the official endurance for the Bristol Fighter, but I knew there was a little more fuel in the front tank and I had left a small amount in the rear tank so that when the front tank ran out I could switch over to the rear, giving me a few minutes to find a suitable field to land in. Back at the aerodrome, I heard later, Flt Lt Gardiner had already used up the whole of his descriptive vocabulary on pupils' stupidity and had just decided — after I had been away for 2 hours 40 minutes — that I must have landed somewhere. At that moment I appeared in the circuit. Just as we are told that there is more satisfaction over one lost sheep being found than over all the rest of the flock, so I found myself fairly popular or at least not as unpopular as I had feared I would be. In fact the Flight Commander was quite complimentary when he heard the whole tale, but he warned me that I would have been in for a packet of trouble if I had had an accident after landing in a field and taken off again. As a result of this long flight of 2¾ hours altogether I came out way above the other pupils in total solo hours flown on Bristol Fighters.

Navigational training now became the main issue and three of us were sent off separately to fly a 70 mile circular tour of Sleaford-Woodhall Spa-Lincoln-Newark and back. The weather around the eastern part of this tour was not at all good with low clouds down to about 600 feet and some rain. I was the last to go off and did not like the look of the weather around Woodhall Spa at all, but since I had not seen the other two coming back I thought they must have gone on through it, so I pressed on through the rain and low cloud. I had been flying just below the clouds at 1200 feet but as I approached Woodhall Spa I was down to 800 feet in light rain. I was soon down to between 200 and 400 feet in heavier rain but, seeing a glint of light towards the south east, I turned that way and flew almost to Boston which I recognised by the 'Stump'. Here the weather improved and I turned north and managed to get round the worst of the weather before turning west for Lincoln. It was this experience that taught me the cheering fact that, on the whole, bad weather exists in blobs not in long straight lines. If one maintains general direction by compass and avoids bad patches of weather one can generally get through. I assumed the other two had done this or else — a thought lowering to my morale — they had pressed on in the

41

rain and got through. I had weakened.

By Lincoln the weather was much better and I was flying at 1200 feet again with no rain. I completed the round tour, landed and reported to the Flight Commander. In his office were the other two pilots being closely questioned. They were rather red in the face since the weather which turns one back never seems to have been so bad when viewed in retrospect and in the rather critical atmosphere of the Flight Commander's office. It looks much worse when viewed from the cockpit of a Bristol Fighter flying in rain only 200 feet or so above the ground with tree-tops looming up every few hundred yards (there were no electric power lines and pylons in those days). I gathered afterwards that the two pilots had been justifying their abandoning the mission by giving a mutually corroborated description of the 'appalling' weather they had encountered. I did not know of this when I arrived in the office and I would certainly have turned back myself had I known that they had. But I still thought that they had gone through it and were perhaps being blamed for doing so. The Flight Commander turned and glared at me:

'And what happened to you?'

I temporized, trying to find out which way trouble lay:

'Well, I went round all right sir, I had to avoid some rain near Woodhall Spa but the weather was much better after Lincoln.'

The glare was turned on the other two and intensified:

'There you are. Wheeler got round all right. Why couldn't you?'

I then realized which way the trouble did lie, and tried to intervene:

'It was pretty bad, Sir.'

'Don't try to make yourself out an experienced bad weather pilot — you went and lost yourself on a clear day.'

That shut me up.

'All right you can go you two. Wheeler, I want to talk to you.'

When the door was shut, Gardiner said:

'Now tell me what the weather was really like. I was flying out that way myself.'

I was clearly cornered, so I told him exactly what it was like. He asked me why I went on through it, so I told him quite frankly that I had only gone on because I thought the other two had. Gardiner's comment, though abrupt, was said not unkindly and it was absolutely full of truth:

'That's just how pilots kill themselves.'

It was just about 5 years later that (by then promoted) Squadron Leader Gardiner led his Squadron in an over-determined effort to get through a dust storm in the desert between Baghdad and Amman. They failed to get through and most of them got lost and landed in various parts of the desert. They were all found and were unhurt but Gardiner was ordered to report to the AOC. I was PA to the AOC and ushered Gardiner in: I thought of Gardiner's talk to me five years before, and hoped the AOC would be as kind and forgiving. Fortunately for Gardiner, he was.

7 Fire!

Since we had no parachutes in those days, fire was a very real risk if it occurred even in a small way at any height above about 1500 feet. There were no automatic fire extinguishers located in the engine nacelles aimed at risk points such as the carburetter, fuel feed or oil breathers as is done in modern aircraft. Therefore if a fire should happen to start in the engine nacelle the pilot could only turn off the fuel, open the throttle wide to use up any fuel left in the carburettor and fuel line, put the aeroplane into a side slip to divert the flames from the cockpit and fuel tank (which was usually situated immediately behind the engine) and pray.

There was a fireproof bulkhead in every aeroplane then, between the engine and fuel tank, but it could only delay the spread of the fire which would get round the bulkhead along the side of the fuselage. If it got round the bulkhead, fire could spread very rapidly indeed in an aeroplane which was mostly made of wood and fabric, the latter being painted with a cellulose paint or 'dope' as we called it. It was true that all aeroplanes had a fire extinguisher held in clips and located close to the cockpit floor but it was unlikely that a pilot would have a hand free — and two hands were necessary to operate it — or indeed be prepared to put his head down into a cockpit which was full of smoke and flames. From my own point of view I was only reminded of the presence of this fire extinguisher on two occasions. The first was when it came adrift at the top of a very bad loop and appeared before my eyes floating in mid-air like a yellow object on the morning after a guest night, and I managed to catch it before it fell back into the cockpit and perhaps jammed the controls: the second occasion was when I felt a 'lumpiness' in the elevator controls and traced it to the fire extinguisher which had also come loose and was rolling about the floor of the aircraft and getting caught up every now and again with the lower part of the control column. Although fire was a significant risk in the aeroplanes of those days I was almost more worried by the presence of the fire extinguisher.

On the whole we tried to forget both and it was, therefore, a nasty reminder to us all when one of our number had a fire break out in a Bristol Fighter and he got badly scorched. Fortunately for P/O Howard, the pupil who was flying the Bristol, the fire only started as

44

he closed the throttle to come in to land. It was, in fact, closing the throttle which resulted in a small 'pop' in the exhaust pipe that started the fire. Investigation after the event showed that there were two defects which combined to start the fire: there was a leak in the fuel supply line which allowed fuel to seep out on to the fabric of the fuselage just behind the engine. This alone might not have caught fire since the exhaust pipes on the Bristol Fighter extended well back along the fuselage almost to the tailplane, but there was also a small leak in the exhaust pipe just behind the engine where it ran along the fuselage and only a few inches from it. When the pilot had closed the throttle there was the inevitable outflow of a slightly over-rich mixture down the exhaust pipe as the engine slowed down, followed by a normal flow of incandescent exhaust gases which ignited the previous unburnt over-rich mixture, giving rise to the familiar 'pop' one gets in any car exhaust system which has a leak in it. This particular explosion ejected a small tongue of flame out of the exhaust pipe directly on to the fuselage fabric which was soaked in fuel. Had the two defects, one in the fuel pipe and the other in the exhaust pipe, not been adjacent to one another there would have been little chance of fire breaking out. However, it did and P/O Howard suddenly found himself at about 200 feet, fortunately heading straight for the aerodrome, with smoke and flames coming up out of the cockpit. With great presence of mind he put the Bristol Fighter into a side-slip so that the flames tended to be blown away from him and the rest of the fuselage and within 30 seconds or so he landed the Bristol and, as it slowed down on the ground, he switched off the engine and scrambled out of the cockpit. Although badly scorched on those parts of his face which were not covered by helmet and goggles he was relatively all right. His overalls were burnt around the legs. The fire, for some reason, went out almost as he touched down, perhaps because it had burnt up all the petrol soaked fabric, but it is doubtful if it would have gone out so quickly had he remained in the air.

For the next week or so we all had the possibility of fire at the back of — if not further forward in — our minds. It was only the next day I was detailed to do my height test. This was for us quite exciting since we were sent off on a clear day with good visibility to climb to 16,000 feet. This involved using the altitude control on the engine which was a lever alongside the throttle lever which weakened the carburettor mixture: one used it progressively as one gained height. For many years now this control has been made automatic, although such classic aeroplanes as the Tiger Moth with the DH Gipsy engine still have the hand operated control, which is often wired shut to prevent pupils fiddling with it.

During the climb to 16,000 feet I was very conscious of the need to operate the altitude control, and still more conscious that if I operated it incorrectly I might cause the engine to get the wrong mixture, backfire and perhaps start a fire. I felt very much alone and very far from the ground as I approached the 16,000 feet mark. Although I was longing to start on the descent as soon as possible I felt, for self respect considerations, that I must exceed the 16,000 feet mark by a little, so I added a couple of hundred feet to the score before I let the nose of the Bristol Fighter drop to a shallow dive at about 140 m.p.h. This indicated speed, corrected for altitude, would have given a true speed of about 175 m.p.h. Only then did I relax and enjoy the magnificent view on that 28th day of August 1925. It was a view that few people in the world ever saw in those days unless they lived in remote and romantic places like Switzerland or Tibet. Almost directly below me was Lincoln, looking almost like a village with, it seemed from that height, an unnecessary number of roads and railways radiating from it. Far away to the east I could see most of the coastline of Lincoln and Norfolk with the clear-cut line of the Wash and the fading remoteness of the North Sea beyond. To the west the industrial areas of the Midlands were, as usual, shrouded in a yellowy white haze which hid the ugliness of William Blake's 'dark satanic mills' but also hid the loveliness of the Yorkshire moors and the impressive outline of the Pennines.

The height from which I was descending was, by modern standards, a modest one of only 16,200 feet, but in an open cockpit with no oxygen or heating it felt very different to the same altitude in a closed and heated cockpit. I had momentarily forgotten the possibility of fire, but very soon I came back to realities and I decided not to close the throttle until I was much lower just in case I might find myself in a similar predicament to P/O Howard, but much further from the ground. However all went well and by the time I had got to 10,000 feet my confidence was high enough to close the throttle, stall the Bristol and spin off 3,000 feet of remaining height. It gave me a renewed confidence in the Bristol and in myself and with this confidence, perhaps augmented by lightheadedness induced by a slight shortage of oxygen, I threw a loop at 5,000 feet and then dived into circuit.

One sequel to all our anxieties about fire caused a somewhat amusing incident a few days later, the funny side of which was appreciated by all of us except the Flight Sergeant, who lost a beautifully polished Bristol Fighter, and the Flight Commander who lost a beautifully creased pair of trousers.

At this time we had reached the stage when we were allowed to take up our first passengers. Strangely there was quite a lot of competition amongst the airmen to go up as first passenger with a pupil. They were stout stuff, the airmen, in those days! They used to find out when the first passenger flights were due and come up to us and say:

'Excuse me Sir, but would you take me up when you first take a passenger?'

Looking back on these apparently foolhardy requests I believe they can only have been inspired by a genuine desire on the part of the airmen to boost our morale. They certainly did that.

Apart from taking up passengers we had also reached the stage when our Flight Commander decided we should be initiated into the elements of formation flying so on 1st September he led a formation of three of us on a cross country flight which was intended to follow a course to Lincoln and then Newark and return to Digby. To say that our ideas of formation flying were nebulous would be an almost exact statement of fact if the word nebulous were used in the same sense which is usually applied to Heavenly Bodies. We were metaphorically 'light years' apart. In all our previous training we had concentrated on avoiding close proximity to other aeroplanes — except in the rare case when we observed some unimaginative fellow pupil drifting along doing nothing in particular and decided to 'liven him up a bit' by flying close past him. But these exploits did not prepare us for the highly controlled form of flying which is required for close formation work. Apart from that most of us were imbued with the absolute necessity of treating our Rolls-Royce engines with very great respect and close formation work makes that impossible — certainly for pupils. As a result both I and P/O (Daddy) Holmes, who was the other 'formator' kept at a very respectful and safe distance of about 300 yards from our Flight Commander. All was very quiet, relaxed and peaceful at that distance. It was so quiet and peaceful that the airman in the back seat of P/O Holmes' Bristol started admiring the scenery and was particularly struck by the beauty of the midday sun shining on Lincoln Cathedral spire. He commented on it; leaning forward with his mouth close to his pilot's ear he shouted:

'Look at Lincoln SPIRE, Sir.'

P/O Holmes thought he heard the ominous words:

'FIRE, Sir.'

He immediately shut the throttle and dived for the nearest large field he could see. The airman, realising that his message had been misunderstood, but not knowing why, shouted:

'It's only the SPIRE, Sir.'

'Daddy' Holmes pushed the nose of the Bristol further down. By this time his passenger realized that the pilot was worried by what he

47

had said and guessed that he might have misunderstood the word SPIRE, so he yelled still louder:

'SPIRE, Sir, SPIRE.'

'Daddy' Holmes went into a steep side-slip towards a large field. By any standards the field would have been big enough for a Bristol Fighter to land in had it not been divided in half by a barely visible fence of iron hurdles. The Bristol Figher touched down a few yards before the fence, ran into it and was neatly but forcefully tipped on to its nose doing it quite a significant amount of damage.

Flying on the other side of our leader I had watched this performance with interest and concern since I thought 'Daddy' Holmes' engine must have cut. I followed him down, saw the accident and with relief saw Holmes and his passenger climb out unhurt. I waved to them and they waved back. I then rejoined the Flight Commander who had become aware that we had both left him and wondered whether it was mutiny or an amazing coincidence of two Rolls-Royce engine failures within seconds of one another. We flew back to the aerodrome and I told Flt Lt Gardiner what had happened. He told me what he thought of our attempts at formation flying. Within a few minutes we were both airborne in a dual Bristol and Gardiner told me to fly it and find the field where Holmes had landed. I had foreseen this requirement and found the field fairly easily with it's additional feature of a Bristol fuselage standing up almost vertically in it. I had warned Gardiner about the railings which were difficult to see and he, very boldly I thought, allowed me to land the Bristol. I taxied close to the accident and switched off since we had plenty of 'hands' to start it up again. Gardiner got out of the back seat and walked towards a rather subdued P/O Holmes and an extremely worried airman. They were standing the other side of the broken fence. Gardiner walked up to it and asked what had happened. In some confusion they told him their story badly, and it all sounded too utterly ridiculour to be believed. Homes finished:

'... so when he said "Spire, Spire" I thought he was saying "Fire, Fire".'

'But you didn't have to land on this damned fence! Anyone can see it! It stands out clearly enough....'

Gardiner rushed forward to get over the fence but at least one piece of the fence did not stand out clearly enough for him to see. He caught his trouser leg in one broken bit, stumbled over another, fell forward and split one trouser leg right up the whole length of it. After that the damage to the Bristol Fighter seemed of lesser importance, even though his Bristol Fighters were a source of great pride to him and any loss or even damage of one, was a great sadness.

Only a few days later a brand new Bristol Fighter was issued to the Bristol flight to replace the damaged one. Flt Lt Gardiner adopted it as his own. No-one, not even an instructor, was allowed to fly it. Airmen working on it had to change their shoes before they got into the cockpit. A corporal complained that they had to wash their hands before they worked on it. Every metal fitting was either glossy black or polished silver: the tyres were blacked and polished with a special grade of shoe polish — too valuable to waste on pupils' shoes. The streamlined bracing wires between the wings were polished with a brand of metal polish too expensive for pupils to use on the buttons of their No. 1 dress: the tail-skid shoe was polished so that it should not pick up or kick up too much dust.

At last, on one clear sunlit day when the aerodrome was just wet enough to prevent dust flying, and just dry enough to prevent mud being flung, Flt Lt Gardiner took off to show an instructor friend at Cranwell this really beautiful Bristol Fighter. He was wearing, as always, spotless white overalls with a brand new silk scarf. On his hands were new chamois leather gloves.

He delayed his take-off until all the pupils at Digby and Cranwell were sure to be on the ground for lunch, so that no 'incidents' were likely to occur, then he flew this immaculate Bristol over to Cranwell. He walked over to the Mess for lunch. All through lunch he expatiated on the beauties of his Bristol and after coffee and a cigar he and his friend walked back to view this piece of absolute perfection in British Aeronautical Engineering. As they walked round the corner of the last hanger and came in sight of the aerodrome, the Bristol Fighter was there in all the glory of illumination by a red wintry sun picking out its beautiful lines enhanced by the incomparable polish on its every surface.

To complete the scene came the sound of an Avro 504K not yet in view, making that typical (and now nostalgic) 'BRRP — BRRP — BRRP —' sound of a rotary engine taxiing on the ground under the control — or nearly under the control — of a pupil.

Flt Lt Gardiner stopped his friend for a moment in their advance to point out the ineffable beauty of the scene:

'But' he said 'Wait 'til you see it close to.'

They walked on towards it.

As they approached, the taxiing Avro appeared round the corner of a hanger. With, it seemed, almost relentless purpose driving it, it went straight into the Bristol Fighter and wrecked it.

The shock and dismay of the two instructors lasted all of five minutes as they surveyed the wreckage and as the unfortunate Avro pupil clambered out of the Avro. He clearly felt some form of explantion or apology was required. In a stuttering voice, normal but

49

rendered more emphatic by his nervousness, he said:

'I'm sss-sorry bbb-but I was tuttuttut-taxing into the sss-sun.'
He was meticulously and furiously corrected by Flt Lt Gardiner.

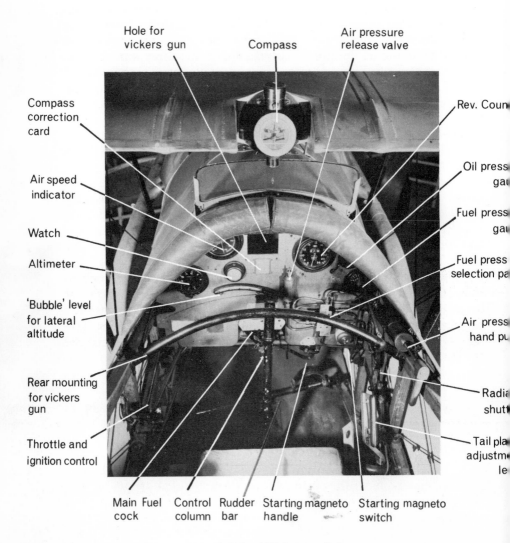

A Bristol Fighter cockpit

'Taxiing into the sun be damned; you were taxiing into my beautiful Bristol Fighter.'

He added:

'What can I do with it now?'

It was a rhetorical question, but his friend answered it:

'Put it on the scrap heap and draw another out of Stores.'

On the whole we had few accidents on the Bristol Fighter and there was only one fatal one in which both the pupil and instructor were killed. They were practicing spinning and for a reason which was fairly well established later, they failed to recover from a spin and went into the ground not very far from the aerodrome boundary. Some of the pupils saw it happen and there was a general gloom around the Flight Office as we knew all too well that when a Bristol Fighter spun in there was virtually no possibility of survival for the occupants. As was traditional in the Air Force — then and now — we carried on with the day's programme although we were not much cheered by one of the other instructors saying:

'Well, that's what I always say; one day a Bristol will come out of a spin and another day it won't.'

Subsequent investigation into the cause of the accident seemed to prove that when the pupil was doing the spin the instructor had taken his feet off the rudder bar and rested them on the floor: as the rudder bar moved over one of his feet had followed it and then got jammed between the rudder bar and a fuselage strut, thus locking the bar over almost on full lock. The pupil only knew that the rudder bar had jammed and tried to force it back, thus holding the instructor's foot. With plenty of height they might have sorted the situation out, but in this case they had insufficient height. Remembering this accident through the years I have always either kept my feet on the rudder bar in dual control aeroplanes or kept them well back out of the way.

The Bristol Fighter was not very forgiving in a crash

I have never known whether it was sheer bravado, a wish to give others confidence, or just a desire to give myself confidence, but when I was detailed immediately after the accident to do half an hour's aerobatics and the order was not changed, I took off and did as told. Amongst the manoeuvres prescribed for aerobatics was a spin. I did not relish the idea of a spin at that moment but I decided to do one, in full view of the aerodrome. There was such an atmosphere of gloom around the place that it seemed to be almost a public duty to dispel it. I took the precaution of doing only two turns of a spin and then, very quickly, took recovery action. To my immense relief the Bristol came out of the spin quite normally. It certainly gave me confidence having done the spin at that time and recovered.

When I landed one of the instructors came up to me and said:

'You'll tempt providence too far one day, but I think it did us all good to see you do that spin.'

I wondered at the time whether it was in good taste to do it then. I still don't know. But two other pupils followed my example.

From then on our training consisted largely of cross country flights which, on occasions, included landing at another aerodrome, usually Spittlegate near Grantham where there was another Flying Training School. We also improved our aerobatics which included loops, half rolls, flick rolls, spins and the 'falling leaf'. Inverted flying was not allowed on the Bristol Fighter. We also practised landing in the 'circle', which was a large white chalk circle in the middle of the aerodrome and could be used to simulate a landing in a small field. One of my last flights in the Bristol flight was as observer in the back seat with no dual control when Gardiner led a formation to land in a field owned by some farmer friends of his about 30 miles away. My pilot was one of the Sergeant pilot instructors from the Avro flight who was putting in time on a Bristol Fighter to keep his hand in. When we landed in the field he approached rather too slow over some trees and sank heavily on to the ground: he was also unfortunate in actually touching down on a rough patch in the field. The result was a badly bent axle and a damaged centre section strut. I had to stay the night at the farm house where I was made very comfortable. In the morning the Bristol was repaired and Gardiner was so indignant with the Sergeant pilot that he made him sit in the back seat and told me to fly the Bristol. As a parting shot at the unfortunate Sergeant he had said to me:

'Wheeler, you had better fly it back: we haven't got too many spare axles left in the flight.'

I was by then a favoured pupil in the Bristol flight. Two days later I was by no means favoured.

8 Flying the Sopwith Snipe

The circumstances of my fall from grace in the Bristol Flight were not really dishonourable. Due to various factors, including one or two pilots not making the grade on the Sopwith Snipe, it was decided that three or four pilots from the Bristol Flight who had completed their training on Bristols should be allowed to transfer to Snipes and get in some training on them as well, thus fitting them for posting either to fighter or Army Cooperation squadrons. Flt Lt Gardiner called us all in to the Flight office and explained the situation but made it fairly clear that he did not like the idea of his pupils 'deserting' his flight. He then called for volunteers and I suppose I stepped forward with indecent − certainly tactless − haste. Two others followed suit and we were told we could GO, in a tone of voice which implied that we would not be missed either. We went hurridly. I was sorry to appear disloyal to Gardiner whom I had come to respect and like, but the opportunity was too good to be missed.

On 28 October I reported for flying to the Snipe Flight Commander's office and again I was lucky in my instructor. I was allotted as pupil to Sergeant Snaith who, like George Lowdell, and a great friend of his, was a brilliant pilot and a most able and inspiring instructor. Snaith retired from the Air Force some 30 years later after becoming Commanding Officer of the Experimental Flying Department at the Royal Aircraft Establishment at Farnborough in which post he followed me after my second appointment in that position.

The Sopwith Snipe was a delight to fly − when one had mastered the art of flying it. It was direct descendent of that other famous fighter, the Sopwith Camel, which came from the Sopwith firm at Brooklands where the British Aircraft Corporation now design and build supersonic air'iners. It was from the same aerodrome at Brooklands that the Vickers V Bomber, the Valiant and the V C 10 airliner took off on their first flights. The problem for pupils at No.2 F T S at Digby in 1925 who had been posted to the Snipe flight, was to master the art of flying it. Fortunately all of us had done our earliest training on the Avro 504K with its rotary engine, so the Snipe's Bentley Rotary Mark II was not a great surprise to us. But it was a slight surprise all the same. The Mono engine of the Avro

504K was only 100 h p and there was only one power lever to fiddle about with. The BR II engine of the Snipe was 230 h p engine and it had two power levers to fiddle about with. That just about doubled the chances of mishandling. One of these levers opened and shut the air supply to the engine, the other opened and shut the fuel supply. It was up to the pilot (pupil in our case) to achieve the right mixture so that the engine would give the power required. As on the Mono engine, if the mixture was allowed to get too rich it took a long time for the engine to recover and it only recovered if the right corrective action was taken. As on the Mono engine, one could run up the BR II engine on the ground and find out where the maximum power setting of the levers was on the quadrant. One could also find out where the minimum power setting was which gave about one quarter of full power; one could also 'blip' the engine on the magneto cut out. Having established these settings one tried to remember — or at least find — them whilst one was in the process of taking off, coming in to land, or just flying.

As in the Avro, if one could manage the engine one could manage the Snipe. Structurally it was so strong that one could not break it in the air, and this went for all the Sopwith aeroplanes I can remember right up to the Hunter. Its landing speed was only about 40 m.p.h. but at touch down it was at a fairly high angle of incidence so that if one misjudged the speed and moment of landing a lot of things started happening fairly quickly; this included all one's friends near the flight office starting to laugh.

Having got the Snipe into the air it became, on the whole, a very straightforward aeroplane, but on the way to getting into the air it behaved just like the bird from which it derived its name. That is to say, on take off it darted from side to side in the pilot's endeavour to counteract the gyroscopic kick of the large Bentley Rotary engine. Although the Snipe (as a bird) does not have a rotary engine, it may well be that its habit of darting from side to side as it takes off is due to similar characteristics to its namesake in the aeroplane world. Both are undoubtedly endowed with a very high power/weight ratio.

The trouble with the Sopwith Snipe lay in its heavy and powerful rotary engine which gave a gyroscopic kick at right angles to any turning force applied to it. This meant that if the pilot pushed the stick forward to get the tail up on take off the Snipe immediately tried to do a smart turn to the left which needed a significant rudder force to correct it. As one came off the ground and pulled up to a climbing angle the Snipe tried to turn smartly to the right. All this correction ultimately became instinctive to pupils if they were ever to make the grade on Snipes. Some didn't.

When once one had got used to these peculiar characteristics the

54

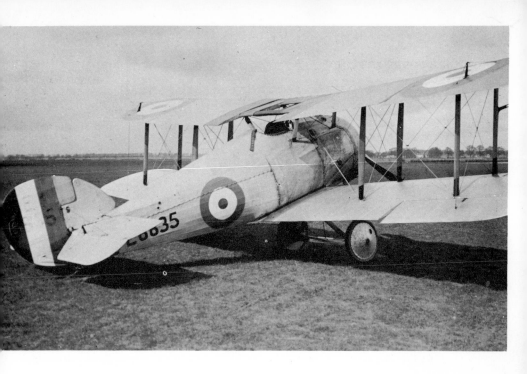

A Sopwith Snipe, powered by a 230 h.p. Bentley rotary engine

Snipe was a delightful aeroplane to fly with light and effective controls and a performance which was only barely exceeded in another 5 years of fighter development. Its top speed was 121 m.p.h., a Service ceiling of 20,000 and it could climb at nearly 1000 feet per minute. For a pupil converting to Snipes the major problem lay in managing the engine when coming in to land. The technique was to reduce power until one got a reasonably steady idling speed at a very weak mixture. With the two levers (air and petrol) this could be achieved at quite a low power setting. One then switched off the engine on the magneto switch which was located just above the throttle on the left hand side of the cockpit. One then forgot the engine and concentrated on gliding in at the right speed and the right angle of approach. If all went as planned and the Snipe touched down smoothly one then switched on and the engine came to life and was thereafter controlled on the magneto 'blip' switch on the control column. If all did not go well on the landing and one bounced badly one still switched on the engine and the engine power at the previous setting was then sufficient to smooth out the landing — if one managed the controls properly.

Since we had all done our earliest training on rotary engines and had never known an easier engine — except for those transfering from the Bristol Fighter — this complication in engine handling seemed reasonable. In any case when one got it right the engine ran a lot better than the engines in the motor cycles some of us owned in those days.

After 5 hours and 20 minutes conversion under the able instruction of Sergeant Leonard Snaith, which included a check test with the Flight Commander, Flt Lt Harrison, I was judged sufficiently skilled to be sent off solo. About three quarters of this time had been taken up in getting the landing technique right. Snaith used to say to me on any bumpy landing:

'There you go: you'll have us up-side-down if you do that too often.'

I had learnt the correct reply to this comment from my friend John Noel who was also a pupil on my course, and had also been Snaith's pupil. The reply was:

'What happens to you if we turn over?'

'Shut up', said Snaith.

It was well known that the instructor, with his head and shoulders well out of the rear cockpit in the slimming rear fuselage might, if unlucky, have his neck broken in a violent nose-over. That made the instructors careful.

I don't remember any of the dual Snipes turning over on their backs during our course, but it was quite common to see solo Snipes up-side-down on a gusty day. We were all warned that if we turned over we must not be in too much of a hurry to get out. One pilot on the senior course forgot this and, as soon as things had stopped happening on his rather careless inversion, he pulled his Sutton Harness release, dropped out on to his head and knocked himself out. It was, in fact, quite dangerous since the distance was about 3 feet. The correct action was to get a firm grip on something first so as to lower oneself gently. The actual damage to the Snipe was not extensive and they would normally be back in service in 48 hours. This was just as well in view of the number which turned over. On one very gusty day I asked a pupil returning from the early schedule what the weather was like and he replied in a matter-of-fact voice:

'Not too bad. Bit gusty. Couple of Snipes on their backs.'

I felt quite a veteran on first solos by now and the Snipe gave me no surprises. About half of the 5 hours 20 minutes dual conversion had been taken up in getting my reflexes trained to deal with the gyroscopic 'kick' of the big rotary engine under all types of manoeuvre. I also had to go through the full training for stalling, spinning and recovering from a spin.

By the time I was flying solo on Snipes with reasonable confidence my friend 'Scruffy' Purvis was under close arrest for paying a visit to one of his recent educational establishments. Unfortunately for 'Scruffy' the establishment was only about 40 miles south of Digby on the Great North Road and the temptation to re-visit it was irresistible. The obvious way to pay the visit was by air in a Snipe so he went that way. The educational establishment, a crammer run by a dear old parson, was located in the broad main street of a village (then) on the Great North Road. 'Scruffy' Purvis flew up the main street about level with the chimney pots of the houses each side. A lot of people came out of the houses to see what was going on so it seemed essential to 'Scruffy' to come back and fly between the houses to see if his friends were there also and had noticed his arrival.

Reports of this visit might not have been made if 'Scruffy' had not returned a third time to have a better look: it was difficult to get a really good look at the people who were waving if he flew the right way up, so he flew up the main street on the third run up-side-down and very close to the main street. By that time the local policeman had been alerted and local public opinion forced him to take action. Even if the locals had not got the number of the Snipe — which they had — there were no other Snipes near to the scene of operations except those from Digby, and 'Scruffy' was the only individual there who was likely to attempt and successfully achieve this feat. He was put under close arrest, which meant being confined to his room with an officer always on duty to see that he remained there. He was however allowed recreational periods within the camp confines when the officer on duty had to accompany him wherever he went. During one weekend, on a Saturday, I was on duty from 6 p m to midnight. It seemed to me that 'Scruffy' was getting depressed by this long confinement. He admitted to me that he would love to get out of camp to the great wide world again, with a special predilection for a visit to his old crammer where the trouble had occurred. The difficulty was to get him out of camp when the guard room knew perfectly well that he was under arrest and not allowed out. At the time I had a 1921 Riley car. It was a 2-seater with a very small sort of boot behind, hardly big enough to take a suit-case. With the help of a large tyre lever I got 'Scruffy' into the boot, shut it down with some difficulty and drove out of camp. Ten miles out of camp I stopped and managed to get him out of the boot again and we drove the rest of the way to Wansford village in comparative comfort. His parson friend greeted us doubtfully but very hospitably and we had an excellent supper. We did not mention the rather questionable methods by which his ex-pupil had managed to make the visit, since it might have weighed too heavily on the ecclesiastical conscience. The visit did 'Scruffy' a lot of good and he became his own cheerful self again. I got 'Scruffy' back into camp safely and no-one knew he had been out. In this respect we were more fortunate than another pupil who was not under arrest but confined to camp. Finding this

57

confinement rather irksome he dressed up in a nondescript raincoat with a felt hat pulled down well over his eyes and a muffler covering his mouth and rode his motor cycle out of camp to Lincoln. Returning late in the dark he found the first gate into Camp closed, with a sergeant on guard, so he continued up the road for a few yards to the second gate — a single bar gate — which was normally left open. In the dark he failed to see that this gate was also closed. Although the motor cycle passed freely underneath he was left on the gate bar. Fortunately he was only doing about 5 m.p.h. so was more or less unhurt, but he had to explain why he had been out of camp.

A few days later a message came through from Group HQ to say that P/O (on probation) Purvis could be dealt with summarily by his Commanding Officer and no Court Martial would take place.

I don't remember what the Commanding Officer's sentence was, but offences of this kind on a really brilliant pilot were often treated as lightly as possible — always bearing in mind that *some* action had to be taken to discourage other less accomplished pilots from trying the same evolutions. The normal punishment by the Commanding Officer for this type of offence would have been 'confinement to camp' and as 'Scruffy' had already been under close arrest that punishment had already been inflicted. If it had come to a Court Martial the Court would either have sentenced him to be dismissed the Service — and he was much too good a pilot to lose — or ordered loss of seniority by dropping him perhaps a 100 places in the Air Force list, but as Pilot officers on probation were already at the bottom of the list they had very little to lose.

Purvis then celebrated his return to the world of flying by doing a new manoeuvre in sight of the aerodrome which he had been perfecting for some time. It was an inverted falling leaf, which although done nowadays by very experienced aerobatic pilots — in the right type of aeroplane — was a novelty to us then. He executed the manoeuvre beautifully much to the astonishment and envy of some of the Snipe instructors. Some of them said it was a foolish and dangerous manoeuvre for which the Snipe wasn't stressed, but most of them were observed later practising in remote places away from the aerodrome. Only one or two really got the manoeuvre perfected. Since the Snipe had the advantage of a rotary engine which would continue to run for a short time up-side-down, quite a number of inverted aerobatics could be done more precisely in it than in the later generations of fighters with radial engines, unless they were modified considerably to allow for the fuel and oil supply to continue with the aeroplane on its back.

As the winter of 1925 drew on the weather tended to get cold and

58

misty. On one rather marginal day I was sent off to do aerobatics which included flying inverted as well as the normal full range. After 20 minutes in the clear sunshine of that late October day I descended into the thicker haze below 1500 feet where the visibility was little more than a mile at best, and could not find the aerodrome. I instituted a square search and found myself over Cranwell aerodrome, so set course for Digby, but this time my calculations must have been out because I missed the aerodrome. I then flew along the Lincoln main road and made a dart away from it a right angles when I thought I must be close to Digby, but again it eluded me. I then could not find the road again so started looking for Cranwell. I failed to find Cranwell but found Digby unexpectedly and quickly adjusted my flight direction to make it look as though I had just flown back to the aerodrome naturally: no-one was deceived. In any case I had been away from the aerodrome for over an hour when my flight was authorized for only 30 minutes. My mistake then, as Flt Lt Harrison pointed out to me, was in descending into the haze to look for the aerodrome. I should have remained above it looking down through it when the haze was only about 400 yards thick viewed in all directions over quite a wide range of country. As soon as I was down in it whichever way one looked the haze became impenetrable beyond about 1500 yards. The Flight Commander had been a bit worried because if I had got really lost he might have been held to blame for letting me go off in that sort of weather. I explained that I had not been worried since it wasn't I that was lost it was simply that the aerodrome would not appear at the right place when I got there. Flt Lt Harrison said:

'More dual for you tomorrow. Pupils who lose aerodromes are careless.'

I managed to regain the Flight Commander's confidence in my flying but not in my responsibility a few days later, just before we finished our course. On that day some air gunners were doing ground-to-air firing with the practice camera guns we used then. These were in fact cameras installed in a frame of the same shape and weight as a Lewis gun, which was then standard armament for air gunners in the air, and also for ground gunners for aerodrome defence. On the ground, as in this case, the camera guns were mounted on a swivel on top of a post which was out on the aerodrome just in front of the Snipe flight office. Some of the instructors were diving on the gun position and pulling up in a climbing turn so as to give the gunners practice shots coming and going. The pupils, in turn as they were sent up for other practices, were told they were not to dive on the gun position. The Flight Commander forgot to tell me as he detailed me to go and fly and he also forget to tell 'Scruffy' Purvis, who was sent off at the same time. We both decided that it was an opportunity not to be missed, but I suggested to 'Scruffy' that since his reputation for misunderstanding orders would hardly stand up to investigation it would be better if I did a couple of dives on the gun position first and established the fact that it was me and then he could join in and they would still think it was me. The plan worked out well enough so far as 'Scruffy' was concerned and he was never suspected of having been in on the act. I made my first dive along the line of the hangars with them on my right. I came in rather steeper and faster than I had intended and went rather lower than I had intended since the windscreen was covered with castor oil. The result of this was that I had to pull up much more abruptly than I had meant and this resulted in a considerable gyroscopic 'kick' from the engine for which I was only barely ready and that put the Snipe into a steep right hand climbing turn over the hangars. I was told afterwards that it looked most impressive and frightening. I shared in the latter emotion. However, this was essentially the manoeuvre we had planned and I disappeared from sight behind the hangars, sorted myself out and came in for a second but more controlled dive. I could see several instructors coming out of the Flight office so I again disappeared as quickly as possible over the hangers. Then 'Scruffy' took over the next dive and we alternated for three more dives until I left 'Scruffy' to it for another three on his own. Whereas my dives and pull outs might — with the exception of the first — have been considered safe for an experienced pupil, 'Scruffy's' dives would have been hair-raising even by instructors' standards. In every case he pulled right up to an almost vertical climb before he rolled over and dived behind the hangars. All good things come to an end sooner or later and in this case we wisely flew away for another 20 minutes to let things cool down. I then landed first and taxied in. As I stopped the engine one of the other instructors who was quite a friend of mine came up and said "Flight Commander wants to see you." I put on an innocent puzzled expression and said:

'Oh, do you know why?'

'I can't imagine!'

I kept my innocent expression on my face as I went into the Flight office but it was wearing a bit thin by then:

'Sir, you wanted to see me? I've just landed Sir. Do you want me to go off again Sir?'

'No I don't. You disobeyed orders.'

'Disobeyed orders Sir?'

'Yes. You were told not to dive on the gun position.'

'No Sir. No-one told me not to Sir, and I saw a lot of other pilots diving on it Sir. I thought you wanted us to give the gunners practice Sir. Did I do any harm Sir?'

'Your first dive nearly gave me heart failure.'

'I'm sorry about that Sir.

I didn't tell him that it had nearly given me heart failure too.

'Well, I won't say any more this time. I think I did forget to tell you — all right. . . . .'

As I left the office he said:

'As a matter of fact it was a good bit of flying, but you'll kill yourself that way sooner or later.'

This relieved my mind since he clearly did not know of Purvis' part in the exercise.

As I emerged from the office the other instructor was waiting with a questioning look on his face. I smiled and said:

'Yes, not much trouble.'

He also complimented me on Purvis' flying:

'It was a good show.'

By the time 'Scruffy' had taxied in and was looking rather apprehensively towards me as I left the Flight office. I nodded reassuringly and he called to me:

'Weather's not too good around Newark.'

I suppose it was as good an alibi as he could produce under the circumstances. He got away with a most enjoyable 'beat-up' and I got away with a reputation for brilliant, albeit rather dangerous, flying which I did not earn or deserve.

Sadly, Flt Lt Harrison's final admonition to me proved prophetic so far as 'Scruffy' Purvis was concerned. He was killed about a year later at RAF Hawkinge flying a Gloster Grebe. I heard he was approaching to land doing a series of half rolls or stalled turns to left and right. On almost the last one before he straightened out he saw another Grebe coming in below him and in trying to avoid it he hit the ground and was killed. It was a sad loss of someone who would undoubtedly have been one of the great aerobatic pilots of the Air Force.

In mid-December 1925 we left Digby and dispersed on leave for Christmas, and then to our respective postings either to a Fighter squadron, Army Cooperation unit, or, in a few cases, to a light day bomber squadron, which meant a further conversion to the then standard DH 9a. Before we left, the Station Commander, Wing Commander Tedder, interviewed us individually to ask what we thought of the course and also to give us advice for the future. His last words to me at the interview were:

'I shall watch your future with interest.'

I wondered whether he said that to everyone — which proved on

A DH 9a, powered by a 400 h.p. Liberty engine

enquiry amongst the other pupils not to be so — or whether he had heard about the Snipe episode and thought he might not have to watch for long, or whether it was general and sincere interest. I decided to choose the third possibility and Tedder certainly had one or two incidents — like Air Council Displeasures — to interest him so far as I was concerned in the not distant future.

We were all told where we were going next and I knew that my final destination was No. 2 Squadron on Army Cooperation work at Manston near Margate, but I had first of all to do a 3 months conversion course on that type of work at Old Sarum near Salisbury.

I went to my home for Christmas leave where our friends still looked upon flying folk with mixed feelings. Amongst our friends the teenage girls mostly said:

'Why didn't you join the Cavalry.'

and didn't understand my reply when I said:

'Because the Cavalry don't fly.'

A few friends said:

'Isn't it terribly dangerous. If the engine stops where are you?'

I explained one was very soon in a field waiting for a car to take one back to the aerodrome. They didn't believe this. If the engine stopped in an aeroplane it fell to the ground like a stone!

However, I was not subjected to this type of questioning to any great extent. Most of the general conversation in those days had a sort of basic theme connected with horses and no-one was particularly interested in aeroplanes.

There was one very dear old lady, an old friend of the family, whom I met in Ludlow. She had a different outlook on the fact of my having joined the Air Force. She could remember fairly clearly the excitment over the Reform Act of 1831; in her youth her parents were still talking of Trafalgar and Waterloo, not as historical events but as recent news. She summed up her view of my future career in simple, direct terms:

'If I were a young girl today I'd go for that blue uniform every time.'

It was an entirely new thought to me and I could see my mother, who was present at the time, was a little doubtful of the wisdom of putting such ideas into a young man's head.

I was not, of course, in uniform at the time, but she must have seen a picture of it somewhere.

9 Army Cooperation

In early January 1926 those of us who were selected to go on Army Cooperation work assembled at the School of Army Cooperation at Old Sarum Aerodrome near Salisbury. Our ground training consisted of some technical (mostly radio) instruction, but it was mainly composed of lectures on Army Formations and Operations. Our practical flying work included finding our way about over the countryside, seeing what went on there and reporting it back to base. All this came under the main general heading of Reconnaissance (recce for short). During the 1910 manoeuvres of the Army an aeroplane had brought back information to the General Headquarters of one side which was of supreme importance. It was disbelieved, largely because it had not been brought back on a horse. In 1914 a very similar situation had arisen when the main German thrust had been observed and reported by an aeroplane. Again this information lacked the equine ingredient which alone could assure credibility by the General Staff, so it was treated with reserve if not ignored. By about 1916 when the war had become absolutely static, when cavalry could not move at all within a mile of the front line, aeroplanes were used for reconnaissance in the lower strata of the air whilst other aeroplanes fought for air supremacy above them.

So long as air supremacy was assured, or even in doubt, the Army Cooperation aeroplanes could carry on with their ordered jobs, which consisted essentially of photographing large areas of front line trenches, rather hurriedly observing troop movements just behind the front line and observing the result of artillery fire. Occasionally a relatively long range reconnaissance was ordered when strong cover was supposed to be provided by the fighter squadrons. On the whole all this was a leisurely affair, albeit dangerous for the pilots, but it could afford to be leisurely since the front line for most of the First World War only moved a few yards one way or the other every month — if it moved at all. Reporting artillery results was done rather more speedily since Wireless Telegraphy (W/T) was used. This meant that the pilot of an aeroplane reported back to the artillery by morse code, according to a prearranged code which he knew by heart.

The procedure developed in the First World War was for the

artillery observation aeroplanes to fly at between 2000 and 3000 feet between the guns and their targets. This height was chosen partly because it was convenient for sighting, but also because it was just above the range of rifle fire and too low for effective heavier anti-aircraft fire. It was also lower than enemy fighters liked to come down to if there was any danger of enemy fighters being in the locality. On the whole the observation aeroplanes could have a fairly peaceful existence under these conditions except for the occasional heavy shell passing them on its way to more remote targets.

The 'shoot' would usually have been prearranged with the pilot knowing where the guns were and also knowing the location of the various targets they would be shooting at. He therefore signalled when he was ready and then watched for the muzzle flash from the guns. Having seen the flash he could count for the correct number of seconds and look for the shell burst. Then he informed the gunners where this was by a form of clock code wherein the centre of the clock face was the target, 12 o'clock was directly over the clock face remote from the gun and the distance from the target was recorded by judging concentric circle distances, each circle having a code letter. When a direct hit was recorded the pilot would signal "GO, GO" meaning 'go on, go on' until he judged the target destroyed. On practice 'shoots' when the weather was bad and the pilot wanted to get home, the target was usually found very quickly, obliterated two shots later and the guns were quickly ranged on to another target which was dealt with in the same way until all the targets were finished and the pilot turned for home.

For practising this procedure, after pilots had memorized the general idea and the code, there was a primitive form of simulator in a hut where a typical Salisbury Plain area was represented, small lights simulated a muzzle flash of the gun and a puff of smoke showed where the shell had fallen. The puff of smoke came from an individual crawling about below, smoking a cigarette and puffing the smoke up through the painted sacking which was used to illustrate the area. The pilot doing the "shoot" was up in a balcony working a morse code signaller. After the pupil pilot had mastered the procedure on the simulator he could start doing more realistic 'shoots' from the air. In the early stages he flew over the area which had previously been laid out with 'puff bombs' which could be touched off with electric wires from a central control panel. The pilot then reported the positions of the puffs according to the clock code. As we became proficient we might have been allowed to do a real 'shoot' with a real battery, real shells and a real target, but in fact the Royal Artillery were so restricted in the number of shells they were allowed to expend that these real 'shoots' were so rare that only very

experienced pilots were employed to do them. The nearest approach
to a real 'shoot' we ever got to was when the Army actually got their
guns out and waved a yellow flag by the muzzle to simulate the flash:
a few seconds later a puff bomb would go off somewhere, if the
month's quota had not been used up already.

One has to remember that the period 1926 onwards, for almost a
decade, was one when political parties were vying with one another
in their enthusiasm for reducing the size of the Navy, getting the
Army back to pre-1914 size and abolishing the Air Force —
particularly the bomber force. It was only a year or so later that a
one-time girl friend of mine wrote and asked me to come and help
her fiance in his election campaign. That seemed to me to be asking
me to be very broadminded but when I opened my morning paper
and read that his particular party's main election cry was 'Abolish
the Air Force' I felt the obligation of 'Auld Lang Syne' was being
stretched a bit far. In any case we tried to be as non-political as
possible in the Services.

Our practices on reconnaissance could be more realistic in some
ways since we did not offend the tight political control through the
'Auditors' (more about them later!) by using up shells or puff
bombs. Reconnaissance reports were done by the simple process of
the pilot writing out (in triplicate) on a pad, what he had seen. He
then put it in a message bag, which was a long strip of multi-coloured
canvas with a lead weight on the end, and flew back to Army Group
HQ where he expected to see a white cross on the ground. He then
threw out the bag and the Army picked it up. Since there was
considered to be some danger of these messages falling into enemy
hands there was a requirement, occasionally observed, for the
messages to be encoded before they were written down. The code
could not easily be retained in the pilot's memory so he had a code
book with him. This was not supposed to fall into enemy hands. The
pilot, or observer, if he was not fighting off enemy fighters, was
expected to encode a message on the way back to Army HQ.

The whole process probably took at least one hour from the
moment the pilot saw something interesting and reported it till it was
decoded and laid reverently on the Army Commander's office table.
In the static war conditions of 1916/1917 this system probably
worked well enough, but we at the School of Army Cooperation at
Old Sarum in 1926 were preparing for the next war. In 1940 the
same system of Army Cooperation was essentially in force and the
German armour was moving at approximately 20 m.p.h. By the
time an Army Cooperation pilot had reported seeing a Panzer
division (if he ever got back to do it) the Panzer division was
probably 30 or 40 miles further on. It was largely this factor that

meant that most of the useful information obtained about the German advance in 1940 came through the R/T of Fighter squadrons with messages like:

'For God's sake don't try and land on "X" aerodrome — it's full of Panzers!'

But the 1916/17 system was the only one fully understood then (in 1926) and we were taught it down to the last detail. It was no fault of the staff at the School of Army Cooperation that there was no live Operational Plans Department anywhere in existence to think ahead.

It is probably fair to say that we pupils on the course had two main worries: one was the intense cold of those January days in the open cockpits of the Bristol Fighter, and the other was the fact that every alternate trip we had to sit in the back seat behind another pupil pilot in whom we might have very little confidence. Learning to report fictitious happenings to a disinterested and often non-existent Army HQ in an entirely synthetic situation offered little in the way of thrills, interest or excitement. But we ploughed on through the course and if one or two of us — as I did — felt some boredom at this synthetic, uninspiring existence, we might not have been wholly to blame. My partner in this, P/O Hayes, shared a somewhat similar view to me on the work. He was fortunately a very good pilot and he seemed also to have confidence in me. We flew very happily together. Within a couple of weeks we had mastered the art and whatever mystery there was in recce work and artillery 'shoots' as they were called. Thereafter we flew around looking at interesting towns, cities, forests, coast lines, etc. and duly reported imaginary troop movements on deserted parts of Salisbury Plain. On one occasion when I was flying in rather murky weather we went down to Southampton to see if any big ships were in the harbour and then returned following a small river which should have led us back to Salisbury Plain where we were supposed to be. We were busily sending W/T messages giving our position on the Plain and what we could see. By some careless error of navigation I got on to the River Avon and only noticed my error as I approached Christchurch. I observed, by looking at the weirs, that the river seemed to be flowing the wrong way. By then we had not the slightest idea where we were and decided we had better land and ask someone. We soon found a field but my old trouble with the Bristol throttle control recurred and I kept floating across the field which was only marginally large enough anyhow. Hayes was remarkably philosophic about these attempts and was even sitting up on the side of the cockpit giving cheerful advice. After three attempts I remembered what had happened before and, on the fourth, I shut the throttle with such a

SCHOOL ᴼF ARMY CO·OPERATION
OLD SARUM
12ᵀᴴ R.A.F. OFFICERS' COURSE
11ᵀᴴ JAN 1926 TO 3ᴿᴰ APRIL 1926.

F/O A.R.HAMILTON   F/O A.H.WHEELER.   P/O R.J.ADAMS.   F/O R.J.BETT.   P/O J.F.NICHOLAS.

F/O J.PHILLIPS.   P/O C.K.TIGHE.   P/O.F.C.ROWLAND.   P/O.C.A.BELL.   P/O.J.HOLMES.   P/O.N.K.HOWARD.   P/O.E.ADDIS.   F/O.F.S.COGHILL [R.C.A.F.]

P/O R.L.BURNETT.   P/O.C.P.VINES.   P/O M.HAYES.   W/DR.A.S.BARRATT.C.M.G.M.C.   S/LDR.A.W.F.GLENNY.M.C.D.F.C.   P/O.A.M.LOVE.   P/O.J.Y.K.POWLE.   F/LT.A.X.FLOWER.

F/OX L.K.GOUGH   F/O N.V.MORETON.   F/LT.E.R.B.PLAYFORD.   LT.COL.F.A.MILLS.D.S.O.M.C.   LT.COL.E.R.B.PLAYFORD.   P/O.A.ROWAN.   F/LT.A.ROWAN.   F/LT.J.K.A.JEAKES.D.F.C.

School of Army Cooperation, 12th course, Old Sarum, April 1926 slam that there was no doubt about it and we landed all right. Hayes found a local inhabitant who told us where we were. I offered to let Hayes fly the Bristol home after his nerve-wracking experience in the back, but he said he was confident enough with me so we took off and hurried back, arriving just as it was getting dark. We explained that we had got lost because 'one part of Salisbury Plain looks so like another!'

By the time we were half way through the course I had decided that Army Cooperation work was definitely not for me and Hayes said that if we failed the course we would be sent on fighters. We concentrated on failing and in due course succeeded but the desired result was not achieved. I applied to go to fighters and said I was not interested in Army Cooperation work. The Air Council said I had incurred their displeasure and I would go to No.2 Army Cooperation squadron and continue with my training there until I became proficient. This was the first of my three Air Council Displeasures, which I think must still be a record for any officer in the Service.

Hayes and I enjoyed the better weather in late March when we took to exploring the old disused aerodromes on the Plain. Boscombe Down was then closed with a care and maintenance party, and its hangars were full of SE 5as, which were subsequently put in a heap on the aerodrome and burned. One sunny afternoon we landed there and investigated the hangars and then we lay on the grass listening to Bournemouth Broadcasting Station which we could get on the Bristol's R/T. One of the aerodrome guards came up and asked us what we were doing and I said I wanted one of the SE 5as if I could have it. He told me I could have the lot so far as he was concerned. They were not on his charge and there was no record of how many there were. In 1927 I bought one from the Service for £50 and sold it again 2 years later for £125. Today an original SE 5a in that condition would be worth £10,000.

I left the School of Army Cooperation at Old Sarum on 1 April 1926 with few regrets. Both Hayes and I had been called before the Air Officer Commanding just before we left to be given a 'rocket' for failing the course and then we both got another for saying we had done it deliberately to get away from Army Cooperation. That was not the end of it since, as recorded, I then got the first of my Air Council Displeasures when the news reached the Air Ministry.

I was a little hurt to find my flying assessment had been down graded to 'Average' but subsequent enquiries revealed the fact that all the pupils seemed to be assessed that way since it was assumed that no pilot straight from the School could be an above average pilot on Army Cooperation work. An additional comment in the report was:

No. 2 Army Cooperation Squadron, Manston, 1926

'Flying satisfactorily but requires constant practice.'

This comment was also on almost all the pupils' reports but I used the comment for years afterwards when I had any difficulty in getting hold of an aeroplane to fly.

I went from Old Sarum School of Army Cooperation straight to No.2 Squadron and was put in a flight commanded by Flt Lt Noel Desoer who had previously been in charge of me when I was on probation. He greeted me with every appearance of pleasure but was a little worried about my report from Old Sarum. I explained the situation and said I was sorry but I really did want to go on fighters. He said he was sorry too but he could not do anything about it. He promised, however, that he would try and make my work in the Squadron as interesting as possible. We had always been, and remained, great friends and I worked as hard as I could in his flight. Although I had officially failed the Army Cooperation course I did know the work thoroughly and within three weeks my Squadron Commander, on the recommendation of Flt Lt Desoer, reported to Group H Q that I was entirely proficient. I was then in a quandary: I did not want to let my Flight Commander or my Squadron Commander down by doing careless work, but equally I did not want to achieve a reputation for being a good Army Cooperation pilot. I just waited to see what would turn up, but kept working efficiently.

During the first four months in No.2 Squadron from April until the end of July, I did just about 100 hours flying on Bristol Fighters, mostly on Army Cooperation work, but as promised by my Flight Commander, I was given jobs to do which were as interesting as could be found in Army Cooperation work. One must emphasize again that doing synthetic 'shoots' reporting imaginary shell falls to a non-existent gun battery, or even an existing one which couldn't afford to fire the guns, was a boring process and, on one very hot afternoon, I actually dozed off whilst buzzing through imaginary 'corrections' in morse code to a battery which was actually in existence but also doing a lot of make-believe down below. The airman observer in the rear leant forward and shook me, shouting:

'Sorry to wake you up Sir, but the battery won't make much sense of that last message.'

He was nearly as drowsy as I was.

Reconnaissances were better since we could fly up and down the crowded beaches to amuse the crowds or land at disused aerodromes to see what went on there. Sometimes we had cameras fitted, either vertical or oblique, and we usually took a few extra, more interesting photographs than the standard ones of old trenches on disused Army training grounds.

In July we were livened up for a fortnight by the undergraduates

71

in the Oxford University Air Squadron spending their summer camp on Manston Aerodrome. They were an enthusiastic lot and for those two weeks it seemed as though we were doing something worthwhile in showing them the workings of the Air Force at first hand. Many of them must have joined the Air Force or the Auxiliary Air Force and been part of that invaluable reserve we called upon in 1939. They flew with us in the back seat of the Bristol Fighter and enjoyed every minute of their time in the air, not least perhaps when we did a bit of low flying or some aerobatics, or came in to land over the Margate Road which ran straight across the old (extended) aerodrome and gave us the legitimate amusement of side slipping steeply down towards the cars and pedestrian holidaymakers who always stopped to watch the flying in spite of road signs forbidding it. Most of them seemed to enjoy it as much as we did, but we got occasional complaints. Some of these came through the Station Commander's wife, who was closely related to a very senior officer in the Air Force, and on occasions almost tended to assume the same rank and position herself, much to the embarrassment of her husband.

On one dull day when we were not on the flying programme we rang up our own Squadron Adjutant, assuming a high-pitched feminine voice which we hoped resembled that of the Station Commander's wife, and said:

'Pilot Officer Cannon, you've got to stop it — at once — your pilots are flying low over the road and frightening the crowds there. I shall tell my husband when he gets back but I'm coming up to your office now to see you do stop it. Understand I won't have it.'

Then we rang off and dropped in on P/O Cannon and started a rowdy party in his office, which got him still more worried as he begged us to move somewhere else as 'the old man's wife is on her way up.' We didn't get quite as far as sending in someone to impersonate the woman, who probably got credited with a lot more interference than she ever perpetrated. Our Squadron Commander was particularly annoyed by any interference of this kind since he was, or pretended to be, a confirmed bachelor.

Phoney telephone calls were a permanent amusement on our Station, as on many others, but with us they were abruptly curtailed after a famous one when the Station Adjutant on a very busy morning, and having been pestered by three practical jokers, answered the fourth with:

'Oh, for God's sake shut up. If you haven't got any bloody work to do I have.'

The voice at the other end — a voice of obvious authority said:

'Do you realise who you're talking to? It's the AOC here.'

The Adjutant thought quickly and replied:

'Do you know who *you* are talking to?'

The AOC said:

'No I don't.'

The Adjutant replied:

'Well thank God for that.'

Then he put the telephone down and went and flew in a Bristol Fighter to establish an alibi. Anyone might have been in his office when he was out!

Apart from the amusement we derived from coming in to land over the holiday crowds in a way which gave every appearance that we were completely out of control we also got some anxiety over the security aspect. There was literally no barrier or fence between the Margate Road and the aerodrome where our aeroplanes were parked. On one occasion, after lunch, I walked back to the flight from the Officers' Mess and found a civilian sitting in the seat of the Bristol Fighter I usually flew. He had two boys with him who were standing up one on each side looking in. I went up and pointed out to him that he was on Government land and sitting in a Government aeroplane. He replied that he was a taxpayer and therefore the aeroplane, or at least part of it, belonged to him. Before I had time to think up a reply to this he finished off his talk to the two boys, who were his sons. The talk was clearly meant for me as well:

'... well, that's how the controls work son, and they're good aeroplanes – or were when we used to look after them in 1917 – but mechanics today aren't what they were. Bit o' rust here ...'

He pointed to a minute speck on the exhaust pipe:

'... that split pin is spread the wrong way.'

He was right there too.

'Well, well, things aren't what they were in my day in the RFC.'

Then he turned and addressed his remarks directly to me:

'So you fly these things do you?'

He climbed out of the cockpit and cast an obviously expert eye over the rigging:

'Well, it's all yours.'

Apparently he had given up his taxpayer's share as not worth having.

This aspect of security was to become a very significant one almost immediately when the General Strike started and the Air Force, along with the other Services, was alerted. No.9 (Bomber) Squadron equipped with twin-engined Vickers Vimys, which was also on Manston Aerodrome, was allotted the task of flying newspapers around the countryside. This consisted mostly of flying the British Gazette which was published by the Government. As the weather was very bad a large number of the No.9 Squadron pilots lost

themselves and delivered the papers at diverse unintended desti-
nations. One load came back to Manston and we all collected copies
as souvenirs. The Commanding Officer of No.9 Squadron was told to
put in a report in writing to Group HQ explaining why his Squadron
could not navigate properly. He took a long time writing the report.

We in No.2 Squadron were kept in readiness doing nothing so our
Squadron Commander went to Group HQ to ask why the 'best'
squadron in the Air Force was not being used in this national
emergency. Perhaps to make him feel better he was told that No.2
Squadron was being kept ready for any really important work since
the Air Ministry knew they could be relied on. He came back purring
but was still a little worried at this inactivity; airmen and officers
tend to get restless under such conditions. So far as I know the
airmen in those days were completely apolitical and were prepared to
do just as they were told. Any decision they had to make about
obedience and discipline had been made when they decided to join
the Service. On the whole that is not a bad outlook since one can
hardly have a situation where Service personnel start arguing about
orders once 'battle's begun.' But admittedly there could be some
very worrying moments when they are used 'in support of civil
power' as the Manual of Air Force Law and King's Regulations
describe it. To while away the time we all read up the appropriate
sections and paragraphs so as to know all about them. We were not
allowed to fly since there were doubts about fuel supplies if
communications broke down. We took a lot more trouble about
guard duties since there were alleged to be Bolshevik elements in
Ramsgate and Margate. There certainly was one since he turned up in
the Canteen distributing leaflets and free beer to the airmen there.
When he ran out of money and could buy no more beer they threw
him out of the Canteen, but kept some of the pamphlets and framed
them because the officers wanted to keep them as souvenirs too.
There was one memorable phrase at the end of the pamphlet:

'. . . so if any snotty little officer gives you an order, don't obey it,
REMEMBER McCAFFETTY.'

By a strange coincidence the Station Commander at Manston, who
was rather worried about the whole situation, had an A/C 2
McCaffetty up in front of him on some small charge the next day.
Before the airman was marched in the Station Adjutant, who had a
highly developed, perhaps an over-developed, sense of humour, had
handed the Station Commander one of the pamphlets to read just
before the 'orderly room charges were taken'. The Station Commander read the pamphlet through with an increasingly perturbed
expression on his face. As he came to the end he said to the
Adjutant:

74

'Flt Lt Tomlins, what's this about McCaffetty. Who was Mc-Caffetty?'

'Private McCaffetty, Sir, shot his commanding officer in 1897.'

The CO almost jumped out of his chair.

'But this is incitement to murder!'

'Yes Sir. Will you take the charges now Sir?'

'Yes, yes. All right. I'll take them.'

The Adjutant opened the door and said:

'Bring in the first charge Mr Brown.'

The traditional procedure ensued and the Station Sergeant Major (Disciplinary) went into action:

'Atten-shun. Quick march. . . .right wheel. . . .mark time. . . . . Halt. Left turn.'

'A/C 2 McCaffetty, Sir.'

We were never told of the final outcome of this interview but popular opinion held that the discussion went something like this:

'What's your name?'

'McCaffetty, Sir.'

'McCaffetty have you had any relations in the Services?'

'Not now Sir, but my father did very well in the Army in 1897 Sir.'

'Case dismissed.'

The General Strike fizzled out soon after and we all returned to normal, except for the CO of No.9 Squadron who was still trying to write his report. One of his least efficient young officers, who had also disgraced himself in some minor way, came in for a lot of trouble and was awarded seven extra duties as Orderly Officer, which incidently is against Regulations since duties cannot be assigned as punishments. Indeed, in certain cases assigning further duty to a delinquent can be argued in Military Law to condone the offence since one had (in effect) shown further confidence in the individual. Rather far-fetched but the plea has nevertheless proved a successful defence against any further punishment. In this case the young officer, P/O Simpell, bolted in panic. He had been a variety performer before so he went off and rejoined the troop where his young wife was also performing. He was found fairly easily, brought back under close arrest and in due course of time he was Court Martialled for desertion. Many of the junior officers at Manston were appointed to attend 'under instruction'. There was a lot of sympathy for the accused since he was rather pathetic case of a weak and unintelligent young officer who, due to his characteristics (or lack of them), was always in trouble.

The Court room, as frequently happened, was in a large room in the Officers' Mess. The Court sat at a table at one end of the room.

A Vickers Vimy bomber, powered by two 285 h.p. Rolls-Royce Eagle engines

Opposite them and on each side of the room were the Prosecution and Defence, the latter being close to the accused. Witnesses were brought in one at a time by a Court orderly. At the back of the room, remote from the Court, were the officers under instruction. All officers were dressed in No.1 Dress *i.e.* breeches and puttees, but Field officers (Squadron Leaders and above) wore Field Boots instead of puttees. These had been abolished as well as puttees by the time I achieved Field rank so I never found out which of the two were the most uncomfortable. All the tables in the room were covered with the standard medium dark blue cloth which did not show spilled ink too badly, but still bore some evidence of stains from previous hearings.

As the Court Martial opened the President asked where the Defending Officer was and it transpired that the accused had not asked for one. The President said he must have one as he was clearly incapable of conducting his own defence. This caused consternation since there was likely to be a long delay whilst a suitable officer was found. The problem was resolved by one of our number, Flying Officer Barlow (later Air Commodore Sir Richard Barlow, Bart.), himself supposed to be under instruction, jumping up with King's Regulations and the Manual of Air Force Law in his hands and announcing: 'I'll defend him, Sir.'

This was unusual, if not irregular, but Barlow had a force of personality which was difficult to resist and there seemed to be no alternative anyway. In some doubt, the President agreed and Barlow

76

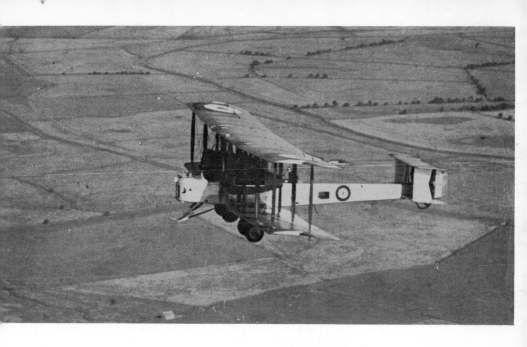

A Vimy of No. 9 Squadron in flight near Manston, 1926

conducted what is often described as a 'spirited defence'. It was just unfortunate that of the two complementary factors available for the defence, one of them was the argument of victimization by his Commanding Officer, culminating in an illegal punishment. The other line of defence against the charge of desertion, which is a very serious offence, was the argument that he was, in fact, only 'absent without leave', which is a relatively minor offence. The usual acid test to distinguish between the two, apart from what the accused himself says at his trial, is whether his action in leaving and after he left indicates any intention to return sometime. For instance, if the chap pushes off with all his belongings, sells his uniform, changes his name and takes a permanent job somewhere, the evidence is against him. In P/O Simpell's case he had left his uniform and service equipment in his room, he had not changed his name, and no-one in 1926 could claim that employment in a third-rate travelling troop of variety artists was a permanent job. The prosecution argued that the accused had probably forgotten to take his belongings with him, had meant to change his name but could not think of another one, and assumed the job to be permanent. They may have been right but F/O Barlow was a very able and persuasive defence Counsel. Having disposed of those points he called P/O Simpell's Commanding Officer — who was also his own C O — as a witness and proceeded to put him through a gruelling cross-examination which brought out clearly some indication of victimization. When Barlow got on to the question of the illegality of the punishment, the President of the

Court stopped the cross-examination. The sight of a junior Flying Officer indicting his own C O was too much for the Court. Barlow gracefully gave way, but the points had been made. A verdict of 'Absent without leave' was brought in and P/O Simpell was allowed to resign his commission and get that portion of his gratuity which was owing to him. We all hoped *Mr* and Mrs Simpell would live happily ever after. F/O Barlow received rather guarded congratulations on his defence from the Court. As the heir to a baronetcy and a very efficient and conscientious officer he did not worry what his C O might think about him after the case. In any case, the C O still had his report to write and F/O Barlow was one of the few pilots in his squadron who had not lost himself delivering newspapers during the General Strike.

A few weeks later Barlow was in mild trouble on a cross country flight at night. The route took him West and then North of London and back over the Thames east of London. He was not supposed to take the shortest route back since it would have been across the Thames Estuary at a fairly wide point. However, it was a clear starlight night and the lights of ships and navigation aids in the estuary were so beautiful that Barlow decided to take the wide crossing. After all, he had two Rolls-Royce Eagle engines and they gave little trouble. It was unthinkable that both would stop during what was only about a 12 minute crossing. What Barlow did not know was that one of his main fuel tank cocks had been turned off immediately against the tank itself during an overhaul. The cock was normally wired on permanently and the pilot controlled the flow through other cocks. Almost exactly in the middle of the estuary both engines quit together. Barlow made a perfect 'alighting' on the water into wind, touching down at a forward speed of only about 30 m.p.h. but he wasn't where he should have been! As expected of him, his immediate action was exemplary in every respect thereafter, even to recording the rate of sinking of the Vimy as the wings and tanks slowly filled with water. When daylight came they were quickly seen, still just afloat, in that busy sea lane. They were all rescued but the Vimy sank. Barlow had to answer a few questions on the navigational aspect of the occurrence but he was warmly commended for his action on the sea. Some months later a letter came through from Group H Q pointing out that the Vimy must have been seriously overloaded and giving a list of the items which were alleged to have been on it when it sank: the list had all the weights annotated alongside. There was in it an incredible assortment of Service equipment aboard — the list, if carefully checked, would probably have included every item which members of No.9 Squadron had found missing from their individual inventories. Everything was on it except the proverbial kitchen stove. That, of course, would have been a fire risk!

Fortunately someone in Group H Q had a sense of humour even if they lacked that over-meticulous sense of administrative responsibility which nearly lost us the war in 1940.

1 0 Flying new types

In one of those rare bursts of accurate appreciation of future requirements by defence Committees and the still rarer let-ups on financial stringency by the Treasury, it had been agreed some 3 to 4 years earlier that a new type of Army Cooperation aeroplane was not only required, but would actually be provided. The decision might not have been made so promptly but for the fact that the rate of wastage of the Bristol Fighters, coupled with the limited numbers left over from the war stocks, made it apparent that the Army Cooperation Squadrons would soon be short of aeroplanes. This would result in the Army not getting the cooperation from the Air Force which had been promised. This, in turn, would have resulted in the Army again raising their demand for a separate Flying Corps under the control of the Army and would have been bound to touch off a demand by the Navy for a reversal of the recently declared Government policy of an independent Air Force, so that the Navy could again have its own Fleet Air Arm under absolute control. Any circumstance which could have touched off such a train of events was highly undesirable from the Air Force point of view. Accordingly a specification had been put out detailing the requirements for a Bristol Fighter replacement for Army Cooperation. As in the case of all such specifications, particularly in time of peace, the specification required a new type to be able to do everything which a staff officer in the Operational Requirements Section could think up. Although these requirements were almost more than all-embracing, fortunately they did not make it impossible for the new aeroplane to fly properly, and four firms competed for the contract with four very different but very reasonable types. In any case, it was tacitly accepted, though probably not stated, that the new aeroplane must perform better than the one it was to replace. The Bristol Fighter was a very good aeroplane. The aeroplanes produced to compete against one another were the Atlas, designed by Armstrong Whitworth's, the Boarhound designed by the Bristol Aeroplane Company, the Hyena designed by De Havilland's and the Vespa designed by Vickers (see illustrations on pages 82, 86, 90 and 91).

The competing companies had, of course, interpreted the requirements of the specification in slightly different ways giving more

80

emphasis to one requirement than to another. But it is fair to say — with the reservations mentioned later — that any one of these aeroplanes would have performed reasonably well in its intended operational role, although none of them, as it turned out, ever had to pass the acid test of a serious war.

The essential requirements were for the aeroplane to be able to operate from the same size of field as a Bristol Fighter, but to have a better speed and climb. It had to carry rather more in operational load than the Bristol, including such items as Radio (R/T and W/T), guns, bombs, message picking up devices, and all the operational oddments like Verey pistol signalling devices, map pockets, etc. which were then fitted in every operational aeroplane in the Royal Air Force.

By 1926 the four aeroplanes had already been tested for acceptance (provisionally) by the Aeroplane and Armament Experimental Establishment at Martlesham Heath on the Suffolk coast and all four had been found to come up to their specification requirement. It was then decided to send them to the operational squadrons to get the squadron pilots' opinions.

The first one to arrive was the Vickers' Vespa which was flown in from Martlesham Heath on 9 August 1926. We all crowded round the gleaming silver-doped Vickers' designed aeroplane with admiration and wonder — admiration at the gleaming newness of it, wonder at its size. It had a very considerable span which, a few years later, enabled it to achieve the World's height record with the Bristol Test pilot, Cyril Uwins flying it. However, this possibility was not then apparent to us, nor indeed relevant to our operational needs. The Vespa was, however, a very fine aeroplane and in many ways it fulfilled our requirements exactly. Two factors ultimately eliminated it from the selection, neither of which was likely to have been written into the original specification. Firstly, its sheer size made it impossible to get a Squadron of them into the existing size of hangars available to the Army Cooperation Squadrons, and having squeezed the money for the aeroplanes out of the Treasury it was unlikely that the Air Force could then have squeezed still more money out of them for enlarging the hangar space. The second factor was an obscure one which only became apparent almost by accident when we were trying to fly close to another aeroplane to take a photograph of the Vespa for Squadron and personal record purposes. The position of the upper wing made it extremely difficult for a pilot to fly in formation with another aircraft and continuously to keep it in sight. This could have been a serious handicap in the operations normally undertaken at that time. However, these factors became apparent later in final assessment of the four contenders. At

A Vickers Vespa, powered by a 425 h.p. Jaguar engine, at Manston,
1926

that time on the sunny afternoon of 9 August 1926 we were all
standing round looking at it and wondering which of the Squadron
pilots would be chosen to do the first flight on it. Our Squadron
Commander, Squadron Leader R. E. Saul, had been very reticent on
the subject although it was known that he had been in conference
with the Flight Commanders, particularly with Flt Lt Desoer, who
was the senior Flight Commander. Some of the older and more
experienced pilots, some of them war time pilots, felt they had a
good chance of being selected since, apart from their experience,
they had flown quite a number of types of aeroplanes besides the
Bristol Fighter. On the other hand, most of these older Squadron
pilots were not much in favour with the present Squadron
Commander for one reason or another.

We were all in deep discussion on possibilities in a group in front
of the hangars not far from the Vespa. Not far away, but out of
earshot, the Squadron Commander was talking to my Flight
Commander. This meant little to me since I could hardly hope, as a
newly joined pilot, to do the first flight, or for that matter even get a
chance to fly it later. At last the Squadron Commander walked
across to our group. As he came close he called to me to come over. I
walked across and saluted very smartly indeed, hoping at least to get
sufficiently into his good graces to be allowed to fly later. He said,
quite loud enough for the other pilots to hear:

'Wheeler, I want you to do the tests on these aeroplanes first. You
have had experience on Snipes and we can't take any risks with
them.'

He glanced at some of the pilots who were badly out of favour and

82

then went on, more quietly with, I thought, not inconsiderable anxiety:

'Don't try and be clever. Just fly it round for a few circuits, and see how it handles, then land and report to me.'

I was so surprised I just stood with my mouth open with a look which must have been an all-high in inanity. For a moment I think my Squadron Commander doubted the wisdom of his decision when he saw me look so bewildered, but my Flight Commander was nodding reassuringly to me behind him and I recovered quickly.

'Yes Sir. Thank you very much Sir. I'll go and get my flying kit, Sir.'

I saluted and rushed off to the Flight Office. It occurred to me that he could hardly change his mind after I had got my flying kit and returned. In any case I knew my Flight Commander would use all his influence on my behalf — as he had clearly done already. They were certainly keeping to their promise to give me interesting jobs.

When I came back with my flying kit on there was a little delay whilst mechanics were checking the Vespa over and ballasting her to represent a passenger. I spent some of this time making my peace with the older officers in the Squadron. Tactfully I went up to them and said:

'I don't know why the old man has done this, I shall probably break the thing!'

But they were good fellows and did not seem to grudge me the job. In any case only one of them could have been lucky. They all wished me well:

'You'll be all right.'

'Good luck.'

'She'll probably come in a bit faster than the Bristol.'

'Open up slowly in case she swings, but she'll be much easier than a Snipe.'

I felt more confident after that and walked over to the Vespa. My Squadron Commander was having quite a few qualms however. He came up to me and repeated:

'Don't try and be clever. You have flown Snipes haven't you?'

I tried to look confident and reassuring:

'Yes Sir. I am sure I shall be all right on this.'

I climbed in and looked over the controls. One of the Bristol mechanics was there to help. They were pretty simple in those days with no special complications in the Bristol radial engine.

Manston aerodrome was very big by 1926 standards and there was no trouble in operating from it. The engine started easily and after warming up I ran it up, checking the magnetos, oil pressure and maximum r.p.m. as I did so. There was nothing else to check in those days. The Vespa was already parked almost at take-off point which, in some ways, was not a help since I have always found it easier to taxi a new type at least a little way to get the feel of it on the ground. But I did not want to add to my Squadron Commander's anxiety by doing a lot of (apparently) unnecessary taxiing: in any case he might still change his mind.

To prevent any possibility of that I opened up the engine carefully but determinedly and took off. There were no surprises and I flew around at 2500 feet trying out the slow speed end of the speed range with particular attention to gliding turns and side slips. I stalled it two or three times to be sure of the feel before she 'went'. When I felt absolutely sure of the handling I came in to land carefully checking the approach speed. To my surprise the Vespa seemed to float much further than I expected after I had levelled out to land. She would not settle down and I floated on and on across the aerodrome. I put the throttle on and climbed away wondering why I had come in too fast. At 1000 feet on the circuit I checked the stall again: it was as I had expected. I worried, and if I worried I was pretty sure that both my Flight Commander and my Squadron Commander would be worrying even more. I wondered if the idling speed of the engine had been set too high. Then suddenly it dawned on me that my old fault of over-gentleness on the throttle had again caught me out. I tried it, and sure enough there was that hard spot on the throttle near the closed position. One did not feel it when one was shutting the throttle with confidence, but my gentle hesitant 'feeling' back of the throttle had resulted in my failing to close it. I came in again and as I started my final approach to the aerodrome I slammed the throttle shut. Fortunately I had anticipated a much steeper glide so I came in with a little spare speed — 7 m.p.h. for my own and my Squadron Commander's peace of mind — and the Vespa settled down very well. I taxied in, switched the engine off and reported to the Squadron Commander who wanted to know why I had floated across the aerodrome the first time. I explained that it was my fault in not giving the throttle a good pull to close it. He only remarked that I had better make a point of that when I was giving the other pilots dual as they might damage the aeroplane. He probably wished they could have heard that remark. For myself I could see even more embarrassing times ahead if I were to give instruction to the older pilots in the Squadron, some of whom had at least five times my experience. I took the Vespa up again the next day with an airman as a passenger and tried it out thoroughly in all operational manoeuvres, including aerobatics. It behaved very well for the big aeroplane it was, but some of the manoeuvres were a little unwieldy because of its great span. It went into a spin and came out again very safely. The spin itself was rather flat and gave one the impression that even if one spun into the ground it would hardly do more than break the undercarriage. This was certainly an illusion created by the apparently flat attitude of spinning and the very low wing loading which gave it such a wonderful performance at high altitude. One of the criticisms I had of it was the difficulty one experienced in flying near the ground: the position of the upper wing almost level with the pilot's eye-line made it very difficult to see obstructions like trees and houses and low flying was a definite requirement for an Army Cooperation aeroplane. At high altitude it handled better than the other three aeroplanes but we only went to 20,000 feet on these tests since we had no oxygen. But we did have parachutes in these new aircraft and they took all the worry out of high altitude work.

On the day after the Vespa arrived the Armstrong Whitworth Atlas arrived also from Martlesham Heath, and the pilot who brought it gave me a very quick superficial explanation of the various controls and then remembered he had urgent work back at Martlesham. None of the test pilots seemed to relish the idea of giving any flying instruction to us with the very rudimentary and minimal flying controls available in the back seat. In fact we did not need any instruction since none of the aeroplanes had difficult characteristics. The Atlas was probably the least easy to fly of the four aeroplanes. But it had the best performance all round. It like to be landed properly whereas the other three could more or less be thrown on the ground. Its controls were also just a little bit more sensitive with a slight feeling on the tail controls that they might become over-balanced at certain conditions of speed and manoeuvring: but in fact they never did. Thus aerobatics and quick manoeuvres were a joy on the Atlas. It was probably for this reason that I, early on, became persuaded that it was the one we should select and indeed the one we would all select if war seemed imminent. In 1926 there was, of course, no foreseeable chance of a major war anywhere and for this reason some of the older pilots preferred either the Vespa, which was very easy to fly, or the Boarhound, which was very warm, draught-free and comfortable.

I took up the Atlas soon after it arrived and felt quite confident in my ability to handle it. After all I had now flown FOUR different types of aeroplanes! I was not, however, by any means over-confident. I was very well aware that if I damaged anything I would very likely be taken off the testing work. In the case of the Atlas my first flight lasted an hour. I quickly sensed that it needed more careful handling than the Vespa so I practised every attitude which might be involved in the approach and landing before I came in for the first time. Then I practised landings and take-offs so that I would

Armstrong Siddeley Atlas, powered by a 375 h.p. Jaguar engine

feel confident when I was taking up the other pilots.

So far as any of the aeroplanes needed to do aerobatics, which was not a very important function in their operational life, the Atlas came out best. This ability to perform aerobatics was a great help in low flying where quick manoeuvres to avoid obstructions were important, although it was still of secondary importance to the ability of the pilot to see the obstructions. If forward and sideways view was restricted any sensible pilot flew well above likely obstructions.

The qualities of the Atlas quickly spread throughout the Station and several pilots, including the Flight Commander of another flight, joined the queue to be taken up and shown how it flew. Within a week F/O Barlow of No.9 Bomber Squadron asked me to take him up. I knew Barlow for a pilot who wanted to get all he could out of every aeroplane he flew. Normally he was flying the twin-engined Vickers Vimy bomber with which his Squadron was equipped, but they also had an Avro 504K in the Squadron so that the pilots could keep their hands in on light types. On several occasions I had met this Avro in the air around the aerodrome and it was nearly always being flown by F/O Barlow. On these occasions it invariably 'attacked' me. Although the Avro had not much chance against a Bristol Fighter, since the Bristol could always get away, climb up and then come back to the attack from above, I learnt to respect the

86

Avro when F/O Barlow was flying it. There were many interesting encounters between Barlow and myself when the Avro, in his hands, proved a worthy adversary. He certainly flew it to its limits. For this reason I was not very keen to take Barlow up in the Atlas in case he found out there was a form of dual control in the back which could be rigged up. Fortunately the control column was clipped up under the cockpit cowling where it could not easily be seen, and even if found it had to be fitted into a not very obvious socket. The rudder bar likewise was not very apparent since it was located forward of the observer's seat almost under the pilot. The throttle was in the normal place on the port (left hand) side of the cockpit but even the most lighthearted 'observer' could not do much with the throttle alone unless he rigged up the other controls. But Barlow was the sort of chap who might find all these controls, rig them and then ask to take over. I was taking no risks so I said I would love to take him up but unfortunately I had orders not to take up anyone without my own and their own Squadron Commanders' permission. I felt this was fairly safe since Barlow was still slightly *persona non grata* with his C O over the Court Martial cross-examination and there was such a queue of pilots in No.2 Squadron wanting to fly the Atlas that I felt a pilot from No.9 Squadron would be so far down the queue that he would not stand a chance. I was wrong. Within a day Barlow had put forward a complicated theory whereby it seemed essential to the whole Air Force strategy, training and morale that F/O Barlow should go up in the back seat of the Atlas. His theory was accepted.

I resigned myself to an anxious flight but told Barlow that it would have to be a short one since there were other pilots who wanted to fly. He said a short one would be quite enough. How right he was! I did not tell him about the dual controls and we took off and climbed to 3000 feet so that I could show him how well the Atlas manoeuvred. As we were doing a steep turn the engine suddenly cut. I was not deceived by this since I always did, and still do now most of the time, have my hand on the throttle (relic of rotary engine days) and I felt the throttle move back. Barlow had found the throttle. I turned round to remonstrate and saw he was waving the stick in his hand above the cockpit cowling. He held the throttle shut to reduce the noise and shouted:

'I'll fix this and fly her a bit.'

I shouted back:

'No you won't.'

He hit me fairly gently on the head with the stick and said:

'Won't I?'

I said:

'No, you won't.'

He hit me much harder on the head and repeated:
'Won't I?'
I said:
'All right.'
His head disappeared into the cockpit whilst he pushed the stick into its socket, then he shouted:
'I've got her.'
Thereafter we went through a series of manoeuvres, starting gently but with ever-increasing diversity and enthusiasm until we were down to 1500 feet. At that height Barlow dived to 1000 feet for a third loop: as he pulled up from the dive I felt a sudden dip of the Atlas's nose and it continued in its dive at a fairly steep angle. Barlow was shouting at me and I guessed his control column had come out of its socket. There was no trim control in the rear cockpit. I pretended not to understand what he was saying and just looked back and smiled inanely, holding my hands up to show I still conceded control to him. He waved his stick at me — not hitting me on the head this time — and shouted:
'You take over, the stick's come out.'
I shouted back:
'Yes, carry on. You've got her.'
Barlow was in a very justifiable frenzy.
'You fool, look.'
He waved the stick at me. I just smiled again and held my hands up to show I was not doing anything. I watched Barlow out of the corner of my eye and we were now down to 700 feet in a fairly steep dive. As I anticipated I saw his head go down into the cockpit as he tried to fit the stick back into its socket. I knew he would be bent almost double with his head right down. At that moment I pulled firmly back on the control column imposing a good 4 g (four times the normal gravitational force) on the Atlas. I looked back into the rear cockpit and there was no sign of Barlow: he was, as I expected, crumpled upon the floor unable to raise his head against the 4 g load. I knew that as soon as I eased the load he would re-fit the control and try a few more manoeuvres but I had had enough and was in no mood for a low flying spree across the Kent countryside dodging trees or, another popular amusement, flying along the Margate and Ramsgate beaches chasing the bathers, first into the sea and then out of it again on the return. Strangely almost no-one seemed to mind this amongst the holidaymakers, who always waved and cheered. If there was the odd one complaining, by the time he had got to a telephone one had time to get back, land, and, best of all, sometimes receive the complaint oneself by answering the telephone and saying — with perfect truth — that no-one was flying at the Squadron.

However, this amusement laid on by F/O Barlow in the back seat with an unreliable control and a desire for the 'last laugh' on me, was a thing to be avoided. I kept a load of about 2½ g on as I turned for the aerodrome and then came in to land in a series of tight gliding turns and a few violent side-slips. By the time Barlow had recovered himself we were on the ground and I was politely asking him how he liked the flight. He said it was a pleasure and invited me to come up in the back seat of the No.9 Squadron Avro, but there was a look in his eye that persuaded me to decline the offer. Barlow remained a good friend and was always a great pilot and a famous navigator. It was a tragedy when, after the 1939/45 War he was killed in an accident in South America when an aircraft, which I heard he was not piloting himself, flew into a mountain.

Soon after my flight with F/O Barlow those of us testing the aircraft were due to check the maximum speed at ground level of the first two — the Vickers' Vespa and the Armstong Atlas. We arranged an early morning flight for these to avoid undue turbulence and at 7.15 a m I took off with F/O Hadden in the back to check the speed. I recorded an indicated speed of 134 m.p.h. on the Atlas. At 9.55 a m I did the same speed test on the Vespa, also with F/O Hadden in the back, and recorded an indicated speed of 120 m.p.h. These speeds were probably fairly accurate since the instruments would have been carefully calibrated shortly before at Marlesham Heath. They showed that the Vespa had only 10 m.p.h. more speed than the Bristol Fighter, but the Atlas had 24 m.p.h. over the Bristol and 14 m.p.h. over the Vespa. It was not much improvement in any case after almost 10 years' development in aviation, but the fact was that aeronautical development almost stopped after the first World War ended in 1918. I had also taken the Atlas to 20,000 feet on a height test so there was no doubt that its speed had not been achieved at the expense of other qualities. In fact the Atlas was a very similar design to the already famous Siskin fighter from the same firm, which was in service in our fighter squadrons.

The recorded speed of the Atlas was 142½ m.p.h. at 15,000 feet, but at full load it was recorded at 124 m.p.h. This probably corresponds to the speeds we got in No.2 Squadron. The Vespa Mk.VI was credited with a speed of 149 m.p.h. at 10,000 feet, but this was probably a later Mark with a more powerful engine than we had at Manston.

By this time the rivalry between the Vickers Vespa and the Armstrong Whitworth Atlas had become fairly intense and representatives from the two firms arrived on the Station to extol the (already appreciated) virtues of their products. The Armstrong Whitworth representative was Flt Lt (retired RFC) Bennet-Baggs,

who was a test pilot with the firm and a cheerful type. On the Vickers side we had (almost) the heir apparent to the Vickers fortunes in the name of Oliver Vickers. Both Bennet-Baggs and Oliver Vickers were old friends and the rivalry was — and would still be — a model of wisdom and sales decorum. Neither of them stooped to decry the other's product: they both studied our operational requirements meticulously and tried to show how their product met them. If they emphasized their own product's special advantages in design in meeting these requirements over the other product, well it was just a technical matter which could be worked out on a slide rule.

We who were testing the aeroplanes had a very happy association with both, and if it so happened, as it did, that I was offered a job in both firms as a test pilot at a salary about double my Air Force pay, well it was just because both representatives recognized a really able pilot — or so I would have liked to believe! But at the advanced age · of 23 I was just old enough to realize that perhaps other considerations had come into their generous offers. However, these offers lent a useful background to my intention to force through the issue of my being posted to Fighters — even to the point of resignation from the Service.

Left: De Havilland Hyena, powered by a 375 h.p. Jaguar engine

Below: a Bristol Boarhound, powered by a 450 h.p. Jupiter engine, at Manston, 1926

At this stage, on 19 August 1926, the De Havilland Hyena arrived and I flew it in the late afternoon of that day. As one would expect from that magnificent company (Enterprise) De Havillands, the Hyena was a very good compromise of all the diverse requirements which the specification had asked for. It did all of them well, but it was not superlative on any one. Like the two other unsuccessful contenders it had concentrated on meeting the specification rather than building a good aeroplane first and then adapting it to meet the requirements. Famous historic and classic aeroplanes which achieved the latter by concentrating on the former were the Spitfire (originally built to get the world's speed record) and the Mosquito which threw all defensive armament away and was designed for all out speed with a moderate bomb load.

The Hyena was a good all-rounder, but hit the headlines nowhere. However I took a great interest in it. It was the first product I had flown designed by that great firm, De Havillands, and I wanted to check all its characteristics. None of these were outstanding but all were acceptable. At the time one must remember that De Havillands were concentrating on the design, development and sales of the DH60 Moth, which almost revolutionized private flying in England and also in many other parts of the world. One feature of the Hyena struck me forcibly and that was its unusual recovery from a spin. I had made a point of spinning all the aeroplanes since I had then, and still have, a theory that all aeroplanes reveal their basic medium to low speed characteristics best on their entry into a spin and their recovery from it. That, of course, goes for aeroplanes which are expected to do that sort of manoeuvre. I am not suggesting that a BAC VC10 or a Boeing 707, or a Boeing 747, or even a Concorde should be judged that way! But light aeroplanes during stalling manoeuvres reveal their characteristics in a most impressive way. The particular feature which impressed me in the Hyena's recovery from the spin was that if one took the normal recovery action — opposite rudder and the stick forward of centre — the Hyena came out all right, indeed rather abruptly, but in a dive so steep it was almost beyond the vertical. I tried this out two or three times, taking the precaution of doing it at about 5000 feet and found that the Hyena came out very well indeed with opposite rudder but the stick held back slightly nose-up of the central position. It then more or less flew out of the spin without a very steep dive, and the height loss in recovery was only about 300 or 400 feet, as against 700 or 800 feet if it got into a very steep dive.

It was fortunate I made this discovery. While taking up one of the pilots of the Squadron to show him the handling characteristics of the Hyena, he took over the dual controls rigged in the back and very soon got it into a spin at about 1200 feet. I quickly checked his corrective action, firmly holding the stick back to prevent us going into an almost inverted dive. I could feel him pushing on the stick to try and take the normal corrective action but the Hyena came out of the spin and flew away pleasantly before his pressure on the stick became significant. Afterwards he asked me why on earth I held the stick back whilst we were trying to get out of a spin. In answer I said that as he was soon going up solo, he should go to 6000 feet and try the normal recovery action. When he came down after his flight he said to me:

'By God you're right! I have never known an aeroplane do that before. We shouldn't have had much height to spare if we'd tried to come out the normal way.'

In many ways this was no criticism of the Hyena since the normal recovery action for many aeroplanes developed later was to use opposite rudder and hold the stick approximately central. Indeed there have been recorded cases of rather vicious aeroplanes which if the stick was pushed right forward would flick out of a normal spin one way into an inverted spin and the other way. This could cause the pilot quite a lot of embarrassment!

The last of the four new aeroplanes to arrive was the Bristol Boarhound which flew in on 24 August and again the Martlesham Test Pilot who brought it spent little time briefing us on its characteristics but he did remark to a slightly astonished group of us:

'Quite a nice aeroplane, but I shouldn't side-slip it if I were you: the fin breaks off.'

Whatever the evidence may have been for this remark we decided not to take it too seriously and a check up with the firm seemed to confirm that the fin was quite strong enough. Just as a precaution I did a few gentle side slips first, increasing the angle until I had got a full vertical side slip angle. There was no sign of weakness or looseness in the tail bracing wires as the test progressed. Beyond this there was very little of interest in the Boarhound. We were all slightly prejudiced towards it because it came from the same firm as our beloved Bristol Fighters; also it was a delightfully warm, comfortable and stable aeroplane to fly. We heard that several Group H Q staff officers favoured it as did one of the other three Army Cooperation squadrons. But opinion in No.2 Squadron still strongly favoured the Atlas. At this stage an incident occurred which may or may not have had a fatal repercussion connected with it shortly after.

There were two views on it. Several of us were flying these new types by now, although I was on them continuously. One of the pilots in the same flight as me was a very junior Pilot Officer who, although quite a good pilot, tended to have bursts of over-confidence when the risks he took could hardly be termed 'calculated'. He had been put on to do a lot of the testing of the new aeroplanes. One day a Bristol Fighter had just come out of the workshops with a new engine fitted needing the standard air test. Flt Lt Desoer asked this officer, P/O Reid, to do the test but Reid said he was bored with Bristols and only wanted to fly the new types. I realized that Desoer did not want to order Reid to do the test but he was a little put out at the refusal so I said quickly I would like to do it. Desoer was very pleased and, as I had foreseen I got all the flying on the new types afterwards that he could possibly give me. In any case I always liked doing aircraft tests because it gave one a chance to do anything one liked in the air. Some weeks later when all the new types had left the Squadron, P/O Reid was sent on a detachment to a small landing ground near an Army camp. There were only two pilots there and the detachment was commanded by a senior Flying Officer (Holder) who had not been put on testing the new types even though he was a very reliable pilot indeed. One of their jobs on the detachment was to take up Army officers for air experience. On one of these trips P/O Reid was coming in to land very slowly and turned round to speak to the Army officer. With his attention diverted from the approach, he stalled the Bristol Fighter badly and it spun in from about 150 feet. The Army officer was badly hurt, but P/O Reid was killed. In the ensuing enquiry criticism was levelled at F/O Holder in charge of the detachment because it was said he allowed the flying discipline to become lax. F/O Holder indignantly denied this charge and said that P/O Reid should never have been put on to testing the new types since it had made him even more over-confident than he was before. This was a direct reflection on the Squadron Commander, who had made the selection. One will never know to what extent there may have been substance in F/O Holder's statement. There is no doubt that being selected for a special job does increase one's self-confidence, but this need not be dangerous unless one has a tendency to over-confidence anyhow.

We finished testing the new types at the end of August and on 30 August I was told to take the Bristol Boarhound back to the firm, then as now on Filton Aerodrome, near Bristol. My Squadron Commander was a little anxious about my ability to find my way to Bristol in the rather hazy weather prevailing at that season, so he briefed me for half an hour on the route to take, which was to be south of London; first down to Ashford, then along that amazing 50 miles of dead straight railway line to Redhill; thereafter following the railway through the Guildford Gap in the Hills to Farnborough where I could land and stay with No.4 Army Cooperation Squadron if the weather was too bad. From Farnborough I was to follow the

railway north to Reading when I could get on to the main Great
Western line which would take me all the way to Bristol. In those
days many pilots distrusted the compass even though I had already
found the Mk.5/17 compass in the Bristol very good and preferred
trusting it to that other common but rather boring method of
navigating by 'Bradshaw' as we called it. On the day I set off I was
still in two minds — even after all the trouble my C O had taken — as
to whether I would go south or north of London. As it turned out
there really was quite a haze to the south since a slight northeasterly
drift of the wind was carrying the London haze that way. Under
these conditions the visibility was likely to be much better to the
north. I decided to go north-about. The fact that this route would
take me over a girl friend's house was, of course, purely incidental. I
had in the back seat the Bristol Company's Engineer, Mr. Arthur
Suddes, who said he did not mind which way we went and agreed
that if a Royal Air Force officer could not show an attractive girl
friend the newest and best aeroplane in the Air Force, well what
were things coming to! With absolute confidence in my compass I set
off, following the Thames estuary until I could cross it conveniently
by Canvey Island. Since I could just see some haze over London
away to the south I judged it wise — certainly very convenient — to
give London a wide berth and go as far north as Stansted where the
girl friend lived. I flew round the house until the whole family had
come out. What I did not know then, but have a great volume of
experience to prove irrefutably now, was that there is in every aero
engine flown by a junior officer a little tiny imp (later called
Gremlin) with a hammer in his hand and just when the junior officer
is in the most embarrassing position he hits some vital part. My Imp
hit the inlet valve so hard that it jammed open and this put out three
of the nine cylinders of the engine. My first impulse was to get as far
away as I could from the area to create some sort of alibi, but the
state of the engine would not allow me to stay in the air for long so I
put the Boarhound down in a field about seven miles from the girl
friend's house. Mr Suddes, excellent engineer that he was, had a look
at the engine and said that he could get it right by the morning. I
delayed as long as I could before sending a telegram to my Unit
telling them what had happened and saying that I would be on my
way to Bristol in the morning. I calculated rightly that the telegram
would not be delivered until after cease work, so that only the Duty
Officer would get it. As no damage had been done there was no need
for him to take any special action. We got the nearest Air Force
Station at Duxford near Cambridge to put a guard on the
Boarhound. Mr Suddes got the engine fixed late that night and I
stayed at the girl friend's house. I had taken the precaution of stating

95

A Boarhound in a field in Essex where it should never have been

the location of the forced landing field as ten miles east of Braintree, since that name would not, I hoped, touch off any connection with addresses I had given in the Leave Book which were in both Stansted and Dunmow. However, it took my C O just five minutes after he came in the next morning to measure off the distance and then look up the addresses I had put in the Leave Book. It took him less than five minutes to get on to a detachment the Squadron had at Colchester and tell them to send a party out to the forced landing with instructions that F/O Wheeler was to return to his Unit by TRAIN! But Mr Suddes had done his work well and by 9.00 a m we were airborne again on our way to Bristol — but we took off only twenty minutes before the party arrived.

I flew due west and then south round London and picked up the Great Western main line' at Slough. By that time the weather was deteriorating with low cloud coming in from the west. By the time I had got to Reading we were down to only 300 feet and wispy clouds were with us at that height. I picked a field near Reading, by Mapledurham House, and landed to wait for the weather to improve. The farmer was very helpful and Mr Suddes telephoned Bristol and heard that the weather should be clearing in the afternoon. Again I delayed sending a message to my C O for a time (unable to find a Post Office!) so as to reduce the chances of being caught on the ground. The nearest Unit in those days was Farnborough, which was all too close for my liking, particularly with a tie-line between No.2 Squadron and our Group H Q at Farnborough. When I did send the telegram I carefully made the location vague: 'about three miles N.E. of Reading'. Telephoning would obviously have been foolish since I could have been ordered to stay where I was on the ground.

Mr Suddes and I walked to an excellent pub nearby where we had lunch and then walked back to the farmhouse, from which Mr Suddes rang Bristol again. The weather there had cleared and they were beginning to be able to see the Bath Hills, which were our real problem since they rose to 800 feet or more and the clouds must have been right down on them all the morning. At ten minutes to five in the late afternoon we took off again. The weather was still bad at Reading but at least we had hopes of clear weather at Bristol if we could get that far. We followed the railway north to Didcot and then west past Swindon along the Vale of the White Horse, which was quite good since we were down in the valley all the time, but the sight of the clouds down on the hills to the south warned me that we might have trouble as we came to the Bath Hills where the railway we were following went through first a short tunnel and then a longer one. As the ground rose to the hills there was less and less room between the ground and the clouds. Fortunately the land was mostly large open fields, but here and there was the occasional beech wood or line of beech trees which I had to lift over. I became very fond of the Boarhound during this trip; it was wonderfully easy to fly. It could be landed in any reasonably sized field; it had a good fuel endurance which gave me no worries about fuel; and best of all, it always seemed to get away from a forced landing before my C O caught up with me.

We pressed on along the railway as the line climbed towards the high ground. Every now and again the railway went through a cutting and on one occasion the smoke from a train coming towards me filled the cutting and I was in fear of losing the railway, but I saw it again further on where the smoke had drifted away to the side and flew more happily for a mile, when the line went abruptly into a tunnel and I had no line to follow. I hoped the Great Western engineer — perhaps Brunel — had made the tunnel straight. Almost before I had time to lose direction the railway appeared again, but the clouds were now almost on it and I was within 50 feet of the line. I hoped no more trains belching smoke would come along since the line was already in a deep cutting. Visibility ahead was only about 500 yards

97

and suddenly the line went into the long tunnel which would bring it out to the western limit of the Bath Hills. I had no guide-line now but the country on the high lands there was mercifully open. I maintained direction as best I could since I could not spare a glance at the compass. Just as I thought I had wandered from the course I flew over one of the railway tunnel's smoke outlets. I looked eagerly for the next and blessed the tunnel engineer who had built little brick chimney which made them so easy to see. Another and another appeared in front of me at the expected moments and then the ground fell away below me as we reached the western limit of the Hills. I dived to follow the surface and get away below the clouds and suddenly the railway appeared below streaking away before me into a land of watery sunshine and almost unlimited visibility. I closed the throttle slightly as we dived with 500 feet clear above the ground and looked back at Mr Suddes, who called out something to me. I closed the throttle completely to hear what he had to say and caught the words:

'They were quite right about the weather: there's Filton in the distance.'

He seemed quite unperturbed by what we had been through. To me it meant a lot. If I got back having delivered the Boarhound safely, albeit by a roundabout and rather suspect route, the trouble with my C O would be minimized. As on a previous occasion when I was lost at Digby but got back safely, there would be more rejoicing over the safe return than fury over the wanderings and, by any standards, I felt I had done well with very adverse weather conditions. But I was not too optimistic about my reception when I got back to Manston. We landed at Filton at 5.30 p m and were made very welcome. This time I lost no time in signalling safe arrival at Filton but judged it wise to accept a very hospitable invitation by the Chief Test Pilot there, Cyril Uwins, to stay the night and look round the works in the morning. I felt a 24 hour cooling off period in my C O's office after the signal arrived would be a wise precaution.

They looked after me very well indeed at Bristol, my first experience of the Aircraft Industry's hospitality. There was even talk there of a job as a Test Pilot if I decided to leave the Service, which was a great reassurance since I had definitely decided to force the issue about going on fighters and had already put in another letter about it to be forwarded to the Air Ministry.

When I got back to Manston late on the following day it was after working hours so I had a night's rest before having to face my C O.

I I Air Council Displeasure—
Last days in No. 2 Squadron

In the morning, I found that the A O C was visiting the Station so my C O had other things on his mind as well as me. However, he questioned me closely about the extraordinary coincidence of landing close to the place at which I spent my weekend leave. I defended my decision to go north of London because of weather and that was accepted since the weather had been confirmed as very bad to the south. I also pointed out that the last thing I wanted to happen was for the engine to give trouble at that particular moment. I think my C O saw the point of this since he accepted my explanation but remarked that I was due to be interviewed by the A O C in half an hour's time about my renewed application to go on fighters and he added that the A O C did not seem to be very sympathetic to the idea. This, when I saw the A O C in due course, proved to be an understatement. He heard me until I had (nearly) finished and then remarked:

'You'll do what you're told and go where you're ordered and I don't want to hear any more from you.'

But he did. Within a week my resignation from the Air Force was on his desk with a request that it be passed to the Air Ministry.

My C O, now recovered from the Bristol journey episode, had tried to persuade me not to resign and had promised that he would put in a very strong recommendation that I should be posted as a test pilot at Martlesham Heath or Farnborough. This was a very kind offer and might have achieved something: also my C O was taking quite a responsibility on himself in offering this since the A O C was clearly in no mind to consider my case any further. I did not want my C O to get himself involved and also I had no confidence in the A O C doing anything to help, so I thanked my C O but asked him to forward my resignation which, very reluctantly, he did.

The immediate reply from the Air Ministry was another Air Council Displeasure, but I was getting used to them. My chief reaction on reading the letter setting forth the 'Displeasure' was one of an increased feeling of self-importance. In my imagination I pictured a large green baize table in the middle of a dark oak-pannelled room with a number of unbelievably senior officers sitting round it. At the head of the table was the Under Secretary of

State for Air, or if it was my lucky day, the Secretary of State for Air himself presiding. At the other end of the table I visualized a quiet dark-suited but very senior civil servant with his bowler hat and unbrella on a hat-and-stick stand just behind him. He was removing and polishing his gold pince-nez spectacles after reading a long description of what Flying Officer A.H. Wheeler had been doing, saying, and indeed writing, about his job in the Air Force. The Chief of the Air Staff, Air Marshal Sir Hugh Trenchard (not then Marshal of the Royal Air Force) was clearing his throat with his famous bark before saying:

'Gross insubordination.'

The Under Secretary (or Secretary) of State for Air, with eyebrows up and mouth open in shocked surprise, could — almost incredible for a politician — find no words to express himself.

Perhaps the Air Member for Personnel might just have muttered: 'As a matter of fact we are short of fighter pilots.'

But he would be ignored. At last the President would find the words to meet the situation as he looked round the table and addressed himself to the Civil Servant:

'Tell the Comander-in-Chief of Inland Area to tell the Air Officer Commanding of No.22 Group to tell the Commanding Officer of No.2 Squadron to tell Flying Officer Wheeler that we are displeased with him.'

There would then be a few moments of shocked silence before they moved on to the next item which — coming second on the Agenda — might perhaps have been some less important decision such as how many squadrons we needed in India and the Persian Gulf!

That is how I pictured it in my mind. Subsequent reflection over the years has made me regretfully wonder whether my name and offences ever got as far as an Air Council meeting at all. I have an uneasy feeling that it only got as far as a fairly senior clerk to the Council who read the case and then looked up the appropriate action. The only difference between my case and many others was probably that the senior clerk did not have to look very far down the list of 'appropriate actions' before he found a suitable one for me. At the time I treasured the other picture and, under this boost to my morale I wasted no time at all in putting in my resignation again, with a slight hint that an officer had the right, in cases of grievance, to see the Sovereign. Correspondence became fairly rapid after that and I was ordered to report to the Air Member for Personnel at the Air Ministry, who was then Air Vice Marshal Longcroft. I was told to report in civilian clothes. My C O was rather impressed at this reaction by the Air Ministry as also were Flt Lt Desoer and the rest of the Squadron. My C O said:

'Well I hope it comes out all right somehow, but I just don't know what will happen. I've done my best for you.'

There was no doubt he had, since a good special report had gone to the Air Ministry about me and it included the fact that I had probably been offered a job as Test Pilot with some of the firms competing for the Army Cooperation contract. This also may have weighed with the Air Member for Personnel when I saw him.

Punctually at the appointed hour, in my best clothes and trying to look confident, I presented myself at Adastral House, which was then at the southern end of Kingsway and a regular maze of corridors and offices. I was taken up in a lift by a messenger and led along an increasingly impressive line of offices: the final corridor even had a carpet. I was then handed over to a secretary who passed me to a Flight Lieutenant Personal Assistant who had a grin on his face. He opened the door to the great man's office and said:

'Flying Officer Wheeler, Sir.'

He then went out and closed the door. I advanced to the desk where A M P was writing and I went through the motions of coming to attention. This in itself, when in civilian clothes, always looks rather peculiar, almost as though one had got a nervous twitch. I was worrying whether I should then stand at ease again when A M P looked up and seemed to have a perfectly friendly look on his face. He ran through the history of my troubles briefly, but quickly, which showed me that he had read it up completely including my record from when I first joined the Air Force. He asked me first whether I had had any trouble with my Squadron Commander or my Flight Commander, which had influenced my decision to resign. I said very firmly that I had absolutely no complaint at all about them: they had been extremely helpful. Then he said:

'So when we sent you the second Air Council Displeasure you decided to resign?'

'Yes, Sir.'

'You know you won't get on very far in the Service if you resign?'

'No, Sir. I didn't think I would, Sir.'

A M P elaborated on the rather redundant logic of his last remark:

'I mean, we don't want to lose officers we have trained and whom we think will make good officers, but we clearly can't let people go to just any job they want to. If there was a war on you might have to go anywhere.'

I answered quickly:

'If there was a war on I would go anywhere you wanted to send me, and do any job: but in peace time I think I shall be more use to the Service on fighters, Sir.'

'I see. Well, you've caused a lot of trouble.'

'I'm sorry about that, Sir.'

'We may be able to do something for you. Wait here. I'll go and talk it over with the C A S.'

He went out. I could hardly believe that he would really worry the Chief of the Air Staff, Sir Hugh Trenchard, over me: it almost proved my vision of the Air Council's meeting.

A M P was away for a long time so I started looking round his office. Then my eye lit on his IN-tray. I felt fairly sure my own personal file must be somewhere on his desk. It would be nice to know what was in it. I moved halfway round the desk and glanced at the files. Getting bolder I lifted one or two to see if mine was under other papers. I assumed I would hear A M P coming back down the passage, but I had forgotten about that carpet. He was in the room before I had got my fingers out of his IN-tray: but he seemed not to have noticed anything and as I shuffled back round the desk he remarked:

'Well, the C A S has agreed you can go to a Fighter Squadron.'

'Thank you, Sir.'

There was a silence, and as things were going so well I thought it a good opportunity to ask to go to No.111 (F) Squadron at Duxford where my friend John Noel was. I added:

'Could I go to one particular Squadron, Sir?'

Then A M P blew up — or pretended to:

'You can consider yourself very lucky not to be thrown out. What do you think this place is? A Mission House for disgruntled Flying Officers? You're lucky to get to a Fighter Squadron at all . . . asking to go to one of your own choice . . . heh.'

'Sorry, Sir. I just thought it might not matter which one you sent me to. They might all be short of pilots. But it doesn't matter, Sir.'

A M P pressed a bell and a civil servant came in:

'We want to post . . . we are going to post Flying Officer Wheeler to a Fighter Squadron: which ones are short of pilots?'

The civil servant considered for a moment, then he said:

'Well, they're all short at this time since we are waiting for the next courses to pass out from the F T S's. It won't matter much which one he goes to.'

A M P looked at me with a slight twinkle in his eye:

'All right. Where do you want to go?'

'No.111 Squadron at Duxford, please Sir.'

A M P turned to the civil servant:

'Is that all right? . . . Good, well please arrange the posting with effect from mid-October.'

102

A M P thought for a moment, then he turned to me:

'Is there anything else you want?'

I wondered whether he was being facetious, but he seemed to be in a mood to consider further requests. I temporized to get a rather better idea on what his attitude really was:

'I wouldn't like to ask for too much Sir . . . .'

'Oh no, I'm sure you wouldn't . . . !'

But he was still in a friendly state of mind.

' . . . come on, if there is anything you want you are in the right office to ask for it — isn't he Mr Simpkin?'

A M P turned to the civil servant and they were both in a genial mood, so I made bold:

'Well Sir, I would like sometime to go on the Engineering Course, as I'm very interested in that side of aviation and I think you let General Duties officers do that?'

A M P was enthusiastic.

'Yes, I'm sure we can arrange that easily.'

He turned to Mr Simpkin who nodded emphatically:

' . . . in fact it is a policy the C A S is particularly keen on. We want a good proportion of General Duties officers to have specialist knowledge. We will arrange that.'

Again he looked at Mr. Simpkin, who nodded once more — everything was going nicely. The civil servant left and A M P turned to me with a friendly look:

'Well, you seem to have got everything you want. I hope you do well. But the next time I hear your name I hope it will be for promotion.'

'Thank you very much indeed, Sir. I hope it will be promotion too.'

The interview was at an end. I affected that apparently nervous twitch which was meant to imply I was 'coming to attention' and turned to leave his office. I felt I had acquitted myself well and made a good impression. Now all I had to do was to withdraw with dignity. I turned to go and was faced with two identical doors, and could not for the life of me remember which one I had come in by. I chose the wrong one and walked into a cupboard. A M P was again writing at his desk. As I withdrew from the cupboard and made for the other door he just looked up for a brief moment:

'I'm afraid you won't find your personal file there either.'

When I returned to No.2 Squadron with the story of my interview with A M P there was quite a lot of congratulation on my success in getting posted to fighters, but for me there was a little sadness since I felt that I had done very little in return for the breadth of mind with which my C O and my Flight Commander had handled my problem.

Almost 'heaping coals of fire on my head' after all the trouble I had given, Desoer found me a very interesting job with the Tank Corps who had a detachment on Swingate aerodrome near Dover. They wanted to develop and practice a means whereby an aeroplane could pick up messages from a tank. As mentioned earlier, R/T was still in a very experimental stage for aerial work and for communicating with a tank it was non-existent. We already had the highly developed and practised technique of picking up messages from the ground. In this scheme two rifles with fixed bayonets (or just any poles) were stuck in the ground about 5 yards apart and a string was stretched between them with a message tied to it. The Bristol Fighter had a hook which could be let down below from the undercarriage; this hooked up the string as the Bristol flew close between the rifles and the hook was then drawn up until the observer in the rear seat could get hold of it through a hole in the floor. All very primitive but without any form of R/T which could pass such messages it was the only way we could devise.

The development of this message-picking-up arrangement adapted for tanks consisted in an erection of steel tubes bolted to the top of the tank turret and the string across was suspended about 6 feet above the turret. The weakness in the system lay in the fact that if one misjudged the height when picking up the message there was a danger of the aeroplane's axle hitting the tank and there was not much 'give' in a tank. For surface work it did not matter if one came too low since the wheels merely ran along the ground. At first things went fairly well and I picked up the messages about once in every three runs: I would have achieved a better score if I had not been so frightened of hitting the tank. I was in fact doubtful about the whole scheme if applied to operational work. We then decided to try the same operation with the tank moving. The scheme of operations was on the Old Swingate Aerodrome near Dover which was then very uneven. On my first approach the tank was moving at about 6 m.p.h. and the two members of the tank crew were looking out of the turret top. Just at the moment of making contact the tank went over a mound and I was also marginally too low. The combined errors resulted in the undercarriage of the Bristol hitting the steel tubes built on the turret. There was a resounding crash and a jolt which made me think that I had lost my undercarriage, but the Bristol seemed to fly on all right. I looked at the tank and saw that the steel tube erection had disappeared completely and no-one was looking out of the turret top. As I turned slowly round watching the tank I saw two heads very cautiously emerge and when they saw me quite a long way away and not flying towards them they came out shoulder high. I was very worried about my undercarriage: if it was badly damaged it would obviously be better to fly back to Manston and park the accident there with all facilities for collecting and repairing it. But if it was all right I clearly ought to land on Swingate aerodrome and commiserate with the Royal Tank Corps on their damage, although the possibility of an aeroplane damaging a tank seemed rather unlikely. It would have seemed almost facetious for a pilot of one of those 'stick and string contraptions' to apologize for breaking up a tank! I felt sure some damage to my undercarriage must have occurred but by flying 'across sun' and looking at the shadow it seemed that my undercarriage was at least there and possibly undamaged. I decided to land and talk to the Tank Corps who were, in any case, always very friendly with the Air Force since they too had to explain their importance in relation to horses. Coming in very carefully and landing as gently as possible I breathed a sigh of relief as the Bristol touched down, ran 80 yards and came to a halt perfectly normally. I switched off and jumped out and inspected the undercarriage. There was not a mark on it. I looked at the tank: the upper work of steel tubes had been completely demolished. Just how strong was the Bristol Fighter?

I suggested trying out the scheme again but the tank crew were dead against it. They said there were too many elements of uncertainty about it. I was in entire agreement with them.

I had a long and friendly discussion with the Royal Tank Corps officers about tactics in general and then took off and flew back to Manston. The next time I flew from Swingate aerodrome was in a Bristol Boxkite aeroplane nearly 40 years later when I was directing the flying in the 20th Century Fox Film 'Those Magnificent Men in Their Flying Machines' and flew in the Dover cliffs scene.*

Before I left No.2 Squadron, yet another interesting and, in a way, amusing job was found for me. The Royal Air Force Pageant was then an annual event in which later, as recorded, I was fortunate enough to take part in a flying capacity, but apart from these rather glamorous jobs there was a lot of ground work to be done. No.2 Squadron had no part in the flying display in 1926 but a request came through for a junior officer to do duty in the Press Tent during the Display. I think my Squadron Commander must have known that this was an interesting job and indeed an amusing one in some respects. He allotted the job to me and I proceeded to the Royal Air Force Station at Hendon to be briefed. This meant staying there for two nights. We were briefed on the Friday morning; it appeared that I and one other flying officer were to be present at the Press Tent so as to be able to give the various newspaper correspondents accurate information on what was going on. Apart from the technical part of the briefing it was explained to us that there was a free bar in the

105

*Described in *Building Aeroplanes for Those Magnificent Men* (G.T. Foulis & Co. Ltd., 1965)

Press enclosure and although it might be difficult to refuse a drink with some influential Air Correspondent — it was a free bar anyway — we must not, under any circumstances, drink too much. In order to ensure that this stipulation was obeyed an elderly Flight Lieutenant was also appointed to the Press Tent as officer-in-charge and he was told to ensure that all orders were strictly carried out.

On the day of the Display we assembled at 10 a m in our appointed places on Hendon Aerodrome. The Flight Lieutenant was the last to arrive, at about 10.45 a m but he lost no time in impressing on his two assistant Flying Officers that we were all in a very responsible position. We were, he said, literally in the limelight of the press: we must uphold the best traditions of the Air Force. A free bar in our enclosure was, he said, a unique responsibility which we must appreciate. He would be watching us throughout the day. It was a hot day.

The free bar became 'operational' at noon: at 12.45 p m the other Flying Officer and I found the Flight Lieutenant lying on the ground, flat out, in the bar tent. He seemed to be breathing. We held a hurried conference, ably advised by one of the newspaper correspondents who seemed not to be in the least astonished by the episode.

With his help and advice we tried to roll the inebriated form under one of the trestle tables in the Press tent, but we discovered that trestle tables are not designed, leg-wise to receive the inert but rigid body of a fairly large Flight Lieutenant. Again under the expert advice and with the assistance of our friend, we carried the Flight Lieutentant behind the bar and laid him out behind a number of cases of beer. Since he still seemed to be rather eye-catching we covered him up with a tablecloth since our correspondent friend assured us that, without the uniform 'anyone might think it was a journalist!' But this kept sliding off one side or the other every time the 'recumbent' twitched. He had a twitch frequency of about one every three seconds. In desperation we squirted the tablecloth with soda syphons and it then clung snugly round the body — but it looked terribly like a corpse — except for the twitch. Quite a number of junior correspondents kept glancing at this 'apparition' and one or two suggested it should be taken away to a mortuary. We said it was still breathing and certainly twitching. We said it had happened after it's fifth drink and invited them to have another: they declined, not very gratefully, and went out to look at the flying. Even that was not very reassuring to some of the less sober of them since we had the most unusual shapes flying that year.

There was Professor G.T.R. Hill's original design of the Ptero-dactyl, flown by Harold Penrose, which in the air, looked for all the world, like a prehistoric monster and that alone drove some of the correspondents back into the bar — only to be driven out again by the 'apparition' behind the beer cases. When they came out they were faced by the earliest rotary wing aircraft seen in this country, flown by Frank Courtney.

From my point of view it was most interesting and useful introduction to the Royal Air Force Pageant.

I never knew what happened to the Flight Lieutenant. We were told that the Caterer would clear up the enclosure that evening and we assumed it was part of his responsibilities.

On the whole we were useful as information officers in the enclosure since, at that time, the majority of the Press were virtually uninformed on aviation matters. It was, indeed, only a few years earlier that a report was printed in a daily paper describing a very unusual reason for a forced landing by a two-seater aeroplane. The correspondent had repeated the pilot's story and clearly believed it. Unfortunately the pilot had an overdeveloped sense of humour and a lively imagination. Faced with a breathless local correspondent asking what had happened he decided to 'give him a good story'.

'It was his fault'.

The pilot said glaring at his observer:

'Overstoking! He was piling on the coal. I shouted to him to stop but he wouldn't listen; he just went on shovelling it on. The fire went out, the water went off the boil and here we are, down in a field entirely due to overstoking.'

The report was printed in perfect seriousness in a reputable and usually well-informed paper.

I hoped the other Flying Officer and I did a little to improve the air-mindedness of the correspondents. On the Saturday evening we went on weekend leave and returned to our units on the Sunday night. We had learnt a lot: a little more about flying — but a great deal about the almost infinite variety of the pressman's outlook, and the kind friendliness of some of them.

That was the last real job I did in No.2 Squadron. There were other flights giving air experience to newcomers and a final joyful encounter with Barlow in his Avro 504K on the afternoon 28 September. Then I packed up and left. My posting came through so quickly that I had no time to reassemble the parts of my beloved A B C motor cycle, which I still had as well as my Riley 2-seater, so I sold the parts 'as lying' (in my room) to our Squadron Adjutant P/O Cannon, who finally got them together and had a very good motor cycle — some slight return for all the trouble we had caused him by phoney telephone calls.

Flt Lt Noel Desoer kindly gave me a flying assessment of 'Above

107

the average' and my Squadron Commander added in 'A good pilot who, at times, is overconfident', perhaps to stop me getting above myself, or perhaps that landing in Essex was still in his mind and he probably realized that No.111 (F) Squadron at Duxford was only 20 miles from Stansted where temptation for doing all sorts of low aerobatics lay much too close at hand. How right he was!

12 First impressions of a fighter squadron—mainly administrative

In the middle of October 1926 I arrived on the Royal Air Force Station at Duxford, near Cambridge, to join No.111 (F) Squadron. My first impression of the Station was that practically all the officers were under close arrest following a Court Martial. Subsequently I discovered that only about 10 per cent of the Station were in that unenviable position, but another 70 per cent were in the almost equally unenviable position of having to do what was called 'escort duty' on them. That meant that an officers' guard had to be kept on them for 24 hours a day to prevent them running away, committing suicide or in any other way thwarting the due course of justice. Since the guard duties were divided up into eight hour spells at night and four hour spells during the day, and each officer under arrest had to be guarded, a large part of the whole officer strength of the Station was employed. Add to this the fact that normal Station duties of Orderly Officer and Officer of the Watch (Aerodrome Control) had to be done also, and one arrives at the situation − as it actually was − that all the officers on the Station were either under arrest or doing routine duties absolutely unconnected with any form of flying. When I arrived they were, in the parlance of those days 'browned off'. The morale of the Royal Air Force Station Duxford in October 1926 was at the lowest ebb imaginable. This was a shock to me coming from a Squadron like No.2 in which, for all the disinterest I took in much of the work, the morale and discipline were magnificent.

Some of the wiser − or at least more cunning − of the officers on the Station had managed to get appointed to such jobs as Station or Squadron Adjutant in which they were exempted from all escort and Station duties. We had, therefore, the paradox that all the officers in the Flights were too busy on ground duties to fly, and all the officers in administrative posts were flying to their hearts' content in aeroplanes which were standing out on the aerodrome just waiting to be flown. It was no surprise to me to find that my friend, John Noel, was Adjutant of No.111 Squadron and was piling up flying hours at an enormous rate doing just whatever he liked in the air.

John Noel had, in fact, been appointed Squadron Adjutant when the trouble which gave rise to the crisis on the Station first came to light. Since this was due to misappropriation of what are called 'non-public' funds, it was felt that John Noel, with a large private income, was unlikely to be in sufficiently needy circumstances to feel any temptation that way: the few funds which were purely concerned with the Squadron were usually kept by the Squadron Adjutant.

The Station 'non-public' funds consisted of such accounts as the Officers' Mess and Sergeants' Mess accounts and the P S I (President of the Service Institute) account which controlled almost all the various funds for airmen's sports, welfare and amenities generally. This was a considerable fund. Unfortunately, at Duxford, some of these funds had got into the hands of officers who, although they had excellent war records, found peace time Air Force routine intolerably boring. They had tended, therefore, to live above their means. The subsequent decline and fall followed the usual pattern: they 'borrowed' from their particular fund to carry them over to the end of the month, and these borrowings became heavier and heavier. Surprise checks on the bank and cash accounts should have revealed the discrepancies, but these were not done regularly or efficiently, thus others became involved. In some cases the money 'borrowed' had been replaced (in the office safe) by cheques made out to cash so that superficially the accounts might seem to be in order — that is until the cheques were presented to the Bank, when they came back with a curt note to say there were no funds in the Bank to meet them. Then the storm broke. The amount of money represented by worthless cheques was considerable and investigations showed that routine and surprise checks had not been done with the regularity and efficiency laid down in Regulations.

By the time I got to Duxford those concerned had already been tried by Court Martial but the Group and Command H Q and the Air Ministry, advised by the Judge Advocate General's office, were extremely slow in reviewing, confirming and promulgating the sentences. All this time the accused officers remained under close arrest and by December it seemed as though this state of affairs would drag on over Christmas. Urgent representations were made from Duxford and at last the sentences were confirmed. Most of them were reasonably sympathetic considering the mitigating circumstances of excellent war records and, in one case, war wounds in the head which undoubtedly left the officer in no proper state to handle the responsibility put on him.

We all breathed a great sigh of relief as the Station tried to return to normal. The previous Station Commander was posted away and a new one, Wing Commander Barton, was posted in to 'clean up' the place. His method of doing this must remain for all time a model of how this should be done. Throughout my service I have studied the

110

behaviour of newly appointed Commanding Officers: most of them approach the problem in a thoroughly sensible way by studying the special requirements and activities of the Station first over a number of weeks, and then adjusting the running of it in various ways to make it more efficient. Naturally a newly arrived Commander sees bad points standing out more clearly than the previous one who has got used to the Station. There are, unfortunately, a number of individuals whose main aim is to boost their own prestige, build up a reputation for ruthless efficiency with their superiors and thus get promotion. These types usually arrive on a Station and look around for things which can be changed without understanding the workings of the organization properly. They then make sweeping changes which throw the Station into chaos. Such officers pay frequent visits to Group and Command H Q to tell them what a chaotic state they found the Station in, and the carefully thought-out plan of changes they are imposing to rectify the position. They keep up this atmosphere of reorganization for greater efficiency all the time they are there so as to cover up their own lack of understanding — or even disinclination even to try and understand how the place should be run — and as soon as possible arrange for a posting for themselves — if possible with promotion — to some H Q or Air Ministry job where their lack of practical ability is not so easily detected.

This may seem to be an exaggeration of a very rare phenomenon, but unfortunately it is neither exaggerated nor very rare. A lucky restoring factor is that there are usually a number of highly intelligent people in H Q or in the Air Ministry Personnel Department who recognise this type of individual, thus only a few slip through and promote themselves, and when this happens it is entirely due to inefficiency above.

Wing Commander Barton might have had every reason for making sweeping changes at Duxford, but in fact he moved quietly and slowly to put the place straight. Every change was carefully thought out and it was always for the better. Within three months Duxford was a thoroughly efficient Station with a high morale and no-one on the Station could really say where the changes had been made. There was, of course, always the problem of having a Station with three Fighter Squadrons on it, particularly when Fighter Squadrons in those days usually contained a high proportion of Short Service officers, many of them with little interest in the Air Force and a youthful degree of irresponsibility which might be invaluable in war, but tended to be uncontrollable in peace.

It might be thought, from reading this first description of Duxford, that we had no time at all for flying, but in fact I did manage to scrape in 12 hours on the Siskin Mk IIIA between the middle of October and the end of the year, although the greater part of this was done in December. I started off with a 20 minute check test in the Squadron dual Siskin Mk III. This was largely a formality since the Atlas I had flown at Manston had very similar controls and handling characteristics.

Most of my flying on the Siskin was devoted to getting thoroughly used to the handling of it. It had not got the sensitive controls of the Snipe, which I knew well, or the Grebe with which the other two Squadrons at Duxford were equipped, but it was immensely strong and had a good stability which made it suitable for the night flying role in which No.111 Squadron was supposed to become proficient. It was also a steady gun platform for the firing practices we did from an aerodrome called Sutton Bridge near the Wash, conveniently adjacent to the marshes on the sea shore where the firing ranges were located. In fact my second flight on a Siskin was a cross country to Sutton Bridge where I had to do duty marking targets whilst the Squadron pilots fired on them. In this duty we took cover in concrete shelters while the firing was going on and then — very cautiously — emerged when we had ascertained by telephone that the aeroplanes had returned to the aerodrome.

I flew back to Duxford that evening rather glad to get away from the primitive conditions not only on the ranges but also in the Camp, which had only recently been opened. The marshes around the Wash may be inspiring and full of wild life in the summer, but around January the wild life seemed to have moved to a more congenial locality. I was greeted at Duxford with the information that I was to go back to Sutton Bridge for a week's marking duties on the ranges. I got as far as King's Lynn that evening and stayed the night in a 'pub' there, taking the precaution of booking a room for another night in case the conditions at Sutton Bridge were as bad as they had looked the day before. In the morning I drove into the camp and reported to the Adjutant. There was a gale blowing and it was pouring with rain. I had been warned that I 'might possibly need gum boots'. This was an understatement. The Adjutant said I had been allotted tent No.17 in row 3 and his corporal would show me where it was. The corporal and I left the office and squelched gloomily through the mud. On either side of us were officers and airmen in gum boots and oilskins trying to hold down their tents in the rising wind and driving rain. Some were successful, but some were beaten by the wind and then they and their tent took off down wind and usually succeeded in up-rooting another tent as they went on their way.

I asked where my tent was and the corporal said it was difficult to say exactly since tents 13, 14, 15 and 16 seemed to have been blown away. He said he thought it was 'that one', indicating a wildly flapping, rain sodden, caricature of a bell tent 30 yards further on.

'That one there?' I asked.

'The one that was there.'

He said as my future 'home' went the way of the rest.

I went back to the Adjutant and said:

'I don't think there'll be any flying today Sir.'

He replied:

'No. I hope you'll be comfortable tonight. I'll see you tomorrow morning.'

He himself was living in a snug wooden hut.

'I'll be all right tonight Sir.'

I replied, and drove back to King's Lynn.

The weather improved next day, but I stayed in King's Lynn each night that week and claimed lodging allowance, asserting on the claim form that:

'No accommodation was available on the Camp.'

Gloster Grebes of No. 25 Squadron. The Grebe was powered by a
375 h.p. Jaguar engine

That was absolutely true since I had seen my accommodation leave the camp.

By the end of January I had done a total of 18½ hours on Siskins and most of that consisted of aerobatics and what we called Battle Flights, which were simulated interceptions to altitudes around 10,000 feet and distances of around 50 miles. This rather moderate altitude was due to the fact that bombers at that time seldom went much higher and our own oxygen equipment was of a fairly primitive and unreliable nature. Also, with open cockpits and no proper heating, high altitude could be very uncomfortable with pilot alertness at a low ebb.

During December I managed to get a flight on a Gloster Grebe due to the goodwill and a cold in the head of my friend F/O J. H. Mac Reynolds, who was then in the Meteorological Flight at Duxford. His flight Commander was Flt Lt E.H. Fielden, later Air Commodore Sir Edward Fielden, Commodore of the Queen's Flight and previously personal pilot to the Prince of Wales before he became King Edward VIII, and also pilot to all members of the Royal Family.

At the time Flt Lt (Mouse) Fielden was away on leave, and F/O (Mac) Reynolds was doing Met. flights, which consisted of two flights per day to 16,000 feet or to 22,000 feet if the oxygen was working, checking temperatures and weather conditions generally. On this particular day Reynolds had done the morning flight and experienced very considerable discomfort in his sinus on the way down. He was very doubtful about another flight to 16,000 feet in the late afternoon (the oxygen was not working) and was therefore looking for someone who would do it for him, preferably a pilot who was used to flying Grebes. By one means or another I persuaded Reynolds to let me do the flight. He briefed me on the controls and, rather anxiously, let me go off on the flight.

The weather on that late December day was reasonably good but with a distinct haze which promised to become a mist as evening approached. The Grebe was very different from any aeroplane I had flown before: it was pleasant to fly and undoubtedly a beautiful aeroplane for aerobatics, not unlike the Snipe, but aerobatics were not what I was required to do that late December afternoon. The Grebe needed more precise handling than the Siskin but was not basically any more difficult to fly.

I took off just before 4 p m and climbed steadily noting down the air temperatures at each 1000 feet as I went up. I also kept a wary eye on the ground to make sure of my position since I knew I would have little daylight left to find my way back if I got lost. When I arrived at 16,000 feet after twenty minutes of a fairly leisurely climb, I found it was very cold but quite lovely with the wintry, reddening sun shining along the top of a hazy mist. Far below was, I hoped, Duxford, but I couldn't pick it out. I dallied for several precious minutes at that altitude enjoying the beauty of it and also making the classic mistake of assuming that because the sun is shining brightly at 16,000 feet it is also shining brightly on the ground. It was not shining down there at all, having set some time before. By now I had mastered the controls of the Grebe and was in no mood to curtail my flight on that beautiful machine. I checked the stalling speed which was almost exactly the same as the Siskin and amused myself all the way down by doing various aerobatics until at about 6,000 feet I became aware that dusk, if not darkness, was closing in and I only had the haziest idea where I was. But my luck was in as I looked around. I saw the well known — perhaps too well known — terrain around Stansted and away to the North was the easily recognizable landmark of Audley End House with its green coppered roofs. There was a little way to go in the gathering darkness but I knew the way and had the railway to guide me.

By this time Mac Reynolds was in a frenzy. The whole circumstance of appointing me to do the flight when I had never flown a Grebe before might have led to adverse comment if I were lost or had an accident. He decided I was probably not too far away but merely could not find the aerodrome, therefore a few pyrotechnics might help me to locate it. He hurriedly collected three rockets, several flares and an almost inexhaustable selection of red, white and green Verey (signal) cartridges. He let all these off as fast as he could get them lit or fired. At that moment I was coming in to land with just enough light to see the aerodrome, but I was not expecting it to blow up in front of me. Mac Reynolds had not seen me approaching, partly due to his preoccupation with the pyrotechnics and partly to the increasing darkness. To avoid the *feu de joie* I hurriedly veered off and assumed that there had been a crash on the aerodrome and no-one was to land there. I did a careful circuit and watched what was practically a Guy Fawkes celebration going on and I still wondered what it was all about. On my second circuit fortunately Reynolds ran out of either pyrotechnics or matches (or both) and I managed to come in to do my first ever landing in a Grebe, which was practically a night landing. All was well and Mac Reynolds was probably the most relieved officer on the Station that evening.

Finding one's way back after a Met. flight was always hazardous when there was heavy cloud cover which, fortunately, I did not have to deal with. On one occasion a Met. pilot, after climbing through 12,000 feet of cloud with, of course, no radio and virtually no navigational aids except a compass, had found his way down again to see a countryside which, to him, was quite unrecognizable. He landed in a field and walked over to some strange looking yokels to ask where he was. Their reply was unintelligible to him but the language they spoke suggested to him, correctly, that he was either in France or Belgium. On another occasion, Mac Reynolds, perhaps more fortunate in his navigation, came down through 12,000 feet of cloud and saw below him an almost infinite vista of open parkland with no fields or hedges. He landed in a clearing and the first living thing that greeted him was an emu.

'I can't have got to Australia.' He muttered.

He had in fact only got as far as the Duke of Bedford's Park at Woburn Abbey — 20 miles from Duxford — where the old Duke kept a menagerie of strange and exotic creatures.

During the first three months of my time in No.111 Squadron at Duxford I was acting Flight Commander of 'C' Flight. There were two Sergeant Pilots in the Flight as well, so we could just make a formation of three for our formation practices and Battle climbs. One of the Sergeant Pilots was Alan Marsh, who became one of the most expert test pilots on Autogiro rotary wing craft and later he became the Chief Test Pilot for CIERVA. He was doing the test flying on the ill-fated Air Horse 3-rotor helicopter when he was killed. A lightly stressed control rod failed due to fatigue and the Air Horse went out of control.

For some of the time in No.111 Squadron we were also without a Squadron Commander and the senior Flight Commander acted as C O. The result of this was that we were left very much to ourselves and had good opportunities for doing any kind of flying we liked and, subject to Station duties, plenty of it.

As Wing Commander Barton's reorganization went on I found myself getting more involved in all the odd jobs there are on Air Force Stations: none very onerous but all slightly time-consuming. I became Assistant Mess Secretary in the Officers' Mess and was also ordered to take over the inventories of four of the airmen's living huts. In those days all inventories were held by officers but, to a certain extent, one could delegate the responsibility in the actual flights and workshops by putting many items in the charge of sergeants. This could not then so easily be done where the airmen's living quarters were concerned. The actual huts were one-brick-thick wartime huts laid out in rows, and inside they were just a plain dormitory with a coke stove, in the middle and beds and lockers arranged along the walls. I had been warned by a friend that F/O Briggend, from whom I was taking over the huts and who was shortly leaving the Service, was a fairly 'sharp' individual so that I had better take particular care that all the items were really there or I would

116

find myself paying for any deficiencies after the next C O's inspection. We arranged a suitable time at 11 a m one morning and F/O Briggend had said he would then have everything under control. We met at the appointed time and I was rather impressed by Briggend's absolutely open and honest approach to the problem of handing over and taking over inventories. He gave me quite a lecture on the subject before we started:

'Some people,' he said, 'don't take this sort of thing seriously: they just let things slide and then wonder why items get lost. It's just sheer stupidity, apart from the fact that as an officer one is not doing one's duty that way.'

He pulled himself up to his full height, throwing out his chest slightly, almost standing to attention, and went on in a most impressive way:

'Now I don't believe in anything slipshod or underhand. If a job's to be done it's got to be done well. For instance, this inventory — lots of officers forget it until it's time to hand it over, then they try to scrounge and pilfer to get the lost items. I've been round these huts every week — not always at the same time mind you — I just drop in one morning — that keeps them up to scratch. You're lucky taking over this lot from me because it's in perfect order and you take my advice, you keep it like that. Now, let's check it all and if there's any item you're doubtful about don't hesitate to ask. I want you to have everything clear. In fact I'm sorry to hand this over in a way, it's been a joy to me to look after it, and do the job properly.'

By this time I was convinced that the warnings I had had were just due to some misunderstanding. I followed F/O Briggend into the first of the four huts. Everything was perfectly laid out. The beds and lockers were tidy, the broom and brushes were lined up in the order listed on the inventory, the mats were new and in their proper place: even the coke stove and its implements were neatly blackened. But F/O Briggend was not content. He barked out:

'Corporal Evans. What's this? There's only about half a coke shovel there.'

He pointed to the little hand shovel which was used to charge the stove; it was slightly dented where it had occasionally hit the stove. I was fascinated. Even the cadets at Cranwell would hardly have been expected to have a better shovel. I gazed, almost hypnotized, at the offending instrument, and this was F/O Briggend's undoing. I would have recognized that shovel again anywhere and a few minutes later I did — in the next hut but one!

In a flash I realized what was happening and quick action was needed. I remarked casually:

'I think you had one too many brooms in the last hut. Let's check

117

up. You may be down on one later on.'

Before Briggend's reassurances and expostulations could get under way I was out of the hut and on my way into the previous one: it was, by then, almost bare of items and I saw the last of a line of hut orderlies disappearing out of the hut carrying the 'props' out of that hut to No.4 at the end of the line. I went back to numbers 1 and 2 and they were also sadly deficient by then. A check showed me that there were in fact only enough items for about 3 huts at the most. Briggend started to explain a complicated theory whereby it was, he said, better to have a few deficiencies hidden to guard against the embarrassment of suddenly being faced with a lot of surpluses. I explained that, with the deficiencies then revealed, any embarrassment by surpluses was very unlikely to be experienced. I added that I would do the check again in the afternoon and, drawing him away from the airmen, I said that I would see him in the Officers' Mess shortly, where I would need at least a pint of beer: if I didn't get that I might break down with shock at his deception and sob out the whole story in the Station Adjutant's office. I got the pint after a slight misunderstanding as to whose 'book' it should go on, and at the appointed time I arrived at the huts for the second check.

Miraculously all inventory items were present and correct by 3 p m. I don't know who lost the ones Briggend's airmen found, but thereafter I followed Briggend's really excellent advice and dropped in on the huts at unexpected intervals. But the laugh was finally on me. F/O Briggend had, after all, transferred the two pints of beer to my 'book'.

Two years later a brother officer told me he met Mr Briggend (then in civilian life) in a London Bank. He was presenting a large cheque for cashing and giving the bank cashier the same sort of talk he had given me over the inventory. My friend watched the process with interest and was surprised to see that the cashier seemed to know Mr Briggend well. What was even more surprising was that — knowing him — the cashier seemed to have no hesitation at all in cashing the cheque. Mr Briggend seemed to have made good.

With the general suspicion which surrounded all accounts and inventories at Duxford for months after the rather unsavoury disclosures which came out at the Court Martial, the whole business of managing inventories became onerous to the point of becoming almost an obsession.

One day I dropped in on Mac Reynolds to pass the time of day, but also to have a sort of mutual commiseration talk on the whole subject of inventories. On that particular day he was Officer of the Watch which meant that he had to spend all the hours when flying was on in the Watch Office, which was a small brick hut alongside the hangers on the aerodrome side. In this hut there was a normal office with tables, chairs, cupboards, etc., but also another small store room with all the essential pyrotechnics for signalling, such as the ones F/O Reynolds had used with dramatic effect when I was trying to land the Grebe. During the discussion on inventories Reynolds illustrated the iniquity of the whole system by explaining that he was himself officially responsible for all the furniture and equipment in the Watch Office. Somebody had to hold the inventory and the Station Adjutant had decreed that it was to be F/O Reynolds. The fact that he had little or no control over the items seemed not to weigh with authority at all. Someone had to hold the inventory and he had been told to. At that moment an airman came into the Watch Office and picked up a fire extinguisher and started to carry it out of the door. Reynolds reacted:

'Put that down at once, it's on my inventory and if anyone wants it it is going to be transferred properly on a return and demand form.'

'But Sir, it's wanted in the hangar.'

'I'm sure it is. Someone's down on his inventory. Well that's not my worry. He can admit he's lost one and get another. There's a proper Service procedure for this.'

The airman was looking very concerned:

'But Sir, it really is wanted in the hangar.'

'Who wants it, and why?'

'The Flight Sergeant wants it badly, Sir; the hangar's on fire.'

I3 Home communications flight

The hangar fire was put out. Whether the fire extinguisher on F/O Reynolds' inventory was the deciding factor or not I have never bothered to find out. Within a few days I was summoned to the Station Adjutant's office, who wanted to ascertain how many hours I had done on Bristol Fighters. I gave him the answer dubiously wondering whether there was some foul plot afoot to post me back to Army Cooperation. His next remark did nothing to reassure me:

'Group H Q want someone who is experienced on Bristol Fighters to go on a temporary posting.'

I was immediately on my guard but the Adjutant reassured me:

'It is only for a month, to go to the Home Communications Flight at Northolt.'

Subsequent enquiry indicated that the Flight Commander of the Home Communications Flight, Flt Lt Ritchie, wanted to go on long overdue leave, and he had at that time no other pilot in the Flight. The Flight existed for the purpose of providing aeroplanes to transport the Staff officers of Group and Fighting Area H Q on their various duties. Most of these Staff officers flew themselves, but some wanted to have a pilot to fly them since for one reason or another they were not in flying practice. These officers tended to mistrust junior fighter pilots and they wanted an experienced pilot on Bristol Fighters. A search around our Fighter Group revealed the fact that there was only one junior pilot available in the Group who had sufficient experience on Bristol Fighters, and that was me: I had well over 100 hours flying on the Bristol Fighter and an 'above average' flying assessment. This commended me to the Staff officers who did not fly themselves, and they probably had not seen the comment 'inclined to be over-confident.'

I arrived at the Home Communications Flight at Northolt at the beginning of February and my first job was to command the Flight detachment on the working parade at 8 a m each morning. Fortunately it was accepted that the officer in charge only had to be on the Parade Ground for the mustering parade and, having marched the Flight off the Parade Ground he could give the command: 'Carry on Flight Sergeant' or 'Sergeant' or perhaps 'Corporal' and then go back to enjoy his breakfast. There was sense in this since quite

120

A DH 53 (Humming Bird) at Lympne aerodrome

a lot of flight maintenance work had to be done first thing in the morning before the flying started. Most of my flying during February was done on Bristol Fighters and most of this entirely for my own amusement. I went back to Duxford for lunch on one day and also went over to Farnborough on another to inspect an SE 5a which was up for (disposal) sale. I thought it would be rather fun to buy this famous fighter from the War (1914—18) and fly it as a private aeroplane. It seemed to my inexperienced eye, after a very superficial inspection, to be in reasonable shape so I put in a bid of £50 for it.

After a brief overlap of responsibility Flt Lt Ritchie went on leave and left me in charge of the Flight. His last instruction was:

'Don't fly the DH 53 'til it's worn out.'

He had obviously seen my eye on this rather intriguing little machine. It had been built for the Lympne competition in 1923 to a Government specification to encourage private flying. The requirement was for an aeroplane for the private owner which should have an engine of not more than 750 cc capacity which was then the engine size for a powerful motor cycle. This particular DH 53 (Humming Bird) was one of a production order for 12 bought by the Air Ministry to try them out in the Communication role. In fact they were too small and under-powered to be satisfactory for cross country flying, but the one we had was a great attraction to me. I took an early opportunity to fly it just to find out how a tiny little aeroplane like that flew. My first impression was that, even on

121

A Humming Bird cockpit

Northolt Aerodrome, which was then one of the biggest in the Air Force, it would never take off. Its engine was then the inverted 'V' Blackburn motor cycle engine which (in the DH 53) was named the 'Tomtit'. It seemed to have a total power comparable to its namesake in the bird world, but this was partly due to the fact that the engine's maximum power was developed at around 3000 r.p.m. at which speed the propeller was relatively inefficient. I started my take-off run near the hangars on Northolt and hoped that that the downhill gradient in the southerly direction towards the centre of the aerodrome into a light breeze would shorten the distance of take-off run. It may have, but I was well past the middle of the aerodrome when I became aware that the DH 53 was still in no mood to leap off the ground. I raised the tail still further to reduce drag but this seemed to slow it down since the very small wheels were making heavy work of the unevenness of the grass aerodrome. Eventually I got it off the ground and thereafter, so long as I did not try to climb significantly, it behaved fairly well. By the time it had got to Uxbridge about four miles away, I was at 400 feet — and risked a

122

turn back towards the aerodrome, which I reached at the inspiring altitude of 600 feet. Thereafter any attempt at climbing further seemed to be a waste of time, so I contented myself with trying out its handling characteristics in turns and other light manoeuvres. I was immediately struck by the fact that when I closed the throttle the gliding angle of this beautiful looking, streamlined little aeroplane was far steeper than one had imagined. It was, in fact, so light that I had to go into a very steep dive indeed just to maintain flying speed, without the engine. I lost so much height in this test that I only flew on to complete the aerodrome circuit before coming in to land. The landing was easy and straightforward and I ended up only about 80 yards from the hangars. It was clearly entirely impractical for any ordinary flying. Later versions of the DH 53 with the more powerful engines like the A B C Scorpion of 35 h p or the Bristol Cherub of similar power, made it a slightly more practical aeroplane, but the development of the early Moth series by the same firm made it clear that aeroplanes with an engine of at least 65 h p were the minimum practical size for private owners' use.

Another new type I managed to get hold of, which was also in the Flight, was the Fairey Flycatcher. This was a fighter designed to be operated from a ship. It had a light wing loading achieved by its wide span biplane design. Like all the naval (ship borne) aeroplanes of that period, it could only marginally compete with the fighters which the Air Force were using, but it was pleasant enough to fly.

I took it up for about an hour to try it out. There was, of course, no-one to brief me on the controls, but it seemed to be a straightforward aeroplane. An airman showed me where the fuel tap and ignition switches were and warned me not to lower the 'hook' by mistake since if used on a rough aerodrome — and not a smooth deck with arrestor wires — it tended to bounce up and down and might do damage. The airman did not say anything about a knob almost central on the dashboard with a notice against it saying 'PULL'. Two or three times on my flight I caught hold of this knob and thought of pulling it, but each time a sense of discretion discouraged me. When I landed I asked the airman about it and he remarked cheerfully:

'Oh, I ought to have told you about that Sir. You must not pull it whatever happens. It is the fuel jettison control and is only used in emergency when 'ditching'. It is a sort of tin-opener which rips open the bottom of the fuel tank.'

Whilst I was flying the Flycatcher, I went over to Eton to look at the Playing Fields there. I had been appointed Liaison Officer (for recruiting) to Eton and was planning some sort of demonstration which might have been done by landing suitable aeroplanes on the Playing Fields. I wondered if they were large enough. As I arrived

123

over Eton the question had been answered for me. Right in the middle of the most carefully tended cricket pitch was a Siskin. The marks of its tail skid showed as a deep scar diagonally across the centre pitch. Since it was still February no interference with cricket was involved, but the groundsman was already expressing fairly strong views on the subject to the pilot who had landed there. The pilot was F/O T.J. Arbuthnot, who had been at Eton with me and had also flown over to re-visit the place, but his engine had cut out and he had done a really magnificent emergency landing which was appreciated by almost everyone except the groundsman.

Needless to say, his aeroplane was quickly surrounded by Eton boys and he gave them an impromptu talk about flying with the Air Force which did as much for recruiting as any other demonstration I could possibly have organized.

During my time at Northolt I had no occasion to fly any very senior officers. This was partly due to the bad weather prevailing at that time of the year and partly — perhaps — because the senior officers who did not fly themselves preferred going by car to trusting themselves in uncertain weather to a very young pilot from a fighter squadron. They may, therefore, have decided to postpone their visits until Flight Lieutenant Ritchie returned from leave. It was, however, only a little later that I flew a senior officer — an Air Commodore — on a visit he had to make. On that occasion my arrival at our destination was a little embarrassing. As usual in those days all aeroplane movements were signalled so that if an aeroplane failed to arrive some action could be taken to find out what had happened. In some (disastrous) cases there might have been an accident, but usually a rather red-faced pilot had to explain why he had turned up at the wrong aerodrome, failed to report his error, and then returned to his own aerodrome without saying where he had found himself after he had lost himself.

In flights where Air Rank was a passenger, as in mine in this case, a lot of trouble was taken over the flight signal. The time of departure, the estimated time of arrival (E.T.A.) and the name and rank of the pilot and passenger were recorded. Thus the signal went off recording the fact that F/O Wheeler with A/Cdre Brown as passenger were in the Bristol Fighter. Unfortunately the signal staff, with their usual efficiency, abbreviated the signal and, on arrival, it read 'F/O Wheeler and a/c Brown.' were in the Bristol Fighter. The normal abbreviation for Air Commodore was Air Cdre or, at least he was given a capital A and C.

We landed at our destination a little ahead of time with the result that no special reception party was there. I taxied in, switched off, got out and then stood by, awaiting the descent of the Air

Commodore, who was considered, in those days, a V I P, from the rear cockpit. The Air Commodore took a little time unstrapping himself – too long for a corporal who was on the tarmac to receive us and who assumed that a/c Brown was aircraftsman Brown. The corporal grew more and more impatient over the leisureliness with which a/c Brown prepared to disembark, and finally – to my consternation – called out:

'Now then a/c Brown, hurry up and get out. If you're waiting for a footman to let down the carriage steps you've got another thought coming to you. 'Op out – and bloody quick about it.'

The Air Commodore said nothing, but he slowly removed his flying suit as he stood up in the cockpit. As the distinctive blue officers' barathea cloth was disclosed the corporal started worrying. As the broad Air Commodore's stripe appeared the corporal disappeared.

By that time the official reception party were arriving and both the corporal's and my responsibilities were over. The Air Commodore thanked me for the trip and remarked:

'I have often thought we should have our rank badges on the outside of the flying clothing.'

This is now common practice although senior officers – certainly V I Ps – usually travel in a closed, almost air conditioned cabin, wearing the clothes in which they will appear on whatever ceremonial occasion they may be engaged.

Before leaving Northolt I had to fly a Bristol Fighter over to Hendon and back. On this flight F/O Arbuthnot asked to come along in the back seat. I felt rather complimented since he and the other pilots in No.41 (Fighter) Squadron at Northolt had always been a bit uncomplimentary about pilots in other squadrons, and in particular, when I was around, about pilots in No.111 Squadron. I was a little surprised to see that he was bringing with him his Service cane: this was a crook-handled walking stick which all officers carried on parade in those days. He explained the cane by saying he might have to visit the Station Adjutant at Hendon, so he ought to be properly dressed.

We took off from Northolt and climbed to 1000 feet for the short flight to Hendon. As we passed over Harrow the engine suddenly faded. I had not got my hand on the throttle at that moment and in my instinctive reaction to look for somewhere to land I did not notice that the throttle had closed. However, when I felt for it almost immediately I noticed it was closed and pushed it forward to get cruising power again. I assumed the friction nut had become too loose so I tightened it up and proceeded. A few seconds later, as I took my hand off the throttle for a moment to adjust my goggles, the engine stopped again. This time I glanced down and just caught a glimpse of Arbuthnot's crooked handle of his Service cane disappearing rearwards to his own cockpit. I had known that he had no throttle control in the back so had not suspected that he was closing the throttle. He had a satisfied grin on his face which I decided to remove. It was no use doing a lot of violent aerobatics since he would probably have liked that: a more effective form of retaliation for the anxious moment he had caused occurred to me as I looked round at him. Since it was only a short flight to Hendon he had not bothered to put on warm flying clothing. The rear seat of the Bristol Fighter was well known as one of the coldest and draughtiest in the Air Force. The weather that February day was entirely suitable to the scheme. I started climbing. Arbuthnot took little notice of this at first and did not try to shut the throttle again since I had my hand on it. I settled down to a steady climb. Suddenly the Fighter yawed violently to starboard and then, as I corrected it, yawed violently to port. For a moment I thought we must be in some peculiar turbulence but that seemed unlikely. I looked round to see how my passenger was taking it and then I realized what was happening. He was head down pulling on the rudder cables, first one side and then the other. These cables passed through the rear cockpit and were easily accessible to a passenger with a perverted sense of humour. This merely strengthened my resolve to cool my passenger down a bit. We were already at 6000 feet and climbing steadily. I could not tell how cold the outside air was since the front seat of the fighter was always very warm, but I could make a good guess at it by looking at Arbuthnot. His face went pale first and then started going blue: at 8000 feet his teeth started chattering so much that he could not shout: instead he pointed down over the side but as he had no gloves on he soon stopped that. At 10,000 feet I closed the throttle and shouted back:

'No more hooking the throttle back with your cane?'

He nodded.

'No more pulling the rudder cables about?'

He nodded again.

'No more fooling on this trip or coming back?'

I got a third vigorous assent and put the Bristol Fighter into a steep dive, closing the engine radiator shutter as we went down. The Welsh Harp close to Hendon opened out from a small puddle into a wide lake as we dived straight towards it. As always the Bristol Fighter was amazingly quiet even in a steep dive. I pulled out slightly at 3000 feet and headed for Hendon Aerodrome, losing speed so as to arrive in circuit conveniently for a quick landing. When I switched off Arbuthnot got out rather stiffly, still looking very blue. I

126

explained to the Officer of the Watch who met us that he came from No.41 (Fighter) Squadron and in that Squadron they always went blue with fright every time they had to fly.

Our return flight to Northolt was entirely uneventful.

It was during this attachment at Northolt that I struck up a friendship with P/O McEvoy — now retired as Air Chief Marshal Sir Theodore McEvoy. He was then Adjutant to No.41 (F) Squadron and was one of the few officers in that Squadron who did not extol the virtues of that Unit above all others in the Command. It was probably because he KNEW 41 Squadron was the best and was not doubtful about it, so there was no need to state the obvious. This saved a lot of argument so far as I was concerned, since I also KNEW No.111 Squadron was the best, and therefore, like McEvoy, perceived no need to state the obvious.

Instead of arguing on matters of comparatively unimportant tactical details such as the relative efficiency and flying ability of our own squadrons, we discussed matters of strategic importance such as the general organization of the air defences of the country. My recollection is that it was from P/O McEvoy that I got the first clear picture of the Fighter Defence organization of England as the defence was, in its rather primitive state, in those days.

This defence organization had recently had a general shake up when a relatively mild European crisis had revealed the fact that England, having a few years earlier had the most powerful Air Force in the world, had sunk in those few years to having one which ranked fifth in the Air Forces of the world, and was therefore vulnerable to any form of diplomatic pressure her European neighbours might put on her.

The Fighter Defence of the country was, therefore, being expanded very rapidly but Fighting Area, as it was then called, was little more than a Group (by today's standards) in Air Defences of Great Britain which comprised a large proportion of the Air Force at Home. It was at about this time that Air Defence of Great Britain (A D G B) had been formed as a Command with Air Marshal Sir John Salmond as Commander-in-Chief. A D G B in those days included what was later termed Bomber Command, on the principle that Bombers were just as important in national defence as Fighters. In fact this arrangement came very close to the present organization of Strike Command which we have today.

The only part of this chain of Command which was of direct interest to a junior Flying Officer in No.111 (F) Squadron was that the Air Officer Commanding Fighting Area, Air Vice Marshal Sir Robert Brooke-Popham wanted efficient units under his command and knew how to ensure that they came up to the required standard.

In the Home Communication Flight at Northolt I came into contact with a few of the officers on H Q Staff and became aware that, taken by and large, Staff Officers were mostly human beings and some of them were also very good pilots indeed. Most of them knew McEvoy partly because he was adjutant to No.41 (F) Squadron and partly because he had passed out of Cranwell with the Sword of Honour.

On the whole I was glad of this attachment to the Home Communication Flight. I lost little Siskin flying by it since it was a period of traditionally bad weather and it helped to widen my experience of the Air Force generally and Fighting Area in particular. I also saw another Fighter Squadron (No.41) operating and learnt that they had their problems too.

14 No. 111 (Fighter) Squadron —Siskin flying

By the 1st of March I was back at No.111 (F) Squadron and since I was still Acting Flight Commander I took the opportunity to do as much flying as I could, most of the time concentrating on aerobatics. One particular manoeuvre which fascinated me was the upward spin. I had first seen this done at the Royal Air Force Pageant at Hendon in 1926 by (I think it must have been) F/O R.L.R. Atcherley, the almost legendary aerobatic pilot. He was then flying a Gloster Grebe. The ordinary spin downwards is, and was then, well understood: the upward spin is exactly the same manoeuvre except that gravity is not helping, one therefore has to get up sufficient speed to pull up until ascending vertically and still have enough speed in hand to allow the aeroplance to do a spin or 'flick' roll vertically upwards when one applies the correct control forces which are 'stick right back and full rudder'. On the Bristol Fighter one could do a 'flick' roll or horizontal spin fairly easily by flying at about 90 m.p.h. straight and level and then applying the same control of 'stick' and rudder together. The Bristol Fighter then did one complete turn of a spin horizontally and after that would have fallen into a normal spin downwards if one did not reverse the controls and steady it to level flight again. But the Bristol Fighter had not got the engine power compared to its weight to do this in a vertical climb. I felt that if a Grebe could do it a Siskin could too, so I worked up to the manoeuvre by stages. First of all I perfected the 'flick' roll on the level and then I did the same manoeuvre at more and more of an upward angle: as this increased I became aware of the need for more and more speed. After several weeks of trial and error and a vast number of attempts I found that if I dived the Siskin to a speed of around 180 m.p.h., which seemed to be the optimum speed for the manoeuvre, and then pulled up until the Siskin was going vertically upwards − not very easy to judge − and finally put on full upward elevator and full rudder, the Siskin could (usually) do two and a half turns of an upward spin. This was better than the Grebe could normally achieve but the Siskin was so strong that one could dive it to any speed without any fear of 'flutter' and then pull it out of the dive more abruptly than many aeroplanes might have survived in those days. After two and a half turns of upwards spin things became a little confused and I found it best to centralize the controls and leave the Siskin to sort itself out which it always did. I then went into the next manoeuvre pretending that I had had the Siskin under control all the time. Except at the Central Flying School, aerobatics in those days had not been developed to the state of precise sophistication which they have today.

Another impressive manoeuvre of the same appearance, but basically different aerodynamically, was the upward roll. This was a simple aileron induced roll vertically upwards and again it depended on having a lot of speed in hand as one achieved a vertical upward path. As in the upward spin I let the Siskin fall out of the manoeuvre at the top and the result was just as exciting to me as to anyone watching, since on some occasions the Siskin would do a tail slide, having stopped completely in the air still pointing upwards. It was thus advisable to hold the stick firmly back just at the end so that if a tail slide ensued the Siskin would finally fall forwards and remain the right way up: if it fell backwards recovery from the inverted dive would take a little longer.

I concentrated on these two manoeuvres since they were more unusual than the ordinary loops, spins, inverted flying, horizontal rolls and the 'falling leaf' which could all be used as a fill-in if one was giving an aerobatic display. At the back of my mind I hoped I might have an opportunity to do some flying at the annual Air Force Pageant at Hendon, but for the time being I always had an appreciative audience at Stansted or Dunmow!

Much of my practising was, in fact, done above a cloud layer when the weather allowed it, since I could thus judge safely how much height I lost in recovery from any manoeuvre. I used the level top of the clouds as though it was the ground. If I had to dive into it during a misjudged recovery it was softer than the ground!

Apart from aerobatic practice we had the normal formation flying practice, Battle Flights and, by early May, we were practising Squadron formation flying in preparation for the A O C's inspection. Also that month a Flight Lieutenant had been posted to command my flight: he was a serious minded type, but pleasant and helpful. He also took all the administrative duties very seriously. We practised formation flying with him for many hours. This was a serious business since none of us had done much formation flying, even in flights, and keeping in formation when the leader was flying rather erratically to keep station with the leading Flight in Squadron formation made things a lot more difficult. Add to this the fact that in the Wing fly-past for the A O C we were the last of three Squadrons to fly past and we were supposed to keep in formation with the other two Squadrons, and the problem became virtually impossible. In No. 111 Squadron we always thought that the leading squadrons on the Station deliberately made things difficult for us by flying erratically themselves until they were just about to pass the A O C, but the truth probably was that they were out of practice too. The drill was for all three squadrons to take off separately and then form up in line astern as they circled the aerodrome to do a final turn into a straight approach to the saluting base. Usually the leading squadron succeeded in doing this reasonably well, albeit with a lot of speed changes and rather ragged turns. The second squadron was even more ragged with the leading squadron's slipstreams to contend with, and our own Squadron Commander was faced with either having to fly his own course, disregarding the others, and thus risk arriving at the saluting base several minutes after the leaders, or worse still a few seconds in front of them, or else he had to try to follow the others. He chose the latter course and this resulted in his turns becoming more and more like a series of aerobatics which his squadron were quite unable to follow. Thus we passed the saluting base in a sort of gaggle, tossed by the previous squadron's slipstreams, disarranged by aerobatic turns and sudden changes in speed: the result was barely recognizable as a formation. On the actual day of the inspection I heard afterwards that the Station Commander tried to apologize for the apparent confusion of his Squadrons by saying to a senior Staff Officer on the A O C's staff:

'I'm afraid it's a rather ragged formation at the end, Sir. Many of their pilots are new.'

To which the Staff Officer replied:

'Oh, it's meant to be a formation is it? I thought they were having a race.'

The A O C's inspection in other respects went off well enough. The Station Commander, Wing Commander Barton, was an able and respected officer and no-one on the staff wanted to make things difficult for him whilst he was getting the Station properly organized.

There were, of course, minor embarrassments at Squadron level. One of these was when the Group accountant officer asked to check No.111 Squadron's Welfare Fund, which was held by F/O Noel. An inspection of the books indicated that there should be £16. 7. 6d. in the Fund, but Noel was unable to produce more than £15. 1. 6. from the safe out of a rather crumpled buff envelope. the accountant asked where the rest of the money was. F/O Noel took all the confidential files out of the safe and shook them over his desk one by one. The accumulation of small coins arising from this action ammounted to another sixteen shillings. The accountant, now like a terrier down a rat-hole, demanded:

'And now, where's the other ten shillings?'

131

Without a moment's hesitation, John Noel produced a ten shilling note from his trouser pocket and said:

'Oh, I have that: I always keep it ready for any sudden welfare call.'

The accountant reported that 'The No.111 Squadron Welfare Fund was kept in an unorthodox way.'

Some light relief during the inspection was provided by the traditional investigation into fire practice. The Station Fire Officer was accompanying the A O C's party on his inspection. From his point of view things were not going very well. He had been ordered to roll out a coiled up canvas fire hose. This was being done as he gave assurances that it was done every month: as the last coil flicked out of the box an obviously last year's blackbird's nest rolled and bumped across the hangar floor with a sort of jubilant 'I've-been-here-since-1926' look about it that defied any possible explanation. The A O C's entourage waited till the blackbird's nest stopped rolling, then the A O C turned to the Fire Officer and said:

'Do you know your fire orders?'

'Word for word, Sir.'

'Well, we will assume there is a fire here . . .'

Indicating a spot in front of him on the hangar floor:

' . . . Take the appropriate action.'

The Fire Officer immediately came into action. He jumped up and down on the spot indicated and yelled:

'Help, help.'

The A O C recoiled from an apparently lunatic performance and asked what on earth he thought he was doing. The young Fire Officer explained:

'Action No.1. Sir. 'Try to put it out'.

'Action No.2. Sir. 'Call for help'.

'Action No.3. Sir . . . .'

'All right, all right.'

The A O C turned to the Squadron Commander in whose hangar it was:

'Both officers and blackbirds have quick responses in your hangar it appears; blackbirds especially must be quick in their nesting habits.'

Although No.111 Squadron had by now got their full complement of the Mark IIIA Siskin we were still suffering a certain amount of unservicability due to various modifications, and new equipment being delivered. We had, in fact, only recently received all the parts of the gun firing mechanism, which included the 'interrupter gear' which was the control which prevented the bullets hitting the propeller as they were fired. The Siskin, as all other fighters in those

132

days, had its two Vickers guns mounted just in front of the pilot in the cockpit so that he could clear any stoppages which might occur. It was only later with the more reliable guns fitted in the wings of the Hurricane and Spitfire that the old interrupter gear was dispensed with. It was essential in the older fighters since the cockpit mounted guns had to fire through the disc swept by the propeller and the bullets, therefore, had to pass between the propeller blades as they turned. As soon as all the parts were delivered our Squadron Armament Officer, F/O Rhind, who was also a very fine aerobatic pilot, had the job of checking the installation and the interrupter gear timing on the Siskin IIIA. He did this on the firing butts on the Station. In this (normal) procedure the aeroplane was fixed pointing into the butts, which consisted of the usual earth bank heaped against a high, but thin, brick wall: this extended above the earth bank by about four feet to stop stones and ricochets flying over it. The tail of the aeroplane was also raised on a trestle so that it was approximately in flying position and the guns were pointing into the earth mound, rather below the horizontal, so that there was no danger of the bullets ricochetting over the butts. F/O Rhind had got the first Siskin IIIA on the butts for test just as he had done with the Siskin Mark III's, and the armament personnel spent all the morning tying it down and checking the timing of the interrupter gear to make sure that the guns would fire and stop firing at the right moments during the propeller revolutions. First thing in the afternoon F/O Rhind got into the cockpit and started up the engine: after warming it up he ran it up to full power and started his firing tests.

It was at this moment that I walked over from the Officers' Mess, across the main road, to the hangars. As I approached I saw an airman with his head down running very fast. I had been in the Air Force long enough by then to know that airmen only ran under one of two alternatives: either there was a real emergency or they were going on leave. I then saw two more airmen running, also with their heads down; one of them dodged behind a hangar buttress and the other fell flat on his face behind a small mound. I then became aware of the noise of a Siskin's engine running up and the rattle of machine gun fire. Had it been six months earlier on the Station I would have assumed that there was some kind of mutiny afoot. Perhaps the officers under arrest were trying to break out; or there was another raid on the non-public funds; or some other officers found the peace-time Air Force routine boring and wanted to liven it up: but under the new administration none of these things were likely. I paused to think and, being well out of the line of fire, I could consider the matter coolly. A few yards away from me there was a

133

Above: a Siskin Mark III, powered by a 375 h.p. Jaguar engine

Right: a Siskin Mark IIIA

134

civilian builder putting tiles on the roof of a new building. He had just fixed half a dozen in position and bent down to get the next six to lay above them on the roof. As he walked along his scaffolding to place the next six, the previous half dozen shattered in front of his eyes and fell in little russet fragments to the ground below, to the accompaniment of that unmistakeable 'WHEE-EE-EE-' of a ricochetting bullet passing on its way beyond. The tiler was off the roof, down his ladder and behind a wall with a speed that suggested he might have done an apprenticeship on the Western Front in the war which was only a few years back. Whilst I watched this the staccato noise of flying, ricochetting bullets ceased and the sound of the Armstrong Siddeley Jaguar engine died down to the 'idling' sound and finally stopped.

Subsequent investigation revealed the fact that the same tail trestle had been used for the Siskin Mark IIIA that had been used for the

earlier Siskin Mark III, but one of the differences between these two Marks was that they had a different sweep up of the underside of their rear fuselages (see illustrations on pages 134—5) so that the Siskin IIIA, on the same trestle, had its guns pointing above the earth bank into the brick wall above. The first few rounds of the two Vickers guns had burst a hole through the wall and thereafter the bullets sped on their way down the centre of the technical side of the camp. The airmen who were watching the operation at the butts could not warn the pilot what was happening because of the noise of the engine and guns firing, and it was only when an airman climbed up to the cockpit, with some difficulty in the slipstream of a 375 h p Jaguar engine at full power, and tapped F/O Rhind on the shoulder that he realized that something unusual was happening.

It was just one of those oversights which cause worry and anxiety, but definitely liven up what was, after all, a somewhat sedentary existence in the then peace-time Air Force.

Guns firing at random down the main thoroughfare of the technical side of the camp were not the only danger. On the domestic side, particularly around the Officers' Mess, there were other dangers. For instance there seemed to be no restriction on either the number or the temperament of dogs. During the first six months of my time at Duxford we had very little trouble with dogs: that is to say the big ones barked at one — friend or foe — and the small ones tried to bite one's ankles, but fortunateley their mouths were usually too small to get a grip; even then one began to appreciate some advantages for the boots and puttees of No.1 dress. However, one got used to the mild agressiveness of the local canine world until my friend Reynolds obtained a large Borzoi dog of impeccable pedigree. Like all highly bred — perhaps over-bred — dogs, this Borzoi had a temperament. He was broadminded in his way about many things, but he did not like airmen in uniform, officers in flying kit, children on bicycles, postmen either mounted or unmounted, dogs smaller than himself, dogs larger than himself and (in particular) dogs the same size as himself. In all other respects he was entirely tranquil and lovable.

In the first week of his occupation of Duxford — occupation was the word — he pulled two children off their bicycles, fortunately unhurt, one postman off his bicycle, also unhurt, and bit a horrid little mongrel whom nobody liked. The last offence mitigated the other and F/O Reynolds was merely told to control his dog properly. Within two days the Borzoi had pulled the Station Disciplinary Sergeant Major off his bicycle and nipped him where his tunic joined his trousers: this was serious. F/O Reynolds was told he must sell his dog. Three days later the same Borzoi had bitten the postman again.

136

F/O Reynolds explained that he had sold the dog as ordered — to a brother officer on the camp. Whilst this was being discussed and the Borzoi's fate decided, the Borzoi created a major incident in the camp. He had been put out to 'run around' at 7.30 a m from his owner's room — no-one ever quite discovered from whose room he emerged — and he saw, not far away, an Alsatian whom he had not seen before but of whom he immediately took a dislike. He went after him, perhaps on the excuse that wolves were the Borzois' natural quarry, and the Alsatian looked like one. The Alsatian in fact belonged to an elderly administrative Flight Lieutenant who worked to a daily routine developed over many years of service. On this routine he was always shaving himself before an open window at 7.35 a m and he was doing just this — with a cut-throat razor — when the Borzoi had got the Alsatian thoroughly on the run. The two dogs weaved in and out of the Officers' living huts, barking like mad. The Borzoi was steadily gaining on the Alsatian. The latter, in desperation, leaped in through the window of his master's quarters. He landed on his master, still shaving, but the damage done by the Alsation was nothing by comparison with the turmoil which ensued when the Borzoi came in through the same window.

At breakfast we saw the Administrative Flight Lieutenant, with his face covered in sticking plaster, vowing vengeance on the owner of the Borzoi. F/O Reynolds realised that devotion to the canine race had its limits and he sold the Borzoi to a man with seven children who all rode bicycles. Two months later he received a letter from the father of seven — still father of seven — to say how much they all loved the Borzoi — he was so gentle with the family and all their friends — including the postman.

There is always something new one can learn about dogs!

By the middle of May 1927 the Siskin I normally flew (No.8052) had had a new engine installed which was slightly more powerful than the ordinary Armstrong Siddeley Jaguar. It had a higher compression and thereafter the aircraft could get higher than the normal Siskin in the squadron. At this time also we had been sent one suit of experimental heated clothing developed by the Royal Aircraft Establishment at Farnborough. This was essentially a one-piece suit well insulated, and had electric heating wires sewn in to keep the pilot warm. It was very much an experimental suit. The other essential aid to high altitude flying was oxygen. In the Siskin at that date the oxygen supply, which we seldom used, came from a container which was virtually a vaccum flask in which liquid oxygen was stored. This 'boiled off' and came through a pipeline to the pilot's oxygen mask. The oxygen supply was also experimental.

We were asked to test the heated clothing and, since my Siskin had

137

the high altitude engine installed, it was decided that all the rest of the gear should be fitted in it and I should do the test. Thus I had virtually three experimental components to test on the one flight: there was the new engine, the new heated clothing and the still undeveloped oxygen apparatus.

In the bliss of ignorance I set off on the test on a day in the middle of May. It took me about 40 minutes to get dressed, lifted into the (open) cockpit, connected up electrically, connected to the oxygen supply and generally checked for proper functioning of all the accessories. I took off at 9.30 a m on a clear morning and climbed steadily. By 10 a m I was at 21,000 feet, which was several thousand feet higher than I had ever been before and indeed higher than almost any Service aircraft went in those days.

I was uncertain about the temperature up there because my left foot felt very cold, my right foot felt uncomfortably hot, my goggles were showing signs of freezing on the *inside* and my arms and body were fairly comfortable, except for one arm which was marginally too hot and getting hotter. There was a slight smell of overheated fabric which was just detectable in the open cockpit. However the old fear of fire was no longer obsessive since I had a parachute. I believed the oxygen supply was still working since I felt no ill effects from altitude but this did not prove much since I had never suffered from high altitude effects before and, as I subsequently discovered, I could go to over 20,000 feet without oxygen without significant ill effects. In later years I learnt how illusory this feeling of well-being could be at high altitude when lacking oxygen.

I looked around to admire the view as well as I could with clothing which made it difficult to turn my head and goggles which were slowly icing up. There was a wonderful view of the eastern counties of England. Away to the north the Wash looked like a misty mirror with only faintly visible coastlines around it. London to the south was its usual smokey blur for those coal-burning days. I could not see below me since I was intent on maintaining a climbing speed of 65 m.p.h. which seemed to be the optimum at that height. This would give me a true (climbing) speed of (very approximately) 85 m.p.h. It was impossible to look over the side of the cockpit owing to the restriction of my high altitude clothing. In any case I was apprehensive of straining this experimentally electrically heated clothing at all in case it should break one of the heating wires and cause the wire to arc and then, possibly, warm me up even beyond the point of discomfort which I was already experiencing in my right foot.

Apart from all these doubts, fears and worries, I was happy enough. I was venturing up into the then almost unknown world for standard Air Force aeroplanes. I was disappointed over my goggles icing up and thus restricting my view of the really wonderful, and entirely new, world spread out below me. I dared not lift my goggles since I had read in some American magazine of some other pilot attempting a height record whose goggles had also frozen over: he had lifted them and his eyeballs had immediately frozen solid. How true this story was I did not know but I felt it better to accept a temporary restriction of vision — however frustrating — then to risk permanent blindness. I did, however, insert a gloved finger inside my goggles and tried to rub away some of the ice. The result was unsatisfacrory since I merely smeared the slushy ice all over one glass of my goggles. I gave up that attempt and continued climbing with one eye still recording outside events.

By the time I had reached 26,000 feet I realised I was nearing the ceiling since the altimeter was registering practically no increase in altitude over two or three minutes. I kept going but the temperature of my right foot was worrying me and my left arm was beginning to come up to the same temperature. I glanced thoughtfully at the electric suit's plug-in point: the man from the R A E had told me that I could always pull that out if things got too hot. I also reached forward to make sure I could get hold of it if I needed.

At last 27,000 feet came up and we seemed to be unlikely to get any higher. I eased the nose of the Siskin up a little till the speed dropped to 60 m.p.h. and for a time I gained height quite quickly to 27,500 feet, but I realized this was a gain in height at the expense of a loss of speed and that the climbing rate would not be held. However there was still a detectable gain in height. At 27,800 feet I realized I was no longer gaining height at all, even at 60 m.p.h. so I eased the speed up to 65 m.p.h., waited until I seemed to be just holding level flight and then pulled the nose up until the speed dropped to 55 m.p.h. thus squeezing every foot of height I could by sacrificing speed without actually stalling the Siskin. Very slightly I overdid it and the Siskin fell out of the climb at about 45 m.p.h. and I lost 700 feet in regaining control.

Afterwards on the ground the barograph recorded a height of 28,000 feet, so the last desperate climb must have added about 200 feet to the ceiling. This was, of course, not a true Service ceiling since the 'contract' Service ceiling was assumed to be when the rate of climb fell below 100 feet per minute.

On the way down I dropped fairly quickly to 20,000 feet and then started to locate my position. I checked that the Wash was still due north or me and the blurry haze which I believed to be London was due south, and about the same distance away. Keeping on this line I lost height rapidly to 12,000 feet where I flew level for a bit to let my ears adjust for pressure and at that height I could position myself fairly accurately over the now familiar countryside.

At 10,000 feet I pulled out the electric heating plug and thereafter the approach and landing was uneventful my right foot even returned to about 98.4°F which was quite a relief both physically and mentally.

The man from Farnborough was delighted with my report. The uneven heating was a thing they had expected he said. He added that the main thing was that it didn't catch fire! I learnt about boffins from him!

Today 28,000 feet does not seem to be very high for a fighter aircraft, but in 1927 it was some 12,000 feet above any height we normally operated at. Our Battle Climbs seldom went above 12,000 feet, never above 16,000 feet. Our oxygen supply was suspect for very good reasons. Open cockpits and no heating made any height above 12,000 feet very unpleasant.

During the war, fighter pilots, as recorded in McCudden's book *Five Years in the Royal Flying Corps* did occasionally do patrols — without oxygen — up to 21,000 feet, but as McCudden remarked, at that height a pilot could hardly concentrate on anything and his operational alertness was virtually nil.

It was not long after this climb of mine that a letter came round all Squadrons from Command to ask pilots' opinions on the maximum height at which fighters could maintain efficient patrols. Some of the pilots put in reports saying that they thought that a pilot could patrol effectively at heights of 18,000 feet, 20,000 feet or even (one said) 22,000 feet, so long as the pilot kept himself fit by playing rugger, squash, golf and also swimming and long distance running. I claimed that no patrol above 16,000 feet and lasting over 30 minutes could be effective. I got a rebuke from Command for being weak and the rugger enthusiast almost got awarded an A F C. The fact was that none of the high altitude 'experts' had ever been there at all, or if they had they were so anoxic that they did not know what they were doing. One has to remember that it was only on the outbreak of World War II in 1939 that we first started seeing regular vapour trails.

I5 Night flying

In the reddening rays of a setting sun, in late June 1927, I stood outside the Watch Office observing an elderly Flight Lieutenant doing his night flying. He was flying a Siskin III which we used for training purposes and, being a rather sedentary type of officer, he had long since lost my desire to share in the joys and thrills of flying — let alone night flying.

It was part of the service requirements that every officer on the General Duties list qualifying for what amounted to flying pay must do a certain minimum number of hours flying per year, and a very small number of these had to be by night. Experience had taught this officer that, so far as night flying was concerned, he could reduce the risk to negligible proportions if he selected a clear night close to the Summer Solstice. As an additional precaution he chose a night with a full moon. If he then took off before the sun had actually set and landed again when the full moon was well up and the last reflected rays of the sun were still effective, the anxieties and embarrassments of night flying barely exceeded those of normal flying by day.

I was Officer of the Watch that evening and, in order to emphasize the impression that night flying was in progress, I had laid out the usual flare path of 'Money' flares, which were porous lumps of asbestos material about the shape and size of a 2½ gallon (inverted) bucket, standing in a tray. The whole was soaked in paraffin and burnt like a fairly enthusiastic bonfire.

The flares were laid out in the shape of a 'T' though sometimes one arm of the 'T' was omitted, making it an inverted 'L'. The 'T' faced into wind and the pilot could land either side of the line of flares. The actual distance of the flare paths was 450 yards with 5 flares spaced 100 yards apart and one more at the downwind end of the flare path spaced only 50 yards from the rest. Pilots normally landed on the starboard (right hand) side of the line of flares and the left hand side was available for emergency landings such as when another pilot had broken his undercarriage landing on the starboard side. The port side was frequently needed. It was, in fact, the best side on which to land since most pilots looked over the left hand side of the cockpit when landing and therefore, on the left, did not suffer from the glare of each successive flare as he passed it. The extra flare

141

(or two) placed to form the cross bar of the 'T' indicated which way the flare path was laid in relation to the wind.

In some respects this array of bonfires was something of a hazard to anyone landing at night and it was a very definite hazard to the elderly officer then putting in night flying time. He seldom achieved a really safe landing even in daytime and the prospect of making his usual hazardous one in the proximity of a bonfire was not at all inviting. He circumvented this danger by landing in another part of the aerodrome altogether, well remote from the flares, since there was still quite enough day and moon light to guide him down.

When he was safely back the real business of night flying began and this was mainly the task of my Squadron since we were designated as night fighters, not that night flying was a highly developed art at that time; such experience as had been gained during the War, by a very few pilots, was largely forgotten by 1927, certainly so far as fighters were concerned.

We usually started our night flying practice by doing dusk landings which we continued as darkness fell, thus getting used to the sight of the flare path in gathering gloom and the angle at which it was best to approach it. I found it best to approach at a height which allowed me to see all the flares as individual lights in a line, until I passed over the red light which marked a point about 200 yards inside the aerodrome boundary. Then I eased the throttle back and slowly lost height towards the first flare hoping to pass it at about 20 feet flying level. I then closed the throttle gently and waited until the wheels touched, perhaps opposite one of the other flares when one could see the ground. But one was always confused by the fact that the flare gave a bright light as one approached it and immediately one passed it there was inky blackness. Coupled with this the airmen in charge of each flare usually tried to help the pilot by throwing on a tin-full of paraffin as the aeroplane approached. This resulted in a blinding flash of light which completely destroyed any night vision one might have acquired whilst flying around. On really dark nights it was quite a hazardous business landing with the old 'Money' flare arrangement and nothing much better was developed until R.L.R. Atcherley (then Air Commodore) developed the Drem system of continuous shrouded lights early in the 1939/45 War.

Another worry about night flying in 1927 was that one had no effective radio so that if the wind changed the only warning one had of it was the complete confusion which arose on the aerodrome below, whilst the old flare path was extinguished and the airmen tried to carry almost red hot flare containers to lay them out in another direction. In emergency one might have risked a landing whilst this was going on, but at that time the aerodrome was a mass
142

of wandering airmen carrying flares and also transport driving around trying to help. Whatever the emergency, under those circumstances, it was usually wisest to stay aloft if one possibly could.

In those days we made no attempts to intercept other aeroplanes pretending to be bombers coming in. All we had to do, after we had got used to night flying, was to fly patrols over North and East London to give practice to the Observer Corps and the searchlights. We usually flew at heights around 5,000 feet in areas where the searchlights were located. The actual searchlight and anti-aircraft manned areas round London were then few and far between and we merely patrolled where the regulars or, more likely, reservists, were doing their annual training. This was a fairly pleasant activity since the lights of London on a clear night were most impressive, and the sight of the searchlights waving about looking for us was interesting. Two hazards, apart from the possibility of engine failure, occupied our minds in these patrols: one was real, the other psychological. The real one was caused when the searchlights managed to pick us up and when several others joined in we were caught in three or four beams. These tended to blind a pilot if he looked down but also they tended to give a false impression of attitude since the searchlights slowly changed their own angle to the vertical as they followed the aeroplane. Quite a number of pilots found themselves in peculiar attitudes after a few minutes in the beams and then had no horizon to guide them when they finally evaded the searchlights or fell out of the beams.

The other hazard, a psychological one, was caused by the reflection of the searchlight beam running along the aeroplane's wing bracing wires towards the cockpit and giving the appearance of another aeroplane's lights flying straight in on a collision course. This optical, but very worrying, illusion also occurred as one flew round the circuit to land. The reflection of the flares successively ran up the wires towards the cockpit and many a pilot took viloent evasive action to avoid a non-existent aeroplane, and then spent a few worrying seconds getting himself flying level again.

On the ground, during early practice night flying, there was even more chaos than normal. For a start the Squadron Commander was not only nominally in charge of the operation and responsible for seeing no accidents occurred, but H Q might take a dim view of the night's work if he had not himself flown. He therefore had a double worry and this induced an anxiety complex which spread to most of the pilots in his squadron.

On one well remembered night, my Squadron Commander had arranged to fly himself late in the proceedings, and also elected to supervise the earlier flying. He was, understandably, in a fairly

143

emotional state and this was enhanced by the wind changing through 180° whilst four of his pilots were in the circuit wanting to land. The Officer of the Watch that night was well able to deal with the situation alone, but quite unable to deal with it when the Squadron Commander was also giving different orders to all of his. The airmen also knew what to do but were confused by orders and counter-orders and also by the Fire Tender driving around on the aerodrome trying to illuminate the scene with its headlights. Every few minutes one of the pilots in circuit flew low over the aerodrome to try and see what all the confusion was about: this drove the Fire Tender off the aerodrome, but it was ordered back peremptorily by the Squadron Commander. At this stage one of the airmen tending a flare lit it up in what he thought was, and in fact was, the right place, but no-one else knew which flare it was amongst the seven or eight it might have been. The Squadron Commander, on the Fire Tender, drove over to enquire but a swoop at the flare by one of the aeroplanes drove the vehicle away. The Squadron Commander jumped off the running board when he thought he was travelling at 5 m.p.h. but it was in fact doing 15 m.p.h. He was not hurt but his hat rolled away into the inky darkness and took a little time to find. The continual jolting of the Fire Tender caused a failure in the headlamp circuit, so the driver pulled up in what he hoped was a safe part of the airfield and dismantled the headlamp by the light of a torch to get things working again. But he was not in a safe part of the aerodrome since the Squadron Commander found him again and wanted to know why he was not doing as he had been told. The airman had got all the parts of one headlamp neatly laid out on the wing of the vehicle and was about to reassemble them when the Squadron Commander came up. He asked what was happening and to emphasize his need for a quick answer banged his fist hard on the wing: this shook all the parts of the headlamp off onto the ground where they could not easily be found in the darkness. The driver who thought he was well out of the reach of senior officers, assumed that one his mates had caused the interruption and said:

'Ere, 'oose bloody lights d'yer think yer mucking abaht wiv. You go and play spillikins somewhere else.'

The astonishment was so great that the Squadron commander said nothing and left. Indeed the shock was such that he calmed down and took a more logical view of the crisis. Left to themselves the airmen got the flare path laid out in its new direction and all the Siskins came back to land safely.

Although this was just one night, when many troubles happened all at once, it was typical of the sort of confusion which always occurred during night flying in those days, and indeed for years after.

It was worth bearing in mind that night operations by fighters in order to intercept bombers did not become a practical operation until late in 1941 when proper runway lighting was installed, efficient radio had been developed and airborne radar (R D F in those days) had been proved.

However, with our limited resources and even more limited experience we pressed on with our training so that we might win — or at least not lose — some unforseeable war. We knew that fighters alone could not win a war, but pacifists and warmongers alike insisted that with the 'fantastic' £15 million a year the taxpayer was then spending on the whole Royal Air force throughout the Empire, the great British Public should at least have the assurance that they would never be bombed. Eleven years later the Prime Minister offered £100 million to the Chief of the Air Staff if he could guarantee security from bombing within two years. The factories to provide the defence equipment had not then even been built!

Our part in this meagre role was, as said, to provide practice for the searchlights and in the summer months we did as required.

The patrols I did myself were like all others. I took off at 'last light', about three quarters of an hour after sunset, and flew down to the North London area where I flew a pattern over an agreed area. The searchlights came on in ones and twos as the reservists managed to man them and get them going after a full day's work. They were usually fairly erratic but some, perhaps controlled by old war-time crews were quick to pick us up. If we were embarrassed by the concentration of lights we were told we could fire a signal cartridge from our Verey pistol, but I always looked upon this as very much a last resort. We had used these extensively on Army Cooperation work and they were dangerous enough by day, when one or two pilots had accidentally fired the incandescent magnesium flare into the lower wing. At night the hazards were increased considerably. Apart from loading and firing the Verey pistol there was also the problem of disposing of the spent cartridge — quite a sizeable cylinder — and reloading. The spent cartridge was supposed to be put back in a rack, but this was difficult to locate in the darkened cockpit. In any case, 'breaking' the pistol to reload needed two hands and in the emergency envisaged both hands and both feet were fully employed flying the aeroplane. There was also the potential danger of dropping the pistol, or cartridge, or both and either (or both) getting mixed up in the controls on the cockpit floor. Personally I had visions of a dropped live cartridge getting jammed and then fired by the controls so I decided that no emergency would ever persuade me to try and fire a Verey pistol. I discussed this problem with another pilot in the Squadron and he said there was no trouble with the spent cartridges; he always threw them over-board. Since a large part of our patrol area, even then, was covered by glasshouses I wondered how the market gardeners would have viewed this solution to our problem.

When the searchlight crews had had enough they waved their beams about and I usually threw a loop with my navigation lights on to show I had had enough too.

In case of engine failure we had various emergency landing areas marked out with flare paths which we might have been able to reach, but we also had what were called Holt flares on the outboard span of each lower wing which we could fire electrically. These burnt brightly for about three minutes and would have been sufficient to assist in a forced landing in a field, although the proceedings would have been fairly hazardous. Some pilots held the view that one would be better off trying a landing in the dark without the additional hazard of carrying a bonfire at the wing tips. I usually retained one on my starboard (right) wing tip for emergency and let the port one off on my way out to patrol as I passed over Dunmow and did a few aerobatics. The display was always well received.

Our patrols usually ended by about 11.30 p m but we were very unpopular with the ground crews if we landed back too quickly. If the night flying operation continued after midnight everyone concerned in it had the morning off next day. I usually landed at about five minutes after midnight following my patrols to make quite sure we all had a good night (and morning's) sleep.

16 Royal Air Force Display— Hendon, 1927

One morning in late May 1927, I received a message that the Squadron Commander wanted to see me. My first reaction was to search my conscience — or at least my memory — to try and remember what I had done wrong over the last few days which might have been reported. I knew it must have been something fairly serious since I was on excellent terms with the C O whom I liked. He occasionally found that the responsibilities of being a Squadron Commander weighted very heavily upon him but I could not in my heart blame him for this since he had some fairly unreliable material under his command.

As I approached his office my friend John Noel, who was still Squadron Adjutant, bolted out of the office with a thoroughly flustered look on his face. I stopped him and said that the C O had sent for me, and did he know what it was all about? He replied:

'I haven't the faintest idea, but I shouldn't go in now if I were you. He came in a few minutes ago, picked up the telephone, cancelled two seats for "The Constant Nymph" and then sat looking glum. I looked at him wondering what the trouble was, and then he threw the telephone at me and told me to get out of the office and not sit there looking like a boiled lobster.'

This was not very encouraging, but John Noel's face was always very red and with hair the same colour and a steady enquiring look in his rather protruding eyes I felt some sympathy with anyone who had just had to cancel what seemed to have been a very promising engagement. I took a deep breath and walked into the office. The C O was still looking glum and at the sight of me he started looking thoroughly defeatist. But he was not unfriendly:

'Wheeler, I've sent for you because we've had a letter from H Q to ask if we have any pilots to do the individual aerobatics show at the Air Force Display this year. Anyone we recommend would, of course, have to do a demonstration for selection at Northolt first of all, before Air Marshal Sir John Salmond. I don't know of anyone else in the Squadron who might do this, but I thought you might like to think about it? The trouble is they want two pilots. Last year we sent one but he was turned down for dangerous flying. Would you like to?'

Amongst my many failings inability to speak was a rare one, but it afflicted me at that moment. This surpassed my wildest expectations.

'I'd like to try Sir. And I think Sergeant Marsh in my Flight would also do very well. Could you put our names forward Sir?'

The C O looked even more defeatist:

'Yes, I'll do that, but it was a great disappointment to me when they turned down F/O Rhind last year. I hope it won't happen again with you.'

I tried to reassure the C O and went off quickly to tell Sergeant Marsh and then I sought out my friend Rhind. I could not understand why he should have been turned down the year before: he was a magnificent aerobatic pilot. Sergeant Marsh was delighted and I had complete confidence in him. From F/O Rhind I got the full story of his being turned down the year before and he was extremely helpful to me with his advice. Apparently he had been selected to do the individual aerobatics at very short notice the year before, and had asked several pilots at Duxford what sort of a performance was wanted. They all agreed that the main thing was to 'shake them up a bit' and went on to suggest that they wanted something really startling. In his repertoire of aerobatics Rhind had developed two manoeuvres to perfection. One was an exact assessment of the minimum height needed to pull out of a spin and still clear the ground; the other was a near vertical side-slip on the approach to land and a recovery from it which left just a few feet clear as he levelled out and landed. In his case there was no preliminary check up on his performance except for the rehearsal the day before the Display, when all the schools were allowed in free. At this rehearsal Rhind went through the whole range of normal aerobatics, interspersing them with a few spins starting below 1000 feet and pulling out at a proximity to the ground which the watching Air Officers assumed must be disastrous. The fact that Rhind had practised this until perfection was achieved was not appreciated by the audience. Rhind finished his display by approaching in a vertical side-slip which required full control and full engine to place him in a position and an attitude from which he effected a perfect landing just over the crowd barriers. He then taxied to his parking position and switched off. Coming towards him, almost at a run, were the assembled Air Officers with attendant Staff officers. They all had very red faces and from this Rhind assumed he had achieved the desired effect. In fact they were absolutely furious, ordered him to return to his unit at once and they would be considering a Court Martial later for breaking all the flying regulations in the book. It appeared to Rhind that the information he had got from his friends had been inaccurate.

148

In defence of Rhind it should be said that if the officers concerned had been aware of all the painstaking practice he had put into his 'act' they would have realized that it was nothing like so dangerous as they had imagined. A quiet word of advice to lift his display by, perhaps, 200 feet would have been all that was required. But they were not to know this and Rhind returned to his unit with an unjustifiably harsh report. It was mainly this that induced my C O's defeatist look when he spoke to me.

F/O Rhind's advice was invaluable to me and I passed it on to Sergeant Alan Marsh. Between us we spent many days practising our separate 'acts'. We each had five minutes to ourselves in the Display which, to my mind, was quite enough for our engines. The Jaguar engines we had, although very reliable, had a tendency to lose most of their oil pressure under conditions of full throttle and five minutes at that power usually dropped the oil pressure to around 10 lb which was about one third of the recommended minimum. However, we found that if we started our 'act' fairly high and slowly lost height we could use rather less power and still achieve a useful performance.

On 2 June we flew over to Northolt to give a demonstration of our aerobatics before Air Marshal Sir John Salmond who was then C in C, A D G B. My performance covered most of the normal aerobatics and included my (by then) highly developed upward spins. Both performances were approved by Sir John Salmond, but he sent a message to my squadron to suggest that my aeroplane should be thorough inspected internally for any strain to the structure which might have been incurred by the more violent manoeuvres. No.41 Squadron pilots at Northolt, who were watching, said that only pilots in No.111 Squadron would apply that much 'brute force and ...... ignorance' to an aeroplane. They had been assigned to a less glamorous role in the Display so we accepted the fact that any remarks they made were due mainly to pique, but chiefly to a complete lack of knowledge of basic aerodynamics. That was my view anyway.

When my aeroplane was inspected a few day later strained and broken internal bracing wires were found in the tail-plane, but we replaced them and assumed it was due to fair wear and tear: it was unthinkable that the pilots of No.41 Squadron could have been even partially correct in their statements!

On 29 June Sergeant Marsh and I flew down to Hendon in formation to position ourselves for the Display, and the next day we each did a practice five minutes' aerobatics over Hendon Aerodrome. We were very careful not to do anything which might be considered dangerous, and just for the five minutes, starting at 1000 feet and losing height, our oil pressure only fell to about half its stated minimum figure. We prayed for fine weather and a high cloud base for the next two days, the rehearsal day when all the schools came and on the Pageant day. Our prayers were not answered so far as the rehearsal was concerned. It was raining most of the morning and when it stopped the clouds with occasional drizzle gave a minimum height to cloud base of between 500 and 800 feet. The weather was so bad that almost all the flying had to be cancelled and none of the formation flying could be done at all. All the school children, several thousand of them, had turned up and there was nothing to amuse or interest them.

At 10 a m Air Vice Marshal Sir Robert Brooke-Popham, who was in charge of the Display that year, sent for me and asked me if I and Sergeant Marsh would fly around and amuse the children until the weather cleared, or at least for 40 minutes. It seemed to me to be a wonderful opportunity for an officially approved 'beat up' of Hendon Aerodrome, but I remembered the sad story of F/O Rhind. I told the A V M that we would be very happy to do as he asked but with the weather as it was any display we gave was bound to look dangerous and I mentioned that the year before a pilot in my Squadron had been sent back to his unit for doing just that. Air Vice Marshal Brooke-Popham looked at me with an oddly severe twinkle in his eye and said:

'Wheeler, I understand that. I will be personally responsible for anything you do — but don't be absolute fools.'

I wondered how many senior officer in the Service then, or at any time, would have taken on such a responsibility. But it certainly put us on the spot. We had *carte blanche* but, as I told Sergeant Marsh, we must not let the A V M down whatever happened.

Soon after 11 a m we were airborne to the delight of the schoolchildren, who had been waiting a long time for something to happen. The drizzle had by then almost stopped, but the clouds were around 500 feet, which meant that they were almost down on the houses on the hill to the east of the aerodrome boundary. At first we could do little more than fly around in front of the children, but when we saw a chance we did a semi-stalled turn or even a loop. In each case we disappeared into cloud at the top of the manoeuvre but had enough height to get sorted out as we emerged. After 10 minutes my oil pressure had gone down to 5 lb and it remained there for the next half hour, but the Jaguar engine did not seem to mind. Hendon then was not the built-up area it is now, so there were a few fields outside the aerodrome, in which we could have landed in an emergency, and there was also the aerodrome, which we tried to have in front of us at moments when the engine was most likely to seize up. Toward the end of our 'beat up' the clouds had lifted sufficiently for me to do a few carefully positioned upward spins and rolls, but I pulled out of them as soon as I went into cloud to make sure I knew which way up I would be as I came out of the clouds again. On one occasion, emerging from the cloud base, I was horrified to see Sergeant Marsh's Siskin still spinning and apparently only about 50 feet from the ground. In fact he told me afterwards that he was 200 feet up but admitted he had misjudged his recovery badly. He scraped past the aerodrome surface as he pulled out of the dive with about 10 feet to spare and went on straight into other aerobatics. The school children were thrilled. When we landed after 40 minutes and a final low fly round the audience, we were greeted with most encouraging cheers from all the children. Air Vice Marshal Brooke-Popham's reception was different, but quite encouraging:

'Well, thank God that's over,'

he said, and added:

'Thank you. You have saved the day for the children.'

Then he turned to Alan Marsh:

'That spin of yours was a bit low, I thought?'

Alan Marsh hesitated to reply, so I put in a word for him:

'Sergeant Marsh can judge his spin recovery very accurately indeed, Sir.'

'So I saw. Well I shall pray for better weather tomorrow. I hope we have it indeed. I don't want to watch that through again.'

The Air Vice Marshal's prayers were answered. Perhaps rank counted! The next day was fair enough for everyone to fly and, as a result and somewhat to our disappointment, we only got our allotted five minutes in the programme. We did our act just after 2 p m and I then had a late lunch in the Officers' Mess on the aerodrome. I sat between an officer from a bomber unit and an officer from No.41 (F) Squadron. The former, making polite conversation and not knowing who had been flying the Siskins, said:

'Those two Siskins were very good.'

I said:

'Yes. But of course they were from No.111 Squadron.'

The officer from No. 41 (F) Squadron said:

'Pretty awful flying I thought. Nothing clever about it. We don't fly like that in 41 Squadron. We should have been doing the individual aerobatics this year but 41 Squadron have a more precise job to do.'

I hesitated to reply, but the bomber pilot said:

'What are you doing in this Display?'

There was a long pause. Then the 41 Squadron officer started rather pompously:

'I have a very responsible job to do . . . . '

Before he could finish the answer was given for him. Another young officer came in to lunch and said:

'Here, James, you've had more than your time for lunch: they're waiting for you to get back on the job.'

The bomber pilot said quickly:

'What is he doing in the Display?'

The answer came immediately and devastatingly:

'Car parking.'

That evening, when the Display was over, Marsh and I flew back to Duxford and went back into our usual routine.

Within sixteen days — let this be a warning to all enthusiastic young pilots — I crashed my favourite Siskin into a wood within 400 yards of my friends' house (Newton Hall) near Dunmow.

Looking back on this event after forty years I know it was due to over-confidence. Fortunately for me the aeroplanes we flew then were very forgiving.

I was putting up a show over Newton Hall, the home then of a friend of mine of Eton days, Tony Gold and his family, and I felt sure that what I could do over Hendon I could do — and more — over Newton Hall. But many things added up to cause the accident. Newton Hall was 150 feet higher than I had estimated and when I put the Siskin into a spin at 800 feet it was a very marginal height for safe recovery. I should not, at that moment, have looked at the oil pressure gauge and thus lost a few vital seconds of concentration on how low I was. When I decided hurriedly that I must get out of the spin — and quickly — I was already marginally too low. I put on full engine and adjusted my recovery action to what was very clearly an emergency. Siskin No.8052 responded, but I realised I was already too low to clear the ground so I took the risk of keeping the engine full on and pulling the stick back to hold the nose up and thus avoid diving into the ground during the recovery. I held the nose of the Siskin up, but the spin developed into a strange slow, nearly flat, downward spiral. I had never experienced this manoeuvre before but I was sure that if I let the stick forward the Siskin would dive more steeply into the ground. I was still turning in the spiral and only 150 feet from the ground. At that moment in front of me I saw a wood of fir trees. They looked wonderfully soft compared to open ground. I cut the engine, eased the stick forward and dived into the wood. My forward speed was probably only about 70 m.p.h. I rolled myself up into a ball for the impact, which was not too severe, but I couldn't resist raising my head for a second to see what was happening as we went through the trees. This resulted in getting a 3 foot log of pine wood straight in the face; I then ducked down

152

again. The arrival at ground level was uneventful since all the force of arrival had been taken by the fir trees. My first thought was FIRE. I struggled to get out but something was holding me back. Since no fire occurred I could think clearly and I realized that what was holding me back was my safety harness which I had forgotten to release. Had there been fire I wonder if I would ever have remembered it? But with no fire I then calmed down and remembered also to disengage my parachute harness so that I could get out of the cockpit more readily. This was not too easy since the top plane had closed down over the cockpit, but I got out and immediately ran towards my friends' house to tell them I was all right. Their son-in-law, Dick Marter, who was there, ran down to the scene of the crash immediately to help. I passed him within 50 yards as I approached the house and shouted to him:

'I'm all right Dick.'

He glanced at me and ran on. He told me afterwards that he never saw or heard me. He was sure I was dead! When he arrived at the scene of the crash he spent a few worried moments with his hand in the cockpit pulling at the parachute thinking it was me.

I mention these details because they are worth remembering in all cases of minor accidents. Onlookers are bound to assume the worst, but a momentary pause for careful consideration at some brief moment in the situation may be worthwhile. But it is difficult to think clearly in any situation of that kind.

Within a few minutes I arrived at the house and reassured everyone there, but they were still a little worried and sent for a doctor to check me over. In the meantime I got on to my squadron and told them I had 'damaged the Siskin in trying to land it in an emergency'! I thought it would lessen the excitement if the true sequence of events broke slowly.

The next day my Flight Commander was at the scene of the accident looking rather glum and his mood was not improved by a disgruntled 'local' saying:

'Well, what I thinks is it serves 'im jolly well right. Always foolin' around over 'ere: loopin' an' spinnin' and' I'll tell you what 'e was doin' this time . . . .'

He never did tell anyone: at that moment my two faithful and loyal mechanics, fitter and rigger, got him firmly by the arms and walked him hurriedly away from the scene saying that the area was closed to the public. Every time he tried to remonstrate he was accelerated through the undergrowth and brambles.

However, my Flight Commander had heard, and being a conscientious type he reported what he had heard to my Squadron Commander. He only got out a few words before my C O said:

153

'I don't think we need any more reports on this. I am quite satisfied it was a precautionary landing.'

Looked at from the most helpful point of view, that could be said to be an accurate assessment of the reasons for the accident. It was certainly, in view of all the circumstances, the safest way I knew of getting back on the ground at that moment.

Alas, my favourite Siskin, No.8052, was written off, but I had learnt a lesson I never forgot.

Within a week I was back on 'limited' flying duties but I was put in the Operations Room during the air Manoeuvres which took place immediately after. These were the manoeuvres of the whole of the Air Defence of Great Britain organization and included bomber formations which tried to reach targets by eluding fighters. Defences then were in a very primitive state of development and the communications throughout the whole area were even more primitive. We were supposed to have post office tie-lines between all units and Headquarters, also between Observer Corps reporting points and Headquarters. It was, in a way, an embryo state of what we had during the Battle of Britain 13 years later, but in 1927 we had no radar and very uncertain telephonic communications. Theoretically the Observer Corps saw and reported the track of incoming bombers. H Q predicted which way they were going and ordered fighter squadrons to intercept them. The fighters then took off and flew to the predicted height and position where the bombers should have been if they had not changed their heading. Interceptions were few and far between and when made were often purely by chance on a different bomber formation.

Adding to our troubles, the telephone link between the Duxford operations room and H Q Fighting Area, then a Command within A D G B was only working fitfully and at best was barely intelligible. In the operations room I was continually coming in for criticism from both ends of the telephone. The Duxford Squadron Commanders were saying that they were being given wrong instructions, and the H Q operations officer, a Wing Commander, was (when intelligible at all on the telephone) saying that he wished he could be in contact with an efficient station operations officer instead of 'a deaf mute straight from an infirmary for elderly invalids suffering from senile decay'. He was developing this theme when Air Vice Marshal Sir Robert Brooke-Popham, A O C Fighting Area, walked into the operations room. I was on the telephone at the moment listening to a description of what the Wing Commander at H Q thought I probably looked like. The A V M asked abruptly if we had any troubles. I leaped up and tried to stand to attention, still holding the telephone:

154

'Well Sir. Sometimes . . . .'

'Never mind "sometimes".'

'The telephone is very bad, Sir.'

'Let me have it.'

I was all too glad to hand it over to him. The Wing Commander at the other end had already started developing a theory on what he thought my grandparents had probably looked like. The A V M listened to this for a few seconds and then said:

'Who is that speaking?'

The force of expletives must momentarily have shaken up the microphones and loose connections since the message for a short time came through loud and clear:

'It's Wing Commander Testy here and I want to talk to someone who has got a little bloody sense in his head.'

The A V M mildly replied:

'Well, it's Air Vice Marshal Sir Robert Brooke-Popham here, and it won't do any good shouting abuse into the telephone. That gets us nowhere. What were you trying to say?'

By that time, of course, the Wing Commander had completely forgotten what he was trying to say.

Communication with H Q improved thereafter. As he left, the A V M looked at my still heavily bruised face and said:

'Junior officers do that sort of thing often. You're lucky.'

How right he was.

Soon after this I was posted to the Engineering Course at Henlow. The Air Member for Personnel at the Air Ministry was keeping his promise meticulously.

We had a fortnight's leave before reporting to RAF Henlow for the beginning of the Engineering Course year. I spent some of it at my home in Shropshire, some at Dunmow and a few days transferring my belongings to Henlow. Amongst other things I had acquired an SE 5a aeroplane for myself. I bought it from the Air Force by the 'secret' tender scheme then in use, as it still is today. I bid £50 for it and got it. I flew it from Farnborough to Duxford in Air Force markings and with only an oil pressure gauge on the instrument panel, in blissful ignorance of the civil regulations of those days. At Duxford I got it a Certificate of Airworthiness and raced it at Bournemouth in the Easter Races, at Portsmouth in May and again at Bournemouth for the Whitsun races, where I had engine trouble. I did not do much good but I learnt a lot about air racing which came in useful later.

The SE 5a was a wonderful aeroplane to fly. It had beautifully harmonized controls for a 1917 design and its performance was comparable to some of the fighters we had in 1927, although it did not carry the equipment of those fighters. It had a top speed, with full load, of 121 m.p.h. and could climb to a 22,000 feet ceiling starting from ground to 6000 feet at over 1000 feet per minute.

I looked forward to tuning it up for future races when I was on the Engineering Course with all the facilities available there to do the job.

In mid-August 1927 I reported to Henlow.

I7 Officers' Engineering Course at Henlow

The Officers' Engineering Course at Henlow lasted two years and, by any standards, it was a magnificent course of instruction in Aviation Engineering. It gave us all exactly the specialized knowledge in aeronautics which we needed.

The facilities, engineering-wise, were very good and, beside those provided by the course, we were surrounded by the Henlow Depot, which was equipped for, and did, complete overhauls on aero engines and airframes to a standard which compared with the aircraft and aero-engine industry at that date. There was then no question of just stripping down an engine and replacing worn parts with spares from the manufacturers and sending the worn parts back to them. The worn parts were machined or ground back to become serviceable items at Henlow, if that could be done within the limits.

Thus, apart from being taught the basic principles and made to practice them ourselves, we also saw the practical side of aeronautical engineering going on all round us.

That was the technical side of the Course. On the social side our living conditions were primitive by modern standards. It is true that we had bathrooms in our living blocks and did not have to walk 50 yards or so in the open to get to one as we had to do at Duxford, but the living blocks were still only one brick thick and they still felt — in winter — as though the North East wind blew straight through them.

We had a fireplace in each room and a coal allowance which, with care, gave us fires for four days in the week if the coal would burn, but it was of such poor quality that we used to buy a certain amount of the most expensive coal available, then at 2/6 per cwt, to augment — and burn — our normal coal ration. The Officers' Mess was an old wooden hut which had been condemned several years before, but a kindly administrative department decided that we would be better living and feeding in a condemned wooden hut than in no accommodation at all.

It may have been these living conditions which accounted for the fact that a very large number of young officers on the course decided to get married and live out — usually in much worse conditions. But it may, of course, have been due to the fact that some of these

157

officers had by then reached the magic age of thirty which, in those days, allowed one a marriage allowance which added significantly to one's income and, in few cases, covered the additional expense of keeping a wife and — very soon — a child.

The officers who 'joined in Holy Matrimony' under these conditions tried to convince us that they had done this because, in their new state of Service responsibility, they had become imbued with the necessity of leading a stable life in future which would enable them to do their work more thoroughly and with a true appreciation of their obligations to the Service. None of these lofty statements impressed the unmarried officers very deeply and we became even less impressed as the newly married officers asked us, with ever increasing frequency, to do their routine (after hours) jobs for them. We did of course sympathize with them, particularly with those who found themselves with not only a wife, but also a family rather more quickly than might have been expected. However, staying up late on their behalf to 'turn out the guard' after midnight and then getting up early to 'turn it out' again so that they had an extra hour — they said — to feed the baby, tended to take the glamour off their lofty sentiments about dedication to Service duties.

After a few months the Station Commander made an order which was received with understandably mixed feelings. He said that married officers must live in camp on the occasions when their normal duties required it. The unmarried officers wondered, not very sympathetically, how the baby, then, got fed in the morning.

In spite of all these relatively domestic worries most of us enjoyed the Course. Only a few of the married officers found it difficult to reconcile their allegiance to wife and family with their allegiance to the Service, indeed some of them were outstandingly good pilots and good engineers and never attempted, on principle, to get out of doing a routine duty.

For those who were interested in all aspects of flying we had an opportunity for developing our interests which was, and is still more today, unique in the aeronautical world. We were provided with what might be said to be 'a paid-up subscription to a private flying Club' and in this club, membership included full facilities for overhauling and tuning up our own aeroplanes and cars with all the equipment and advice we could possibly want.

The 'Practice Flight' at Henlow had a good diversity of aeroplanes available for our use, including Avro 504K's, Bristol Fighters and even Sopwith Snipes. I flew them all with great satisfaction. If one should happen to damage one it was only necessary to arrange for another to be delivered from stores. It was a wonderful club and one was actually paid to belong to it.

158

There was, however, one important proviso to full enjoyment of the club: one had to be interested in all the technicalities of flying. It was to develop this interest that we were allowed, indeed encouraged, to overhaul our own cars and aeroplanes. One is obviously more interested in shaping a piece of metal as a spare part for one's own vehicle than one is in shaping an uninspiring test piece which, when finished, will be thrown on the scrap heap.

However, we still had to go through the usual and essential basic training of filing up a flat, rectangular piece of metal to the required dimensions: we had to turn up a test piece of mild steel rod to give it two different kinds of screw threads on each end of it; we had to hammer out a piece of copper tube until it resembled some quite different shape; and in the carpenter's shop we had to make up a four-legged trestle with the legs set at the approved angle.

This latter test of the trestle proved to be an embarrassment to quite a few on the course. One student — not a great carpenter — produced a trestle in which he had somewhat misjudged the angle of the legs with the unfortunate result that the trestle, for all the world, looked more like a caricature of a headless and tailless dog standing by a lamp-post than a trestle ready for use in a workshop. Just in case the resemblance might have been missed — and when a deputation of eminent aeronautical engineers was visiting us — another student tacked on a silhouette of the head and tail of a dog to the original 'miscalculation', added a miniature lamp-post to the scene and placed it in a very prominent place. We heard afterwards that the exalted deputation or erudite engineers decided that a pass in the Officers' Engineering Course at Henlow could not be accorded parity with similar achievements in technical Colleges which had been established over a longer period and combined comparable erudition with a less light-hearted approach to their studies. Perhaps the canine caricature had something to do with the decision; but we had other weaknesses in the Course.

One of these included the over-frequent absence of a senior officer on the staff on the Course. He lived on the outskirts of London and thus had a long drive to Henlow. He usually arrived — if he arrived at all — at about 10 a m and he would then be dressed in civilian clothes. The backbone of his orderly room staff consisted of two airmen who were clever to an unusual extent. We used to call them 'Brown and Kennedy' after two famous criminals who had recently been hanged. It was their job to clean the senior officer's uniform, polish his shoes and buttons and prepare a steaming cup of black coffee for him on arrival. There was a theory — never quite authenticated — that they also had to serve him up with two aspirins on a small piece of toast. If the story was not true it was a pity since

159

he might well have been better if he had taken them. On the rare occasions when he went round the activities on the Course he was hampered by two unfortunate omissions in his original creation. He was quite unable to understand the true significance of engineering practice and he was also unable to remember names — or at least to put names to the correct faces. He believed that neither of these failings would be noticed by the pupils, but in this expectation — like many schoolmasters before him — he underestimated the perceptive powers of some sixty pupils of at least average intelligence. We all knew his failings and if any one of us had failed to notice them there were 59 other students who were anxious and willing to provide the necessary information.

Concerning his failure to remember names, partly due to his rare appearances amongst us and partly due to a genetic weakness, we were treated early on in our Course to a scene which by any standards was a memorable one.

The Chief of the Air Staff, Sir Hugh Trenchard, was doing an inspection of our Course soon after we arrived. It was known that the C A S set much store by senior officers 'knowing their men'. This senior officer was well aware of this characteristic of the C A S. He was also well aware of his own failing in this respect and decided he must cover it up by at least displaying recognition in the very few cases where he was sure. Just such a one was a pupil on the senior course called Van Foxin, a name which was difficult to forget. The S O decided that Van Foxin and a few others must be singled out for special attention.

The great day arrived. We had all cleaned and scrubbed the workshops and lecture rooms until they were spotless. The workshops particularly were so clean that they looked — alas — as though no work had been done in them for weeks. With an hour to spare it was decided that the workshops at least must be 'dressed' to look as though we worked there. We ransacked the dustbins and produced little heaps of metal filings for the bench vices, metal turnings for the lathes and wood shavings and sawdust for the appropriate places in the carpenter's shop. As always happens on such occasions, some pupil with a perverted sense of humour placed a large heap of sawdust under the metal-turning lathe of a somewhat dumb friend, but this appeared to pass unnoticed.

As the great man — and he was a Great Man — came round, he clearly paid less attention to our detailed activities than he did to the general atmosphere of the place. He was continually asking questions of our senior officer, who became more and more flustered as he became aware that he was not making a good impression. In the workshops he brightened and steadied as he noticed Van Foxin

160

working at a lathe: quickly he shepherded the C A S over there and with an appearance of casualness (which deceived no-one) said:

'This is Flight Lieutenant Van Foxin, Sir.'

Then, superfluously and quite out of normal tradition in such cases, he indulged in a criticism of one of his own officers on an official inspection. He went on:

'Van Foxin, your practical work has not been up to standard recently. You must do better Van Foxin. I am not at all satisfied with your practical work Van Foxin.'

There was a terrible hush. Van Foxin stopped his lathe so that his words would not be missed. Then he came smartly to attention:

'I'm sorry, Sir. There must be some mistake. I am Flight Lieutenant Rogers, Sir. Van Foxin is out sick today, Sir.'

Van Foxin had put such an unusual expression of worried humility on his face that the senior officer was deceived.

It only needed that to put him into complete panic. He had been certain it was Van Foxin but he knew his weakness and he was not prepared to argue the point. In any case it was not the time or place.

As Van Foxin said afterwards:

'If the — had been decently polite I would have helped him out, but he got just what's been coming to him for years.'

The senior officer did not get on very well in the Service after that. Van Foxin, some years later, came into ownership of his family's brewery. He had never had to worry about his future in the Service, but he had a love for it which persuaded him to take a hand in weeding out useless characters.

Van Foxin was, in fact, a great deflater of pompous senior officers. Very soon after this episode, when he had finished the Engineering Course and was posted to the Engineering Depot, another senior officer was posted in to take over the technical department in which Van Foxin was then serving as an engineering officer. The new officer commanding the section decided, on arrival, that the unit was disorganized, that the officers and N C Os in it were lazy and useless and that he was going to turn the whole section up-side-down to put it right. This after a brief experience of the unit in which he could hardly have seen how thing were going. He suffered from the same fault that many others did and still do.

In this case, on the second day, he called all the officers of the section into his office. He said he considered the section to be the worst run section he had ever known; he said he thought all the officers in it were the laziest and stupidest he had ever had under him. He then outlined the extremely unpleasant regime he intended to impose, starting with P T in the morning at 7 a m and ending with a thorough inspection of every detail of his unit on cease work in the

161

evening, which would probably extend well beyond the normal cease-work time. He added that weekend leave was to be looked upon as a thing of the past and that all married officers would probably find it best to live in in future. He ended this tirade with the remark:

'. . . and if any of you here don't like what I have said you can put on your hat and get right out of my office now.'

He glared round at them. But his glare changed to a glassy look of indecision at Flt Lt Van Foxin stood up, put on his hat, saluted smartly and proceeded to walk out.

There was consternation:

'What on earth are you doing?'

'Obeying orders, Sir.'

And Van Foxin closed the door behind him.

The bubble was pricked.

On the whole the instructors on the Engineering Course were excellent and amongst all of them I would place Mr (later Wing Commander) Whitlock in the RAF Education Branch amongst the best — if not the best — lecturer in Mathematics and Mechanics I have ever known. He had a lucid and amusing way of leading on from one stage to the next in the subjects he taught, which is all too rare in lecturers and can only derive from an absolutely clear understanding of his subject and perhaps an even clearer appreciation of the limitations of his audience. An illustration of this amazing ability can be taken from an incident which occurred later in our Course. Whitlock had, through the first year, led us all through the basic early stages of mathematics and mechanics. We could quote and even understood Newton's Laws. We were thoroughly versed in geometry, algebra, graphs, logarithms and had got to a state with a slide rule when we naturally reverted to its use on almost every calculation. In the second year of the Course we moved on to an elaboration of all this work and almost before we knew we were doing it, Whitlock led us straight into the Calculus. In a bare 30 minutes he introduced us to the theory of it and explained how it could be used to solve problems insoluble by normal mathematics. After 30 minutes every one of us understood it and we almost gasped at the comparative simplicity of it when properly explained. One of our number, Flight Lieutenant Chas Allen neatly expressed the thought in all our minds:

'Well, if it's as easy as that, why do they call it *Calculus?*'

Whitlock was never at a loss for a quick and telling answer:

'I think Chas it is because by the time Calculus was invented, all the other rather dubious words which adorn our conversation had already been given other meanings!'

162

Some of our other instructors on the theoretical side were not so able, nor so inspiring. A temporary instructor on structures of aeroplanes and also on aerodynamics had a tendency to base all his talks on various books with a slavish adherence to the wording in those books which suggested he had never really understood his subject any better than a carefully briefed parrot. He always tried to avoid questions, but we had heard from the senior course – on which were some very able engineers – that even if he made an accurate statement it was usually possible to get him to retract it if sufficient pressure was put on him – he was that ignorant. We therefore amused ourselves by occasionally 'ganging up' on him. One particular instance was when he was 'instructing' us on the (then) standard method of checking the stresses of a wing structure. He explained that this could best be done by hanging the aeroplane up-side-down and loading the wings with sandbags, thus simulating the lift loads of the wings when it was flying the right way up. Sitting beside me was my friend Mac Reynolds, who like all of us was following this particular description with interest, but a doubt entered his mind and he interrupted the lecturer:

'What part of the aeroplane do they hang it up by?'

The lecturer tried to brush it off:

'Really I can't break off in the middle of this explanation to explain trivialities.'

'But what do they hang it up by?'

Came from Reynolds. By this time one or two of the course, who, wanting to stand in well with the lecturer, expressed impatience:

'Oh, shut up. Let's get on.'

But, watching the lecturer very closely I became aware that his apparent impatience was probably due to the fact that he did not know the answer, so I backed up Reynolds. I put in one of those carefully reasoned remarks designed to induce discomfiture:

'I'm sorry, Sir. I don't want to confuse the issue, but it does seem to me to be an important point from the structural point of view to know which part of the aeroplane is subjected to the opposing downward force which balances the force imposed on the wings.'

The lecturer made a last bid to hide his ignorance:

'I am *not* going to be interrupted by these trivial questions.'

But by then nearly everyone in the class had realized that the lecturer was trying to avoid the question and probably did not know the answer. They knew I had an engineering degree at Cambridge and suspected, rightly, that I already knew the answer. They all came in like a pack of hounds. Out of the holocaust came one helpful suggestion from a (perhaps) kindly soul in the class:

'Could you *possibly* find out and tell us next time, please Sir?'

With all the facilities we had around us and provided free it seemed to be a pity not to take advantage of them for one's own convenience. I already had an SE 5a aeroplane, which I set about tuning up for other races, but I wanted a better car than the (then) very common Bull-nosed Morris which I owned — and ought to have kept! I went to London to see a Sunbeam which was advertised, second-hand, at £90 and I came away with a 1911 Rolls-Royce Silver Ghost, for which I paid £65. It would be an understatement to say that, by Rolls-Royce standards, it was not in good condition, but I drove it down to Dunmow in Essex to show it to my friends. On the whole it went very well, except for the fact that a tyre burst just short of Dunmow. The cover came off the rim, bowled away over a low hedge and disappeared into a field of standing corn. I never found it, partly because I had only the haziest idea where it had gone, and partly because an irate farmer turned up and wanted to know what on earth I was doing in his cornfield. His assessment of the damage I was doing compared to my assessment of the probable value of the tyre which had burst persuaded me to leave the cover wherever it was and move on. Presumably it ended up by being reaped and perhaps broke the reaper — there were no sophisticated harvesters in those days or it might have ended up by being distributed in several loaves of bread.

I fitted the spare — which looked as though it would not do a hundred yards — and got to Newton Hall, Dunmow. I got a rapturous welcome which restored my morale.

With another not-so-worn second-hand tyre fitted I got back to Henlow. I then wrote to Rolls-Royce hoping to get a lot of spare parts free under the guarantee: after all the Silver Ghost was only sixteen years old! They did not supply any free parts, but they sent down an engineer who checked over the whole car and I later got a report and a list of spare parts which they considered essential. A quick look at the list suggested to me that it included every single part of the car, except the mascot. In any case I used the list as a spare parts catalogue for the next two years, and still only used about 1 per cent of the list.

I then got down to a major overhaul with the blessing of the whole staff of the Engineering Course. I enlisted the aid of an enthusiastic airman and, together, we took the car to pieces. We laid all the parts out on the floor of a shed I had been allotted for the overhaul, and placed labels against the parts so we would know what they were when we came to reassemble the car.

Things were going very well when I broke my ankle parachuting and went to hospital for six weeks. During that time the shed was urgently needed for another purpose, all the parts of the Silver Ghost were thrown into a few large boxes and the labels were lost. It was quite a job sorting it all out after that! But we ultimately managed it and it ran very well for two years, after which I sold it to a friend for £40 and went to Baghdad.

18 Early parachuting

It may seem strange that I should have been parachuting at that time on the Engineering Course but, amongst other activities, Henlow included the Parachute Training Unit of the Royal Air Force. The history of the use of parachutes in the Air Force, as we were told it then, started towards the end of the war in 1918 when the suggestion that their use should be considered was turned down by certain opinion on the General Staff which stated that, if parachutes were available, pilots might abandon their aeroplanes before it was really essential. This view did not coincide with the views of the front line pilots at that time, or since, but it remained the accepted official view for several years after, until growing pressure in Parliament made the Air Force authorities reconsider the situation. In the United States the use of parachutes in military aeroplanes was standard and the Air Ministry officials were lengthily deliberating the pros and cons of adopting an American type parachute, since no suitable British one had been developed. At this stage the full force of political pressure was brought to bear in Parliament with a considerable background of extremely well informed opinion to back it.

As this pressure broke the Secretary of State for Air was (just) able to say that two officers were already on their way to America to get full experience in the use of the Irvin parachute. The two officers had been put on the liner at 48 hours notice while the answer to a parliamentary question was being prepared.

By 1927 they had returned and already formed the Parachute Training Unit at Henlow and they did very good work indeed in demonstrating the (comparative) safety of using a parachute.

In justice to the Air Staff it must be remembered that all the new generation of 1926 (onwards) military aeroplanes were specified in their design requirements to have parachute type seats. Regular courses were held to teach airmen to pack parachutes and also a number of practice parachute descents were done to give people confidence. Parachute drops were not compulsory for anyone, although there was a feeling in some operational squadrons at that time, where parachutes were in regular use, that they should be made so for certain individuals, never identified, who had stolen the silk

166

canopies from several parachute packs and replaced them with army blankets. The view was that such individuals, if ever caught, should be made to do a drop and given a choice of two parachutes to use on the drop. They would be told that one of the parachute packs had a normal silk canopy, the other had an army blanket. It was further felt that, just in case the individual should choose the 'wrong' parachute, both packs should, in fact, have army blankets!

The method of training for drops in those days was fairly primitive. A Vickers Vimy twin engined (converted) bomber aeroplane was used (see illustration on page 76) on which two platforms had been built on the lower wings at the outer bracing strut. The parachutist stood on this platform facing the tail of the Vimy and clinging to the inter-plane strut. After the Vimy had taken off, gained height and was turning for the dropping run over the aerodrome, an instructor in the nose of the Vimy waved his hands in a circular motion over his head. The parachutists were watching for this out of the corners of their eyes — which tended to be popping out anyway. They then cautiously rotated themselves round the strut — still standing on the small platform — until they faced the nose of the Vimy and could easily see the instructor, who in turn was watching the aerodrome approach as the pilot flew towards it at about 500 feet. When the instructor judged the Vimy to be in the correct position he waved his arms outwards and the parachutists, who should then have been holding the strut with only one hand and gripping the 'rip-cord' handle with the other, would pull the rip-cord and WAIT. If all went according to plan the parachute would fall out of its pack and be pulled out backwards by the slip-stream: the actual time interval between pulling the rip-cord and being pulled off the wing platform varied from about 3 seconds to about 5 seconds. The average interval of 4 seconds was quite long enough for some rather nervous trainees to conclude that the parachute had not opened and they therefore took a firm hold of the strut with both hands just before they were forcibly, but unwillingly, dragged away from it by the parachute. In one recorded case a somewhat muscular trainee clung on so strongly that the strut was pulled out of its socket and the trainee landed on the aerodrome still clutching it. The Vimy managed to fly on and land. In several other cases the trainees would cling to the strut for long enough for the Vimy to be pulled round into an unwilling turn before the parachute trainee's strength gave way and he was pulled off like a reluctant parasite.

After a couple of 'pull offs' trainees were allowed to do a free fall drop from another aeroplane. These were done from about 3,000 feet. In all cases parachute trainees had a reserve chest parachute which could be pulled in emergency.

In later years it was found that free fall drops were in fact more reliable and safer than 'pull offs' since there was a real danger on the latter that the parachute pack, when released, would fall on to the wing and get into an eddy current induced by the wing platform: this tended to roll up the parachute canopy in the long rigging lines. The parachute might then develop sufficiently to pull the parachutist off the wing, but not sufficiently to land him safely thereafter.

We were told to make sure we pulled the rip-cord wire right out, but there was a lightheartedly applied fine of half-a-crown if we then let go of it and lost it.

I had done one pull-off successfully and then arranged to do another, paired off with Mac Reynolds on the other wing. Reynolds had said that he knew a way of speeding up the descent and could get back to the ground faster than anyone else. I disputed that so a bet was made. In those days we thought we could speed up the descent by manipulating the rigging lines so as to close up the diameter of the canopy. If this had been possible by twisting up the rigging lines — and it would have been very difficult — it would have been an almost suicidal procedure, but in the blissful ignorance of a still only partially developed art, both Reynolds and I thought we could speed up our descent by this means.

Looked at from an operational point of view the aim was not as stupid as it sounds since there was always a possibility — in war — of being shot at after one had baled out. In that case the sooner one dropped out of the battle area the better. The ethics of shooting at a baled out enemy were hotly debated. One school of thought argued that there was no sense in trying to shoot an enemy flying an aeroplane if one then did not continue to shoot at him when he had baled out of it: he would merely go back to his aerodrome, get another aeroplane, come back up again and shoot you. The other school of thought argued that it was against the rules of war to shoot at men in their lifeboats after their ship had gone down, and this rule also applied to parachutes.

Somewhere between these ideologies — if one may call them that — there was the middle view that if a pilot was parachuting back into his own territory it was only sense to shoot him, just as the infantry would shoot at a disabled tank crew running back to their own lines: but if a pilot was descending into enemy lines there was no point in shooting at him because he would become a prisoner anyway. A thoroughly practical out-look which was proved over and over again in the air battles of World War II was that if one was in the middle of a dogfight it was not safe to lose height and concentrate on a parachutist when a large number of enemy aircraft were looking for an opportunity to get on one's tail.

168

So there was some sense in the competition in speeding our descent in which Reynolds and I indulged. The outcome was a Pyrrhic victory for me. I came down fastest, fiddling with my rigging lines, but I was a stone heavier than Reynolds anyway and that probably had most effect. As I neared the ground I looked up at Reynolds and called out:

'I've won.'

But I had misjudged the rate of descent, which is much higher than one imagines, and I hit the ground completely unprepared for the landing. One ankle turned over and I broke a piece off the bone of the ankle joint.

The Medical Officer came up, looked at me and said there was nothing wrong and I should get up and go back to work, but later in the afternoon, when my ankle was about twice its normal size, he apologised profusely and sent me off to Uxbridge hospital in an ambulance.

When I came out of hospital some weeks later, parachuting by officers on the Engineering Course was discouraged, but a few free falls were allowed. On one of these another officer on the course got badly mauled. His release had been slightly misjudged, with the result that he found, somewhat to his concern, that he was descending into a field of turnips next to the aerodrome: even more to his concern he realised he was going to land on, or very near to, a yokel hoeing. Still a hundred feet up he shouted 'Hey' to warn the yokel of his impending arrival. The yokel was used to the farmer shouting 'Hey' at him when he was not working hard enough, so after a brief look round, but not UP, he merely redoubled his hoeing efforts. The parachutist shouted 'Hey' again at twenty feet with the same negligible effect and a second or two later both he and the yokel were enveloped in the silk canopy. The yokel, wielding his hoe, started to fight his way out of the canopy. By the time they both emerged the parachutist had a lot of hoe marks all over him.

The Parachute Unit was a continual source of interest and enjoyment to us. Some months after this hoeing incident it was decideded to replace the Vickers Vimy aeroplanes in the unit with a later development of the bomber called the Vickers Virginia. The Vimys were to be flown to Northern Ireland for some purpose. Group H Q called for volunteers from the Engineering Course to do the ferrying. Pilots volunteering had be to be experienced twin-engine pilots. Six of us volunteered and we were all accepted. So far as I know not one of us had ever flown a twin-engined aeroplane before. When the day for the first check flight, before ferrying, arrived we all turned up on the aerodrome to take our turn.

As all twin-engine-trained pilots knew, but few of us did, one only

169

Above: a parachutist on the special platform facing the Vickers Vimy's tail, clutching the inter-plane strut. *Below:* the parachutist has manoeuvred himself to face the Vimy's nose and has pulled the rip-cord

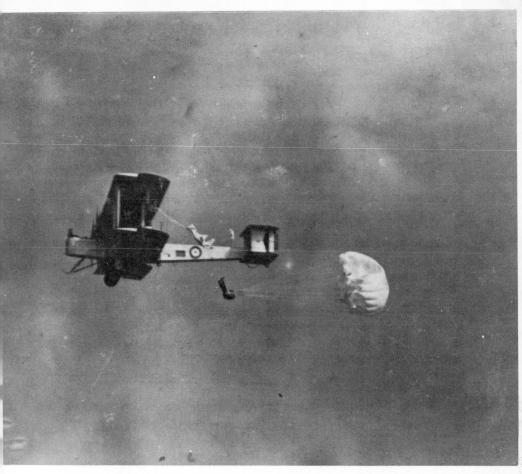

The pull-off is complete and the parachutist falls free of the aircraft

'ran up' one engine at a time on the ground, otherwise there was a tendency for the tail to lift with the force of both engines at full throttle. Unfortunately the first of the six pilots did not know this and he ran up both engines at the same time. The tail of the Vimy came up to an alarming height: two airmen who were trying to hold it down found themselves about 8 feet off the ground and thought the Vimy had actually taken off. The Flight Sergeant watching the engine test shouted vainly against the noise of the engines and the Flight Commander of the parachute flight climbed up into the cockpit and shut down both engines.

After a brief but unsatisfactory interrogation he asked to see that particular pilot's log book to find out whether he had ever flown 'twins' before. He then turned round to us and said:

'And I shall want to see your's too.'

Our little group vanished miraculously.

The Vimys were finally flown to Ireland by proper Vimy pilots. It was a great disappointment to many of us since we had wanted to get a twin-engined aeroplane on our log-books.

The parachute instructors at that time were a gallant lot and they were helped and encouraged in their work by Leslie Irvin himself, who started a factory in Letchworth nearby and took up residence in this country. He used to come to our guest nights and often demonstrated his ability to retain his thinking powers in any attitude in which he might find himself by standing on his head against the piano and playing popular tunes.

Like all groups of gallant pioneers the Parachute School included one or two irresponsible types. One of these got into trouble by drinking too much during a flying visit to various friends at Martlesham Heath Experimental Establishment and also at Hendon. In a state of happy exuberance he flew back from Hendon up the Great North Road at a perilously low altitude, much to the concern of a number of motorists who happened to be on the road. Traffic was not very dense in those days.

His subsequent Court Martial proved to be a classic of a defence Counsel talking too much. It was a difficult case to defend since the prosecution had collected a formidable array of witnesses to testify to the amount of drink the pilot had had, and also to the height at which he had flown up the Great North Road. But whatever the chances of a successful defence might have been, they were thrown away by a superfluity of legal loquacity.

As nearly always happens in such cases, any resentment witnesses might have felt at the time of the offence was lost by the time the case came on, and was indeed partly replaced by a feeling of sympathy for the accused, who always tends to look a bit forlorn in the dock.

Thus the Air Force barmen from Martlesham Heath and Hendon, who had no feeling of resentment at all even at the time of the offence, were entirely sympathetic to the accused. With much trouble and persuasion the prosecution managed to elicit from the witnesses that they had served the accused with two brown ales at Martlesham and two brown ales at Hendon. That was as far as they could be persuaded to go in their evidence until the defence counsel rose to cross-examine them. All he had to do then, if he felt he must do something, was to get each witness to say that he was absolutely sure he was right in what he said: not a very difficult task with witnesses. Indeed, no cross-examination was necessary at all. In the summing up later it would have been an easy matter to persuade the Court that a total of four brown ales taken over a period of about fours hours would not be likely to affect the judgement of the accused, who was quite used to drinking a little beer occasionally.

172

That would have been an understatement!

However, defence Counsel felt he must exhibit his powers of cross-examination and he proceeded to put the two unfortunate barmen, each in their turn, through a searing interrogation in which he insinuated that they were making up a story to damage the officer's career and proceeded to frighten them with threats of perjury. The barmen became harassed and bit by bit admitted under cross-examination by the *defence* counsel that not only had they not overstated the amount of drink taken, but had understated it: the bar books had then to be produced and it became clear that the accused had also consumed four large whiskies at Martlesham Heath and two large brandies at Hendon.

Worse was to follow. The witnesses as to events on the Great North Road had been hard to trace, but a couple of lorry drivers and the driver of an Austin 7 were produced. Of these the lorry drivers were entirely sympathetic and the only danger in their evidence lay in their enthusiasm for the precision with which the accused had handled his aeroplane. This at least could have been used to increase the credibility of evidence of the 'four brown ales' if the defence had not already prejudiced it. Neither the prosecution nor the defence got any more out of the lorry dirvers, who were good, tough, down-to-earth men. They were clearly not going to be bullied and pushed around by lawyers.

A skilful defence counsel, sensing their sympathy might have got them to suggest that the accused was flying really quite high, but — perhaps fortunately — no attempt was made to do this.

The third witness was the Austin 7 owner who had, not unnaturally, been very indignant and frightened at the time, but again his indignation had subsided and the prosecution could get little out of him except to say that he thought the pilot was flying too low. Again the defence counsel waded in where wiser men would have left things alone. The Austin 7 owner was a meek-looking man and perhaps the defence thought he could be browbeaten. He questioned him closely on the height at which the accused had been flying and finally flung at him:

'You stand there, a driver of a small seven horse power car, never flown an aeroplane in your life, ignorant of every basic fact of flying, and you presume . . . you dare to suggest you can judge the height that an aeroplane is flying at. How could you possibly judge the height? I put it to you — you couldn't.'

That did it. The Austin 7 owner felt forced to justify his statement, so the truth — and alas the whole truth — came out:

'Well Sir, I thought he was flying very low when I saw him in the distance, but I got really frightened when I saw that the wheels of his

173

aeroplane were running along the Great North Road coming towards me, and only a hundred yards away. He did lift a bit then, but I don't know how much he cleared the top of my car by: it can't have been much because when I looked back he was down on the road again.'

Probably the accused would have been found guilty anyhow and got a severe reprimand; he might have been dismissed the Service; as it was he was dismissed the Service and sentenced to a term of imprisonment. In a way the latter part of the sentence was not too much of a misfortune, since the case had attracted a lot of attention: the public and newspapers were very anti-dangerous flying in those days and no punishment at all beyond dismissal would have left the way open for a further civil court case, which might well have resulted in a longer term of imprisonment.

Apart from this lapse, the members of the Parachute Training Unit at Henlow were gallant and dedicated people. They laid the foundation of parachute uses in this country and, when they started, parachuting was very much a partially developed art.

An Avro 504K with a Lynx engine. The hood over the rear cockpit is for blind-flying practice

19 Engineering and flying at Henlow, 1927/8

With the various types of aeroplanes which we had in the Practice Flight at Henlow we were able to indulge in all kinds of flying. There was the Bristol Fighter with its (for those days) warm cockpit in which we could do cross-country flights to visit friends on cold days. There was the Sopwith Snipe for aerobatics, and this gave the few of us who could fly the Snipe an added prestige. There was the Avro 504K for circuits and landings and also for local flying, but this was being phased out at that time and being replaced by the later version of the Avro with an Armstrong Siddeley Lynx engine, designated the Avro 504N. This was an almost identical aeroplane to the Avro 504K except for the radial engine instead of the rotary, and a much more soft and sophisticated undercarriage. It was indeed possible to trim the Avro 504N in a glide, with the engine just above idling power, and it would land itself without the pilot doing anything. The landing was, of course, a bit untidy but safe enough: one could taxi in after it anyhow.

Like its predecessor, the Lynx Avro, as it came to be called, was quite impressive in aerobatics, being able to do almost everything that other aeroplanes could do, and indeed one manoeuvre which most other aeroplanes could not do: this manoeuvre we called the Bunt. It involved pushing the aeroplane over into a dive and then further over until it was flying level but inverted. It was in fact half of an 'outside' loop but commenced downwards. There were two schools of thought at Henlow as to the best method of doing this (for those days) new manoeuvre. One school of thought liked to get the Avro to a near stall and then push the control column right forward quickly. The Avro then went into a dive which quickly became inverted, but it seemed to take a very long time thereafter to push the Avro further round until the nose came up to the horizon and one was subjected to a very considerable inverted force, hoping that the shoulder straps would hold it.

The other school of thought held that it was best to fly level at a speed well above the stall and then push the Avro over steadily. Personally I tried both methods and could never quite decide which method gave one least anxiety and discomfort. In both cases there seemed to be an unconscionably long time diving up-side-down almost

176

straight at the ground before the welcome sight of the horizon appeared in front. Many pilots trying this manoeuvre for the first time decided the horizon never would appear and tried to roll out of their dive, which resulted in an almost more frightening vertical (near inverted) dive. Fortunately the Lynx Avro was a high drag aeroplane and one seldom seemed to go much above 180 m.p.h. even in such a dive.

We had tried this manoeuvre in No.111 Squadron on Siskins, but never achieved much success with it, owing to the terrific build-up of speed in the inverted dive, although we heard reports of other Siskin squadrons doing it.

Early on in the Course a letter came from Group H Q to say that the Avro 504K was now considered obsolete and could be 'written off' at a greater rate. The letter meant, of course, that extensive repairs need no longer be done to them, but on the day the letter arrived, almost as though he took the instructions literally, one of our Course taking off in one of the only two remaining Avro 504Ks we had, suddenly saw the other one straight in front of him. Since he could not stop he tried to lift his Avro off the ground to clear it. His Avro staggered up to about 10 feet then stalled and sank gracefully but exactly on top of the other Avro. The letter from Group H Q had been complied with.

Thereafter we had mostly Lynx Avros in the Practice Flight. They were excellent for recreational flying of all kinds — even visiting friends in the neighbourhood, since they could be landed in any reasonable field and left idling for a long time. They were also excellent for the traditional sport of baiting the local brick works, situated about 2 miles from the aerodrome where they had two tall chimneys just far enough apart to allow an Avro to fly safely between them: it also had a Works Manager who objected strongly to this being done, and whose office was situated between the chimneys. He could be relied upon to ring the aerodrome in a fury every time we flew between his chimneys. When the wind was in the right direction it was possible, exerting considerable skill and judgement, to fly between the chimneys just over the roof of the Manager's office, cut the engine, land on the aerodrome so that the landing run ended by all the other parked aeroplanes outside the Flight Office, jump out quickly, throwing away one's helmet and goggles and saunter into the Flight Commander's office just in time to hear him answering the telephone call. As in the case of flying the beaches from Manston one had the perfect alibi.

Apart from the Service aeroplanes I had my SE 5a to fly, although whilst I was in hospital an officer on the senior course asked if he could borrow it to visit some Air Races up north. In a moment of

177

weakness I agreed, since I knew he was a good pilot, but I did not know he intended to enter it for two races; nor would I have lent it to him if I had known. I had got it tuned up for racing by then and I did not want the handicappers to know how much faster it was going than when it had raced before.

The pilot won both races, including two cups and £80 in cash, and then turned the SE 5a up-side-down on Wittering aerodrome on the way back. Thereafter he lost interest in it and he did absolutely nothing to get it back to Henlow. In the end I got a new propeller fitted and did the (fortunately) minor repairs which seemed necessary to fly it back. On the return flight to Henlow it was very right-wing-low, so I later flew it on down to my friend Dudley Watt at Brooklands, since he had all the facilities and spares for repairing an SE 5a. I landed there with some difficulty since I could hardly hold the right wing up at slow speed, and indeed I found I could only land it off a left hand turn. This was not surprising since the rear spar of the right wing outboard of the strut was broken clean through and only the fabric was holding it in position.

I told Dudley Watt the story and he did all the repairs necessary, adding a few refinements in stream-lining until the bill came to exactly £80, which he sent to the 'borrower.' I got a better SE 5a back, but the handicappers then knew that it was much faster. My relations with the 'borrower' were never quite so cordial after that.

During the repairing of the SE 5a the Lynx Avro again emphasized its usefulness as a hack, since it had a capacious rear seat for carrying spares and any goods too long to go in the cockpit could be tied on to the wing roots or undercarriage. The flying speed of the Avro was so low that bits tied on outside made little difference to the handling. The Lynx engine was very reliable and was reputed at that time to have the best reliability record of any engine in the Service. One of its only and rare faults came my way on a return trip from Sutton Bridge aerodrome (on the Wash) to Henlow. Just as I was passing over Waterbeach, flying at 800 feet below low cloud, there was a small bang in the engine and then a worrying silence. I cannot claim any great credit in selecting a suitable field in which to land, since there were very few fields within reach and little time to think about them. But the Lynx Avro was easy to land and, with little difficulty, I landed in a field near a small village. I got out and looked over the engine to see what the trouble was, and at the same time a small crowd of children gathered, apparently from nowhere.

'What's wrong, Mister?'

'Run out of petrol, Mister?'

People, certainly children, were becoming more air-minded in 1928.

'Lost your way, Mister?'

I ignored the insult.

'Will you take me up, Mister?'

I took that as a compliment.

'Why did the engine stop, Mister?'

At last I answered:

'I don't know.'

'I do, Mister — you dropped this!'

A breathless small boy turned up waving a pushrod, the ball end of which had broken off. He had seen it fly off and fall, and he had watched it until it landed on his village green. Now he handed it to me. I took it gratefully and examined it. There was no doubt about the failure. I turned to the small boy:

'That is very useful indeed. Now we will know why these engines give trouble . . .'

I almost looked over my shoulder in case someone from Armstrong Siddeley was listening:

'I will take this part back and we will be able to put it right.'

I then took the boy's name and address, gave him half a crown, which was worth something to a boy of eight in those days, and arranged for him to be written a letter of thanks which, to him, was probably worth far more than half a crown.

Later in the day a new push-rod came up and we fitted it and I flew back to Henlow. The broken push-rod really was useful since it confirmed the reason for failure.

At the end of the first year of the Course we had our various tests and examinations. For the examinations there had always been an argument about how much information one could take into the examination hall. There had for years been a sort of tacit agreement that one could take in as much information as one could inscribe on the back of a slide rule. If one wrote in an enormous amount, very small, one probably could not read it anyhow, so it was useless: but a few important formulae could easily be written in. Since we had also to take in our logarithm tables we argued that we should be allowed to write anything we liked on them. At this point official objections strengthened. But we argued that we would be carrying our slide rules *and* log tables with us for the rest of our working lives: no-one expected us to remember the log tables off by heart, so why not write other useful information on everything we would normally carry with us?

At this stage in the argument we went over to the offensive. Why should we not be allowed to take in any book we wanted? If the exam papers were properly set there should be no objection to this. Clearly one could not start reading through every reference book

179

published to get the answer: one must know where to look. Perhaps this was an early record of a Student Revolt!

One member of the staff, at this point, weakened his case by quoting an analogy. He said that he might as well suggest that divinity students should be allowed to take in the Bible and Prayer books to their exams. We said:

'Yes, Why not? What use would the Bible be to a divinity student in a 2 hour exam? If he didn't know who God was before he went in to the exam he would have an awful lot of reading to do before he found out.'

The argument was an interesting one and ultimately we won through. Largely, I think, due to the influence of Whitlock we were allowed to take any books we liked into our exams. It became a far, far better test when the exam papers were properly written, since we were tested under the same conditions we would be working in in the Service afterwards.

The practical tests were fairly light-hearted and our chief anxiety in this respect was over the requirement to hand in the tool kits with which we had been issued on arrival, and they had to be *complete*. After a year many of the more useful tools had found their way into our car tool kits and we were loth to return them. A certain amount of 'borrowing' had also been going on during the year and this tended to become intensified as the shortages were noted before the final tool kit check. We all kept our tool boxes firmly locked at this time. My own tool kit was good by local standards, but as the vital day approached I was still missing one pair of pliers and they had to be the typical Service type which would grip a piece of wire, or twist it or cut it off as required. No-one on the Course at that stage was likely to leave a pair of pliers lying around. On principle I was determined not to have to pay for them. The cost of pliers (Service type) plus 15 per cent departmental charges, less depreciation was at least six shillings. It was unthinkable. A brilliant thought came to me. There was plenty of lead lying around the workshops. I borrowed — with some difficulty — a pair of pliers and set them in a typical half-open position in a mould of sand and poured in some molten lead. After a little trimming the casting looked just like the pliers I had lost. They were useless, of course, but that would be the problem of the student who drew them on the next Course — not my problem. Since there were two courses it was 60 to 1 against me drawing them again and there was no check to show who had handed them in. I put the lead pliers at the bottom of the tool kit and the whole set went into the stores without comment.

A month later they didn't come out without comment. An infuriated student complained bitterly about being issued with a pair of pliers which were useless. The matter became a major cause of comment — and amusement. It was generally agreed that the student who had perpetrated the deception should either be turned off the course for dishonesty or promoted for ingenuity. I associated myself with the second school of thought.

However, inwardly, I felt a very slight glow of self-righteousness: all the time I was searching for the pliers I held a master key to all the other students' tool boxes. To have used it would, of course, have been cheating or, in strict Service legal language, 'an act unbecoming an officer and a gentleman.'

The circumstances of my acquiring this master key were peculiar. I was working on a part of my car late in the evening in the Engineering Course workshop. With me was a/c Chapman, a young airman whom I employed, and a very able and helpful mechanic he was. That particular evening I had forgotten the key to my own tool box and told a/c Chapman I would walk back and get it although this would have meant a delay of about half an hour. He said:

'Don't worry about that, Sir. I've got the key to my tool box here.'

'But that won't fit mine?'

'It soon will, Sir.'

Chapman studied his key for a few seconds then put it in a vice and filed a few small serrations out of it. He then put it in the padlock of my tool kit and opened it. I was fascinated and asked him how he had known what my key was like. He replied:

'Oh, I didn't, but I just made mine into a master key. You see it now fits all the other locks.'

He demonstrated by opening several other tool boxes. He then made a spare key he had into another master key and gave it to me 'in case I lost mine'. I asked him how he had learnt this art and he told me he had been apprenticed to Chubbs.

He was an excellent mechanic and craftsman, and I asked him why he had come into the Service. He said he wanted to get general experience and then he would go back to 'civvy street' very soon. He said he thought he would always be able to make a living somehow. I thought so too, but hoped his 'art' would not become a 'craft'.

Towards the end of 1927 the first Bristol Fighter fitted with Handley Page 'slots' arrived at Henlow. The slot became a standard safety fitting to a great number of aeroplanes during the next decade. Essentially it consisted of a small aerofoil section which, when an aeroplane wing started to stall, lifted out and upwards from the leading edge of the wing and directed the air forcefully down over the upper wing surface and thus prevented it burbling over the top of the wing in a series of eddies which tended, abruptly, to destroy the lift of the wing. These slots, carefully designed, delayed the stall of the wing to a point at which the elevators were no longer effective, thus preventing the pilot from getting his aeroplane into a dangerously stalled condition. It was still possible to stall the aeroplane by violent application of the elevators but this was not normally the cause of accidents.

The idea of the 'slot' had been developed — and patented — by Mr. (later Sir) Frederick Handley Page, with the very able assistance of his chief aerodynamicist, the late Dr. Gustav Victor Lachmann. Viewing his device historically one can trace an almost direct relationship between the aeroplane wing 'slot' and the jib sail of the sailing yacht, which had been in use for very many years before — perhaps hundreds of years — but no-one had patented it. In any case it was an entirely new application to aeroplanes and it saved many lives. Within twenty years this patent had rewarded the Handley Page company by over £1 million, which at that time was a lot of money. The Company deserved every penny of it — in lives saved.

At Henlow in late 1927 we all tried out this new device and opinions varied from:

'You can't go far wrong now.'

To:

'Takes all the excitement out of flying.'

However, we were soon presented with a new hazard in flying the Bristol Fighter at Henlow. Ever since the end of the the First World War on 11 November 1918, warlike relics had been preserved on Royal Air Force Stations. Perhaps the favourite relic was a bomb: the bigger the better. Most Stations had only been able to collect the 112lb bomb which had large tail fins and could be stood on end. Thus arranged it looked very impressive with a pair, one each side of (perhaps) the entrance to the Officers' Mess. Officers waiting to go on parade used to lean against these, or wipe their boots on the tail fins, or occasionally beat tattoos on the nose of the bomb with their Service canes. About nine years after the end of the war it was discovered that many of these bombs were not only still filled with high explosive, but that the explosive in them had 'deteriorated' to an extent when it was liable to detonate with very little encouragement. The most easily detectable sign of deterioration of the explosive contents was the exudation of blue crystals from the nose. 'Deteriorate' was obviously an armament officers' expression which was a very considerable understatement: in fact the expression was intended to indicate that the bomb was liable to explode with all its original violence, but with far less provocation than was normally given by a detonator.

Orders were issued from the Air Ministry that all such bombs

182

which had no clear history of having been defused and their H E contents evacuated were to be disposed of, and the easiest method of disposal was said to be dropping them in the sea.

Royal Air Force Henlow owned only one such bomb with an uncertain history. It had stood outside the Officers' Mess for over ten years and every year, on the occasion of the A O C's inspection, it had been treated to a lavish coat of whitewash in order to impress the inspecting A O C and staff with the fact that even the most unimportant items on the Station were treated with exemplary care and consideration. When the history of this particular 112 lb bomb was questioned it was clear that no history existed. An airman who had (most recently) administered a coat of whitewash announced — under careful questioning — that he thought he could remember seeing a 'sort of blue colour' around the nose cap, but he had cleaned it off carefully before white-washing. With only this recorded history the bomb became extremely suspect and it was decided that it must be dumped at sea.

A problem immediately arose since none of the Bristol Fighters at Henlow had bomb racks fitted, but the full expertise of the Maintenance Unit was mobilized and within a week one Bristol Fighter was fitted with a bomb rack complete with release gear. It was considered (tacitly) that it would be foolish to use the best Bristol Fighter for this mission: the reasons for this decision were carefully not stated. The oldest and most unreliable Bristol Fighter was selected for the job.

On a date in January 1928 all arrangements for the disposal of the bomb were ready and a volunteer from the Officers' Engineering Course was ready to do the drop. With great care and careful checking the bomb was loaded on the carrier. The pilot took his place in the cockpit. Ballast (no passenger) was placed in the rear seat, for reasons known to everyone but unstated, and the pilot signalled for the normal starting procedure. Nothing thereafter could induce the engine to start.

After half an hour's endeavours the Bristol Fighter was reluctantly wheeled back into the hangar and there were mutterings about the pilot not wanting to do the flight and sabotaging the efforts of the ground crew. These mutterings were silenced when a major fault in both magnetos was discovered. The coincidence of the fault occurring in BOTH magnetos was noted. A week later the Bristol Fighter was wheeled out again and another volunteer pilot actually got the engine started, took off and headed for the selected dropping zone, but had to turn back because of bad weather. He landed at Henlow very carefully indeed. Two days later another pilot from the Engineering Course took off on the same mission, in spite of the fact that the armament officer stated that he thought there were traces of blue crystals on the nose of the bomb. This pilot reached the dropping zone in the bay south of Clacton-on-Sea and pulled the release lever. Nothing happened and nothing the pilot could do would get rid of the bomb. He returned to Henlow and landed even more carefully than the previous pilot!

By this time, 'The Bomb', had become a major interest at Henlow. Airmen had a theory that some kind of jinx was connected with it: they said it was probably waiting for some particular pilot. More realistic, or at least official, views on the situation argued that if the weather was right, if the bomb release gear was properly checked, if the pilot could navigate properly, then there would be no trouble.

These official views were probably right but I was inclined to question them when the Flight Commander of the Practice Flight at Henlow asked me to do the next Bomb Disposal Flight. The day selected was one of those cold, hazy days when one can see reasonably well from 3000 feet and above, but below that visibility is restricted to about one mile. The engine started all right and I signalled to the armament officer present to do a final check on the bomb release to make sure the safety wire, which prevented inadvertent release on the ground, perhaps in the hangar, had been removed. I then took off and headed east, climbing steadily to 3000 feet. At that height I could see such well known landmarks as Bishops Stortford and the parallel road and railway running to Dunmow. I resisted any temptation to dive down over Stansted or Dunmow and 'shoot them up' with a (probably) live bomb with a doubtful history slung on a make-shift bomb rack. After 30 minutes flying the Chelmsford-Colchester parallel road and railway were below me and the hazy outline of the Blackwater Estuary was just discernable. After another 10 minutes I was over the Estuary as it widened out to the open sea. I could see no sign of shipping and felt I could let the bomb go at any time, but for good measure I flew on out until I was only just in sight of land on either side. I had been turning gently from side to side to make sure there was no shipping below. Finally I did a slow circle looking down all the time. There was no sign of shipping anywhere so I headed east again and moved the bomb release lever from the 'safe' position to the 'release' point on the quadrant. I then slowed down to about 65 m.p.h. so as to re-duce the wind pressure on the bomb, which might have induced a hang-up — but should not in theory. Then I pulled the lever over to release. I felt the bomb go, since the sudden lightening of the 112 lb load on one wing was quite appreciable. I then, quickly, went into a tight turn hoping to see the bomb falling and also to see the splash as it hit the water and, perhaps, exploded. I could not see the bomb, but

184

what I could see directly below me was a small fishing boat! I could have sworn the sea was clear before, and the only explanation I could think of was that some drifting patch of sea fog had obscured it.

I watched with a fearful fascination, expecting to see the fishing boat disappear in a cloud of smoke and flame: I counted up to seven slowly, by which time there was no splash, no flash, no concentric ripples spreading outwards — just a small fishing vessel sailing peacefully on through a glassy sea. I then started wondering if the bomb had really gone, even though I felt sure it had from the jerk I got as I released it.

When I landed back it was not on the rack so I put in a report to say it had been dumped at sea and no shipping was seen in the area *before* releasing it. That was quite true.

There *was* something unusual about that bomb.

20 My own aeroplanes—Racing —Posted overseas

The second year of the Engineering Course, from the academic point of view, pursued a normal academic course and from my point of view became more interesting. We were by then exploring aerodynamics and structural aeronautical engineering which were subjects I had not touched on before at Cambridge. With lecturers like Whitlock these were full of interest.

From the flying point of view the course had improved significantly. A Siskin had arrived in the Practice Flight and I had acquired another aeroplane of my own. It was an Anec Monoplane designed by W.S. Shackleton for the light aeroplane competition at Lympne in 1924. It had been crashed by its previous owner and had no engine. After a lot of hard bargaining I bought it for £10. The trouble was to collect the 'bits' from its present location. With great urgency my friend F/O George Green and I built a trailer which we calculated would carry the Anec. We drove over to collect it and everything went smoothly − on the way out. On the way back we managed all right until we got on to the Great West Road, which had then recently been opened. It was a wonderful stretch of road with relatively light traffic on it. Due to some instability in our trailer at any speed over 40 m.p.h. the trailer − with the Anec loaded on it − veered from side to side alarmingly: it swept both lanes of the Great West Road absolutely clear of traffic. It was not so much the sight of a trailer coming towards them that unnerved the traffic, as the sight of an aeroplane on top of it also coming at them − sideways. It must have been this that drove them on to the kerb. Hurried research and a brief conference as we slowed down established the fact that, at 36 m.p.h. the trailer was safe − at 40 m.p.h. it was dangerous to us, to approaching traffic and, to a lesser extent, to following traffic. We completed the rest of the trip to Henlow at 36 m.p.h.

On arrival I got down to the exciting job of rebuilding the Anec so as to get it into the air. The repair was easy with all the facilities, skill and help available on the Engineering Course, but I had to find an engine for it. After a somewhat frustrating search I found an A B C car engine which had been converted for use in the air. As a car engine, designed by Bradshaw, it was a powerful unit, but it developed its power at very high engine speed, which made the

186

The Anec monoplane

propeller inefficient. Designing new engine bearers and installing the engine caused little anxiety since the engine was somewhat similar to one which had previously been installed. After three months' work the great day arrived when we wheeled it out on to the aerodrome for its test. The grass was rather long so we pushed it to the down-wind end of the aerodrome which, by bad luck that day, meant taking off on a slight uphill gradient. We started the engine, warmed it up, pulled away the chocks and I signalled to wing-tip helpers to let go as I opened the throttle to full power. The engine gave all it had and the Anec did not move an inch. My friends and helpers started laughing, but I shouted to them to push. I remembered that with very high revving propellers it was possible to stall the blades whilst standing still, although one would get the thrust as it moved forward. My helpers, still laughing, pushed and to my relief the propeller slowly unstalled and the Anec trundled forward slowly gathering speed. At 24 m.p.h. it lifted off but the air speed was too high for the makeshift rubber tube I had fitted as a petrol pipe: it blew off and the engine stopped, much to my relief since I was trying to decide at that moment whether it was safe to attempt a circuit. Later, after many modifications, the Anec actually got to 700 feet.

The Anec monoplane took only second place in my civil preoccupations. I was industriously preparing the SE 5a for the King's Cup Air Race which was due to start on 4 July 1929, but I was very conscious of the fact that my handicap in the race had been prejudiced by the previous racing when I lent the aeroplane to a 'friend'. As a result of this I knew that I could not do much to improve the speed of the SE 5a but I could at least get the best out of it by accurate course flying. I set about practising on the route which, in that year, went from Heston Aerodrome (near today's London Airport) to Mousehold Aerodrome near Norwich, then down to Folkestone, then Bristol (over my home near Ludlow) to Blackpool, Renfrew in Scotland, and back down the Midlands to Heston. It was quite a circuit of England and, without some form of official organization at every stopping place, it was desperately tiring for a pilot. The petrol companies were extremely helpful and Esso made a most generous gesture in giving me — free — 80 gallons of various grades of Esso before the race so that I could test which gave me the best performance: during the race the selected grade was also provided free.

Practising on the course was easy for me since I took a Service aeroplane round the various 'legs' of the course, even to the extent of going up to Scotland and back. By the time the race started I knew the course pretty well.

Entering for the King's Cup involved paying an entrance fee. In order to conserve my very limited funds at that time I decided to try and find a 'sponsor', someone who would pay the entrance fee. This required a lot of thought. Friends of mine in the Service had got themselves entered by various air-minded Lords, Barons and industrial tycoons. I did not know any of them. However, the editor of the Morning Post, Mr. H.A. Gwynne, lived near Dunmow and was a great friend of my friends at Newton Hall. I asked him if he could suggest anyone who would enter me in the race. He said at once:

'We will enter you as the Morning Post competitor.'

Later it was found that the entrant had to be an individual, not an organization, so it was decided that the owner of the Morning Post should be my entrant: the then owner was the Duke of Northumberland, and I was entered in his august name. My friends in the Air Force who had also entered conceded to me a more aristocratic sponsor!

When the race started at Heston the first leg to Norwich gave us a following wind of which I took full advantage, climbing immediately to 1000 feet. Quite a number of competitors flew at tree-top height because they thought one raced at that height. From Norwich there was a long leg to Lympne, which was almost directly into wind. On this leg the fastest aeroplanes gained considerably and I found I had lost out to the special firms' entries like the Gloster Grebes which were beautifully tuned and flying very fast. The next part of the

188

course took us along the South Coast to Hamble and then Bristol. I was just about holding my own on this leg, but 20 miles short of Bristol I lost pressure in the petrol system and had to hand pump the pressure until I landed at Filton aerodrome at Bristol. Afterwards I found a broken pipe in the pressure feed from the engine pump to the fuel tank. It took me 45 minutes out of the allotted one hour stopping time to mend the pipe with a piece of rubber tube, and another 30 minutes went by in taxiing in after passing the finishing line, refuelling, checking the aeroplane, taxiing out to the starting line and taking off. I lost 15 precious minutes at Bristol and more on the leg to Blackpool with a slightly faulty engine, traced later to a defective magneto. However, I passed over Ludlow at a very low altitude to cheer up members of my family who were waiting and watching.

Blackpool was a night stop, but I spent much of it trying to rectify the magneto fault, without any success. In the morning, which was bright and clear with no weather hazard, I realized I had no hope of achieving anything in the Race. With an undiagnosed fault in the engine and way behind the other runners I decided to retire. I telephoned H.A. Gwynne and he agreed that it was wise in view of my engine trouble.

How right we both were! After the other competitors had left I took off for Heston hoping to see the end of the race. After one stop at Birmingham to try and sort out the worsening engine trouble, I pressed on for Heston, but over Beaconsfield the engine would no longer keep me in the air. I selected a large stubble field just outside the town and made a carefully judged approach to it. Just before landing I decided to make quite sure the engine really had failed and tried opening the throttle. I got a wonderful burst of full power out of it – then a loud explosion, followed by a horrid silence. I decided to land after all, but most of the stubble field had by then passed beneath me and the hedge at the end of it loomed up all too close. I tried the engine again and – God bless it – it gave another faint despairing, but adequate, burst of power. I cleared the hedge by inches and landed in a very small grass field beyond, where I was greeted by a crowd of cherry pickers. One of them said:

'Hey Mister, we though you'm goin' to land in that field,' indicating the stubble, 'but you landed in this 'un.'

I said:

'Well, as a matter of fact I thought I was going to land in that one too.'

'Ah' said the cherry picker 'when you'm oop thar I 'spect you doan 'ardly know where you'm comin' down.'

How right he was.

Recovery action, starting the next day, from my point of view had to be an economy operation. After a lot of checking I managed to diagnose the fault in one magneto which had stripped the gear driving the distributor arm with the result that the magneto was 'firing' at all sorts of odd moments and sometimes not firing at all. Had I known the fault and switched off the faulty magneto I could probably have flown on, but as it was the intermittent out-of-time firing of the faulty magneto caused chaos in the engine.

When I had diagnosed the fault after a thorough check, I went to my old friend R.J. Coley in Kingston who sold aircraft disposal parts (and still does) and bought another magneto for £1. I tried to beat him down, but I think he sensed the fact that I needed it badly so I had to pay his price.

With the replacement magneto I returned to the SE 5a which was being guarded faithfully by the cherry pickers, and started the rather intricate business of changing magnetos and re-timing.

I had not got very far when darkness fell. That was two days after the landing: and I was very short of money. I hired a covered punt on the Thames for the night — for economy not comfort — and had a wash and shave in the Thames in the morning — also for economy not comfort! Feeling a bit low in morale in the morning I treated myself to breakfast in a river-side hotel. It was one of those out-of-the-way pubs to which one assumed no-one ever went: the sort of pub one went to if one did not want to meet anyone one knew. I did not mind meeting any friends that morning, but a friend of mine, charmingly accompanied, had not expected to meet any acquaintances of his at all as the pair came down to breakfast that morning. They sat demurely at the most remote table they could find — about nine feet away from me — and then suddenly appeared to see me. My friend came over and explained that they had left London very early that morning to visit friends. The story sounded a bit thin, as told, but the waiter unintentionally tore it to shreds as he came up to them to check their breakfast order:

'Coffee, grapefruit and 2 eggs and bacon for No.5 Sir?'

In fact I was much too preoccupied with my magneto to worry about their affairs, but I had an extra piece of toast and marmalade after they had gone to celebrate the meeting and to allow for (probably) no lunch that day. I then hurried off to the SE 5a.

By 10 a m I had the magneto fitted and timed correctly but I had no locking wire to secure the magneto bolts. My friends the cherry pickers came to the rescue by producing a piece of barbed wire. They separated it into strands and the leader of the pickers said:

'You look as though you'm done enough on this job. I'll fix the locking wire: it's an awkward job.'

He did just that and no air mechanic could have done a better job. I was wondering how I could reward them for their really invaluable help when a diversion occurred. A friend in No. 41 Squadron had heard about my forced landing and had flown over in a Siskin to see what had happened. He found me and made three attempts to land in the same small grass field I was in. Prestige required that he land in the same field as I had and not in the large stubble field next to it. After the three abortive attempts prestige was lost anyhow, so he landed in the stubble field, left his Siskin ticking over and came to discuss the situation. He asked me particularly why I had landed in the small grass field when there was such a suitable large stubble field next to it. I said I had considered that when the engine stopped but I decided that the grass field with a barn in the corner would be a better place in which to leave the aeroplane for the night. I was relieved when he seemed to believe that I had arrived in the small field by choice!

I had a lot of trouble persuading my cherry helpers to accept any reward: they said it had livened up their lives enormously, and they hoped I would come again. In the end an all too small sum of money went to them and a large basket of cherries was put in the SE 5a. I flew back to Northolt after a somewhat dodgy take-off from the small field, avoiding trees, and a rather sad wave to the cherry pickers as I dived back over them.

That was my part in the 1929 King's Cup Air Race. It coincided with the end of the Engineering Course when we all dispersed to various new appointments. There was some talk of my going on a special course in aerodynamics at London University, which was then under Professor Bairstow. This would have been interesting but it was finally decided that I should go to Iraq, to the Depot at Hinaidi near Baghdad. In many ways this was much more exciting. Only recently the Air Force had taken over control of Iraq from the Army and air control was then in its experimental stage. I started getting organized to go abroad for two years or more. I had two and a half months to fill in. Since the Personnel Department at the Air Ministry seemed to have no particular views on how those two and a half months should be occupied I applied to be attached to my old Squadron, still equipped with Siskins. This was No.111 Squadron, which had by then been moved to Hornchurch in Essex, just north east of London. My application was accepted and I arrived at Hornchurch just when the Squadron was moving to Sutton Bridge for their annual training in firing at both ground targets and also towed targets: the latter were drogues (like long windsocks towed some 800 feet behind an aeroplane). This was one of the most important parts of a Fighter Squadron's training since it involved

191

The SE 5a, powered by a Wolsley Viper engine; a famous fighter and (*right*) a useful aircraft for visiting friends

firing live ammunition at a moving target in the air.

Unfortunately the pressure on this training for squadron pilots was so great that they could not allow me to join in as a supernumary pilot who could not have any effect on Squadron efficiency. However, the Squadron Commander, S/Ldr Soden, did all he could to arrange plenty of flying for me and I was allotted the squadron two-seater dual control Siskin to fly and required to do a regular 'mail' run every day between Hornchurch and Sutton Bridge. On that run I brought up the Squadron mail and any spares required. Apart from this responsibility I had the full services of an Officers' Mess almost to myself and an aeroplane as a private hack. During my time there I made all arrangements for going abroad but, alas, I left

192

No.111 Squadron without their dual Siskin. I broke it up.

On one return flight from Sutton Bridge I found the aerodrome at Hornchurch covered in sheep. Grazing rights had been let to local farmers on most aerodromes, but they were required to clear the sheep out of the way when any aeroplanes were operating. So little was going on at Hornchurch at the time that the shepherd had relaxed and did not notice my return. I was not worried by this since I knew that if one flew over sheep very low down, they always gathered into a flock and then moved clear of the centre of the field.

As I flew low over the aerodrome nearly all the sheep did just that, and I turned to come in to land where the grass was thin and dry, but fairly long. What I did not know was that one sheep was sick and was lying down in the long grass unable to move. By an amazing mischance, for the sheep and myself, I landed exactly on that sheep and it wiped the undercarriage off the Siskin very neatly, but very completely. The Siskin nearly turned over on to its back, but having reached the near vertical position it fell back the right way up. My airman passenger, loosely strapped in, appeared over my head at the critical moment and said:

'Are we all right, Sir?'

And before I could reply with any assurance he disappeared back into his cockpit. A much more important factor from his point of view was the fact that his suitcase had been strapped to the undercarriage and it had been squashed flat by the Siskin and integrated with mutton by the sheep.

I felt somewhat apprehensive about telling the Squadron Commander about the loss of his dual Siskin, and after a lot of thought I sent off a carefully worded signal to him at Sutton Bridge explaining that the dual Siskin had sustained extensive damage due to my landing on a sheep which I had not observed due to the similarity of colour of the sheep to surrounding terrain. I got a somewhat cryptic reply:

'Put Siskin on scrap heap: green sheep should be sent to British Museum.'

My excuse was not considered to be a valid one, but the tone of the signal indicated such accidents will happen, even in the best regulated squadrons.

Whilst still with No.111 Fighter Squadron I had arranged to sell my SE 5a for £125 to a keen private owner. I also did a deal on my Rolls-Royce Silver Ghost whereby I was allowed to use it up till a week before I left for Iraq. The price was £40. I duly handed it over, about ten days before I left, and the new owner went over it with an expert engineering eye: he was *half way* through the Engineering Course. He quickly told me that the backlash in the transmission, which had needed careful clutch operation, was entirely due to the presence of a small connecting link in the rear axle: he had removed it. Just before I sailed he complained to me that the back axle had 'come out' and he wanted his money back. I told him that Royce, so far as I knew, had never fitted redundant members in his cars, but if he thought 'he had a claim against me he could write a full explanation — to Baghdad.

Three days later I sailed, first class, in the Orient liner Orama on my way to Iraq. In my ignorance and inexperience I thought Air Force officers always travelled that way when going abroad! Nearly all my other overseas journeyings were made in very crowded troopships.

Although I did not realize it then, this was about the ideal time for me, or any of my contemporaries, to go overseas. From our course at No.2 F T S at Digby about 23 out of the 30 had survived the hazards of flying and discipliniary action. We had all done about 150 hours solo flying on various types of aeroplanes and should therefore have been proficient in any front line Squadron. So far as one could find active service at that time, it was either in Iraq or in India. In the latter country the Air Force was under the control of the Indian Army and was thus denied a full exploitation of its war potential: the Indian Army still insisted on using their horses on every possible, and several impossible, occasions.

In Iraq the Royal Air Force was paramount, the control and policing of the country was done by the Air Staff. Iraq had, therefore, the nearest approach to the modern conception of a Combined Defence Force.

At home in England the Air Force was in a transition stage of equipment: the old war-time designs of Bristol Fighters, Sopwith Snipes and Vickers Vimy bombers were being replaced by slightly faster and more heavily armed and equipped aircraft. There would be time enough, after two years, to come back and fly these, but operations in Iraq were the last survivors with the old 1914/18 war equipment.

In leaving England I also left behind much of the old 1914/18 war spirit represented by the gallant but sometimes irresponsible pilots who had survived the almost suicidal hazards of flying on the Western Front. In 1929 many of these amusing and gallant types were being retired with a gratuity of about £400, to find their way — sink or swim — in the hard, nearly brutal, world hit by a worsening slump. At this time there was a change, indefinable but I suppose inevitable, from an Air Force which had fought and won a war, to an Air Force which had to struggle to survive a peace. There seemed to be almost a majority in England who hoped the Air Force would not survive.

I left behind that transitional stage in England to see, first hand, what the Air Force could do in what could then still be called the 'outposts of Empire'.

It was a very different life, and another story.

Index